Studia Fennica
Linguistica 12

The Finnish Literature Society (SKS) was founded in 1831 and has, from the very beginning, engaged in publishing operations. It nowadays publishes literature in the fields of ethnology and folkloristics, linguistics, literary research and cultural history.

The first volume of the Studia Fennica series appeared in 1933. Since 1992, the series has been divided into three thematic subseries: Ethnologica, Folkloristica and Linguistica. Two additional subseries were formed in 2002, Historica and Litteraria. The subseries Anthropologica was formed in 2007.

In addition to its publishing activities, the Finnish Literature Society maintains research activities and infrastructures, an archive containing folklore and literary collections, a research library and promotes Finnish literature abroad.

Studia fennica editorial board
Anna-Leena Siikala
Markku Haakana
Pauli Kettunen
Leena Kirstinä
Teppo Korhonen
Johanna Ilmakunnas

oa.finlit.fi

Editorial Office
SKS
P.O. Box 259
FI-00171 Helsinki
www.finlit.fi

Minimal reference
The use of pronouns
in Finnish and Estonian discourse

Edited by Ritva Laury

Finnish Literature Society • Helsinki

Studia Fennica Linguistica 12

The publication has undergone a peer review.

The open access publication of this volume has received part funding via Helsinki University Library.

© 2005 Ritva Laury and SKS
License CC-BY-NC-ND 4.0 International

A digital edition of a printed book first published in 2005 by the Finnish Literature Society.
Cover Design: Timo Numminen
EPUB: eLibris Media Oy

ISBN 978-951-746-636-3 (Print)
ISBN 978-952-222-773-7 (PDF)
ISBN 978-952-222-772-0 (EPUB)

ISSN 0085-6835 (Studia Fennica)
ISSN 1235-1938 (Studia Fennica Linguistica)

DOI: https://doi.org/10.21435/sflin.12

This work is licensed under a Creative Commons CC-BY-NC-ND 4.0 International License.
To view a copy of the license, please visit http://creativecommons.org/licenses/by-nc-nd/4.0/

A free open access version of the book is available at https://doi.org/10.21435/sflin or by scanning this QR code with your mobile device.

Contents

Introduction 7

Appendix 11

MARJA ETELÄMÄKI
Context and referent in interaction
*Referential and indexical dimensions of the Finnish
demonstrative pronouns* 12

EEVA-LEENA SEPPÄNEN
Pronouns, gaze and reference
The Finnish demonstrative pronoun tämä *as a device
for modifying participation frameworks in conversation* 38

RITVA LAURY
First and only
Single-mention pronouns in spoken Finnish 56

LEA LAITINEN
Hän, the third speech act pronoun in Finnish 75

RENATE PAJUSALU
Anaphoric pronouns in Spoken Estonian
Crossing the paradigms 107

ELSI KAISER
When salience isn't enough
Pronouns, demonstratives and the quest for an antecedent 135

OUTI DUVALLON
The pronoun *se* in the context of syntactic
and discursive ruptures of spoken texts 163

PÄIVI JUVONEN
On the pragmatics of indefinite determiners
in spoken Finnish 190

Contributors 212

Subject index. 213

Name index 215

RITVA LAURY

Introduction

The purpose of this book is to make available, for the first time within one volume, some of the most innovative research into pronominal reference in Finnish and Estonian. The articles represent several linguistic subfields and theoretical approaches, including ethnomethodology, interactional linguistics, psycholinguistics, syntax, accessibility theory, and the theory of grammaticalization. In spite of the theoretical diversity the papers represent, all of them are staunchly corpus-based. Most deal with spoken language data, although written language is also represented.

The papers by Etelämäki and Seppänen both analyze the use of demonstrative pronouns in informal conversations in Finnish in the framework of ethnomethodological conversation analysis. Etelämäki's highly innovative paper, strongly influenced by the work of William Hanks (1990, 1992), is based on the assumption that referents in conversation are interactional entities which come into being and are meaningful only in and through verbal interaction and are also identified in relation to the ongoing activity. She proposes that the Finnish demonstratives *se*, *tämä*, and *tuo*, differ in terms of how they reflect and shape the actional structure of the conversation and how they set up a relation between the referent and its context.

Seppänen's paper deals with a feature of Finnish demonstratives which distinguishes them from the corresponding pronouns in languages like English, that is, their use without a nominal head for human referents. Seppänen focuses on the use of the Finnish *tämä* 'this' to refer to co-participants in the speech situation, combining the study of verbal interaction with the study of gaze, and shows how demonstratives are used to modify the participant framework (Goffman 1981, Goodwin 1981) in conversation. A particularly valuable contribution of Seppänen's study is the way in which it challenges the traditional, binary distinction between the second and third person along the lines of speech act participancy, showing that the Finnish demonstratives, although they are third person pronouns, are an important device for navigation in the area between the first and second person, providing a vehicle for paying attention to a person's participant status in the conversation without addressing her directly.

The topic of Laury's paper is the use of pronouns for first mentions of their referents. She shows that, contrary to claims that first-mention pronouns can only be used for generic referents, in ordinary Finnish conversations, such pronouns are also used for referents which are individually identifiable to the addressees, given a sufficient degree of symmetry of the indexical ground (Hanks 1990) shared by the interactants. She also reviews existing research on the Finnish demonstratives to see how well the features proposed for them by various researchers account for their use for first mentions, noting that in particular, the recent approaches which are based on interactional factors are quite enlightening in terms of accounting for the ways in which they are put to use in interaction.

Like Seppänen's paper, the contribution by Laitinen also deals with personhood and participancy in the speech event. Her focus is on the pronoun *hän*, which was developed into a specifically human pronoun in standard written Finnish, although it was and still is a logophoric pronoun in most dialects of spoken Finnish. Laitinen's careful, scholarly paper, reflecting years of research and thinking on the topic, exemplifies and traces the development of *hän* from its logophoric origins to its other uses as the pronoun of the protagonist in narratives and, on the other hand, as an evidential particle of ignorance. The paper also contains a short section on the syntax of person marking in Finnish.

The papers by Pajusalu and Kaiser deal with the factors that influence the choice of pronouns in, respectively, spoken Estonian and written Finnish, adding grammatical features to the chiefly pragmatic ones dealt with in the papers discussed above. Pajusalu's paper, based on a corpus of spoken Estonian, considers the main anaphoric reference-tracking devices of the language, the demonstratives *see, seal, sealt*, and the third person pronouns *tema* and *ta*. Pajusalu's paper is groundbreaking in two ways: up to date, there has been relatively little work done on Estonian pronouns, especially based on actual language use: thus her research, here and elsewhere, fills a considerable void. Another novel feature of Pajusalu's paper is that she combines the examination of the semantic, pragmatic and information flow features which affect the choice of pronouns in Estonian with grammatical features, case in particular. She also shows that, although animacy of the referent is generally thought to be an important factor controlling the choice of referential forms in Estonian, the personal pronouns can also have inanimate referents. Especially interesting is discussion of the interconnection of the paradigms of the pro-forms with morphological case.

Kaiser's paper offers an innovative deconstruction of the factor of the salience and accessibility of the referent, which has often been thought to control the choice of referential form in a relatively straightforward way. She examines the choice between the Finnish pronouns *hän* and *tämä* in two different ways, on the basis of psycholinguistic experiments as well as the distribution of these forms in a written corpus, concluding that a unified factor of salience fails to explain how language users interpret and make use of these two pronouns. Instead, she suggests that the demonstrative *tämä* accesses the discourse level, being associated with the low end of the salience scale, while the pronoun *hän* accesses the syntactic level, and is associated with the high end of the grammatical role scale.

Duvallon's carefully argued paper also proposes a syntactic approach to the use and interpretation of pronouns, but from a perspective different from Kaiser's; like Laury's paper, Duvallon's paper also takes up the issue of first-mention pronouns, but here, too, her perspective is distinct. Using the Pronominal Approach developed by Blanche-Benveniste et al (1987), Duvallon examines the use and interpretation of the pronoun *se* in spoken Finnish. She notes that reference formulation can be an extended process, and that the pronoun *se* can be used for picking out a referent with a minimum of descriptive content even when a lexical description is still in progress, still being negotiated, or even momentarily unavailable. In such cases, she argues, the interpretation of the pronoun takes place inside the linguistic context, by establishing a connection between the host construction of the pronoun and the larger, suspended sequence it is housed in. Duvallon is the first to apply the Pronominal Approach to the study of Finnish, and her work has great promise.

Päivi Juvonen takes up a topic which has so far not received sufficient attention in Finnish linguistics, perhaps due to its complexity, namely indefinite determiners. She discusses the three forms which have been noted to express indefiniteness in spoken Finnish, *yks*, *joku/jokin*, and *semmonen*. Based on their use in a spoken corpus, she comes to the conclusion that the determiners differ pragmatically. Juvonen suggests that *yks* and *joku* differ so that *yks* is used when the referent is specific, but its identity is not retrievable from the context, while *joku* is used with either specific or non-speficic referents. *Yks* tends to imply that the referent will be important in the upcoming discourse; on the other hand, *joku* seems to imply that the exact identity of the referent is not important, or that the speaker is not the original source of the information given. Contrasting with these two, *semmonen* is used when the identity of the referent itself is not in focus, but its type or class membership is.

Put together, these articles represent both theoretical innovation and diversity of approach. It has been a great pleasure to work on this volume with this group of researchers and as the editor, I would like to thank all the contributors for their creativity, flexibility and enthusiasm. Many of us were recently able to participate in a workshop at the Annual Finnish and Estonian Conference of Linguistics in Tallinn, where ideas brought forward in the volume were discussed and expanded upon. The active participation of newer Estonian and Finnish colleagues in the workshop was especially welcome and encouraging, and it is to be hoped that further research and cooperation along the paths opened in this volume will continue across the language boundaries. Auli Hakulinen deserves great thanks for originally coming up with the idea for this volume. I also wish to thank Johanna Ilmakunnas and Pauliina Rihto, the publishing editors at Suomalaisen Kirjallisuuden Seura, for excellent cooperation and expert help in the production stage of the volume, and Pentti Leino, the series editor, for his relaxed attitude about many things.

In Helsinki, June 15, 2004

Ritva Laury

REFERENCES

Blanche-Benveniste, Claire, José Deulofeu, Jean Stefanini and Karel van den Eynde (1987). *Pronom et Syntaxe. L'approche pronominale et son application au français.* Paris: CELAF.

Goffman, Erving. 1981. *Forms of Talk.* Oxford: Basil Blackwell.

Fretheim, Thorstein and Jeanette Gundel. (Eds.) 1996. Reference and Referent Accessibility. Amsterdam: Benjamins.

Goodwin, Charles. 1981. *Conversational Organization: Interaction between Speakers and Hearers.* New York: Academic Press.

Gundel, Jeanette, Nancy Hedberg and Ron Zacharski. 1993. Cognitive status and the form of referring expressions in discourse. *Language* 69:2.

Hanks, William. 1990. *Referential Practice.* Chicago: University of Chicago Press.

APPENDIX

Morphological glosses

ABL	ablative
ACC	accusative
ADE	adessive
ALL	allative
CLT	clitic
COMP	comparative
COND	conditional
ELA	elative
ESS	essive
GEN	genitive
ILL	illative
IMP	imperative
INE	inessive
INF	infinitive
NEG	negation
PAST	past tense
PCP	participle
PL	plural
PSS	passive
PTC	particle
PTV	partitive
PX	possessive suffix
Q	question
SUP	superlative
TRA	translative
COM	comitative
1SG	first person singular (likewise for 2nd and 3rd)
1PL	first person plural

MARJA ETELÄMÄKI

Context and referent in interaction
Referential and indexical dimensions
of the Finnish demonstrative pronouns

Introduction

In this paper, my aim is to describe the referential and indexical features of the Finnish demonstrative pronouns *tä(m)ä*, *toi (tuo)* and *se*, with emphasis on the pronoun *tä(m)ä*.[1] I examine everyday talk as activity, where artefacts are constituted and talked about along with all sorts of other things being done. I assume that conversational referents are best understood as interactional entities (see Etelämäki 1998); furthermore, they only come to being in interaction when referred to. In addition, they are identified in relation to the on-going activity, regardless of whether they are concrete, physical objects, or linguistically created ones (i.e. second or third order entities, Lyons 1977: 443–445).[2] As Heath & Hindmarsh (2000) write, the objects are "inseparable from the environment in which they are located and the specific courses of action in which they figure". Hence, also referential expressions become meaningful only in and through the interaction. Furthermore, the profoundly interactional character of referents-in-interaction is embodied in the grammar of reference forms, particularly in the semantics of demonstrative pronouns.

The acts of reference are profoundly reflexive: the objects of reference are identified in relation to the on going activity, and simultaneously the activity is reflected and constituted through the references to the objects. Therefore, referential expressions themselves take part in indexing the activity, and in that way create their own indexical contexts. When considering referential expressions, the reflexive nature of reference invites us to look at two directions, namely the referential and the indexical. Demonstrative pronouns are referential indexicals, which means that their basic function is to individuate objects of reference in terms of their relation to the indexical ground of reference (Hanks 1990: 36–43;

---

1   The paper is based on my forthcoming doctoral dissertation *Tarkoite ja toiminta. Tutkimus suomen pronominista tä(m)ä*.
2   This is not an ontological claim about the existence of entities *per se*, but a claim about the existence of mutually shared referents in interaction.

1992). The indexical ground is that part of the interactional context that functions as the sociocentric origo for the reference. Since the context is dynamic, the demonstratives function in two ways: while referring to an entity they also organize the indexical ground, and set a relation between the referent and the indexical ground (Heritage 1996 [1984] 236–237, see also Hanks 1992: 53).

I approach linguistic phenomena through ethnomethodological conversation analysis, where conversation is examined as organized activities accomplished in and through turns-at-talk. In conversational data, the unfolding interaction appears as the primary context for the referential acts. The data used for this paper is naturally occurring face-to-face, and telephone conversations. In the next section, I will describe the Finnish demonstrative system. I will then proceed with the analyses of three conversational sequences to exemplify the use of the pronouns, and to empirically argue for the referential and indexical features that I propose in this paper. Finally, I will briefly discuss the idea of indexical context including conversational activities.

The Finnish demonstratives

There are three demonstrative pronouns in Finnish, namely *tä(m)ä*, *toi (tuo)*, and *se*. Besides the three demonstrative pronouns, there are also pronominal adjectives and adverbs, which are based on the same roots.

Table 1. The Finnish demonstratives.[3]

The Finnish demonstrative pronouns
Pronouns:

tää (tämä)	('this')	*nää (nämä)*	('these')
toi (tuo)	('that')	*noi (nuo)*	('those')
se	('it'/'the')	*ne*	('they'/'the')

A sample of other Finnish demonstratives
Adjectives: Adverbs (Locatives):
Adverbs/Particles:

tä-mmönen (tä-llainen)	*tää-llä*	*näin*
to-mmonen (tuo-llainen)	*tuo-lla*	*noin*
se-mmonen (se-llainen)	*sie-llä*	*niin*

The translations above are only approximate ones, since the Finnish reference system is quite different from the English one. All the Finnish demonstrative pronouns may be used either independently or adnominally. There are no unambiguous articles in Finnish, but adnominally used pro-

---

3   The first form is commonly used in southern Finnish vernacular. The standard Finnish forms are in parentheses.

nouns *se* (Laury 1997: 250–263) and even *tä(m)ä* (Juvonen 2000: 196) have been noted to possess features of a definite article.

In my description, I will follow Hanks' (1990, 1992) model of demonstrative reference, first applied to Finnish by Laury (1997). He proposes that the meanings of referential indexicals are composed of three features, namely characterizing, relational, and indexical. The characterizing features designate properties of referents, the relational ones convey the relation of the referent to the ground, as well as ways of access (tactual, visual, discourse) to the referent, and the indexical features organize the indexical ground against which the referent is to be identified (Hanks 1990: 66, 1992: 51–53). According to Laury (1997), the characterizing features of the Finnish demonstratives designate the referent to be either "the one", i.e. a single object, or "the region". The relational features express that the referent is either included in or excluded from the context. The indexical features organize the context to either speaker (+ addressee) or addressee centric (1997: 58-62). My proposal differs somewhat from the ones introduced above, as can be seen from the table below. I have only specified the referential (i.e. characterising) and indexical features in the table, since they are in focus in this paper:

Table 2. The Finnish demonstrative roots.

Roots:	Referential features:	Indexical features:
tä-	open	asymmetric
t(u)o-	open	symmetric
se-	closed	symmetric

For the sake of uniformity, I use the term referential instead of characterizing, when referring to the features that correspond to referential dimension. I suggest them to be "open" (for further definitions) and "closed", for the following reasons. As mentioned above, the demonstrative class in Finnish includes pronouns, adverbs, and even adjectives. They are all based on the three demonstrative roots *tä-*, *to-/tuo-*, and *se-*. The pronouns refer to a single entity, while the adverbs might refer to a region (*täällä, tuolla, siellä*), manner (*näin, noin, niin, täten, siten*), or time (*tällöin, tuolloin, silloin*), and the adjectives to quality[4] (*tällanen, sellanen, tollanen*). In these forms, such referential properties as regional, manner, or temporal are designated by affixes that are mostly frozen forms of

---

4 The pronominal adjectives are often used as determinants for potentially referential NPs, in which case they can be compared to other NP determinants. However, as NP determinants they emphasize the category that the NP expresses rather than the specificity of the referent (see Vilkuna 1992: 132–133; Juvonen, in this volume), which is due to their adjectival character.

original case markers. Hence, it is not the demonstrative root that makes these distinctions.[5]

In addition, the root itself seems to convey some referential meaning. It designates the referent properties that have to do with the issue of definiteness. In the next section, I will propose that definiteness, when understood as "knownness", is not a static feature of a referent, nor is it a dichotomy (see also Du Bois 1980; Chafe 1994: 93–100; Laury 1997: 34–51). The question is not only whether the referent is identifiable, but also whether it is adequately identified for the on-going activity. The pronouns *tä(m)ä* and *toi* express that paying attention to, describing, or determining the referent is somehow relevant for the on-going activity, and therefore the referent is open for further characterizations. That way they also function as pointing. The pronoun *se* marks the referent to be sufficiently defined for the on-going purposes, and therefore "closed" for further identification.

The indexical grounding of referents simultaneously makes reference to, and articulates with, the context in which the reference is performed (Hanks 1991: 254–255). Thus, the indexical component of reference organizes the indexical ground of reference. I propose that the Finnish demonstratives organize it as either "symmetric" or "asymmetric", according to the mutuality of the participants' understanding of the on-going activity, rather than proposing the reference to be either speaker or recipient centric. This is because in my view the indexical ground is profoundly social (see below; also Hanks 1990: 36–43), and based on the on-going interaction. In the next two sections I hope to exemplify the points I have made so far, by analysing three extracts from actual conversational data. I will first discuss the referential features, and then the indexical ones.

Referential features

In this section, the main emphasis will be on the characterizing features of the pronoun *tä(m)ä*, but I will discuss the other two demonstratives, too. I have argued that the pronouns *tä(m)ä* and *toi* convey that their referents are still open for discussion, whereas the pronoun *se* marks its referent as known enough for the on-going purposes. Since *tä(m)ä* and *toi* point at their referents as "observables", their use is parallel to the

---

5   In addition to referring to inanimate referents, the Finnish demonstratives might be used for referring to persons, and even to the participants of a conversation (Seppänen 1998; Kaiser, in this volume). Among other things, they differ from the Estonian demonstratives in this respect (see Pajusalu, in this volume). Since the demonstratives might be used to referring to human and inanimate entities, the referential features do not designate such features as "animate" or "human" either. However, in person references the pronouns do propose particular participant statuses for the referent (Seppänen 1998). In addition, a notion of participant roles is related to the notions of humanity or animacy.

act of pointing. I will exemplify my proposal in the analysis of the following extract (1).

The extract is from a conversation with two participants, Airi and Sisko. They are both artists, and they are at Airi's studio discussing her paintings that are present in the room. The extract is from the beginning of the situation. I will focus on Airi's turns, and show how the demonstrative pronouns function, first, in directing the recipient to look at the painting, and secondly, in organizing the unfolding activity.[1]

(1) (Airi ja Sisko)

```
 1  Airi:   ensin puhutaan tosta?.hh
             first let's talk about that one?

 2  Sisko:  mm:.
             mhm.

 3          (0.5)

 4  Airi:   h::$(h)y(h)y  k(h)yl  se on  aika  kaamee.hh$.hhniin
             h::$(h)i(h)i  it(h)   is    quite  awful indeed.hh$

 5          totah (2.4) se nyt jatkaa sitä lootustee°maa°?
             so:h (2.4) it now continues the lotus theme?

 6          (3.2)

 7  Sisko:  mitä lootusteemaa
             what lotus theme

 8  Airi:   sitä mitä mä tein (.) siihe viime näyttelyyn
             the one that I did (.) to the previous exhibition

                                        |SISKO......
 9          sen pallon (.) pyöreen jos oli se valkonen
             that ball the round one that had that white

                 ...................... |PAINTING....................
10          loo[tus keskellä?  (0.5)     (0.2) mut]ta: (.) se on
             lo[tus in the middle? (0.5)|(0.2) but] (.) it has

11  Sisko:      [NODDS REPEATEDLY]

12  Airi:   (.) jostain syystäh  (.) ruvennu mua kiinnostamaan
             (.) for some reason (.) begun to interest me

13          tää (0.6) pelkän tumman ja vaaleen (0.4) #niin#ku
             this (0.6) pure dark and light (0.4) #like#

14          vaihtelu?
             variating?
```

15   (.)

16 Sisko: mm.
            mm.

17   (0.4)

18 Sisko: krhm

19   (1.6)

20 Airi: ja silleen että (.) toi ei niinku (.)tavallaan ois
            and so that (.) that would not like (.)in a way be

21   mitään ainetta toi kukka. (4.8) et et sillon se ei
            any like material that flower. (4.8) that that then

22   oo niinkun mikään esine. >tai se ei oo< kukan
            it is not like any object. >or it is not< a picture

23   kuva oikeestaan vaan sitä on vaan
            of a flower really but it has only been

24   sitä kukkaa käytetty (1.2) niinku tohon
            that flower used (1.2) like for the purposes of that

25   (1.4) sommitteluunh
            (1.4) compositionh

26   (2.0) ((Sisko walks towards the painting and
            stops (3.6)))

27 Sisko: °$heh eh$° (.) [°$mheh$°

28 Airi: [mitä raati sanoo
                           [what does the jury say

In the extract, Airi introduces the first painting to be discussed about. It begins with Airi pointing at the painting (line 1), and ends with an inquiry after the recipient's opinion (line 27).[6] The introduction can be divided roughly in three parts. In the first part, Airi points to the painting and proposes it to be the first one to be talked about, and Sisko aligns with the proposal (lines 1–2). Then, Airi gives subsidiary information about

---

6   Apparently, Sisko's movements (line 23), and faint laugh (line 24) prompt the actual question. However, both the movement and the voice can be taken as expressing her orientation to the situation, i.e. the introduction being taken to its end, and thus to a transition relevance place.

the painting (lines 4–10). Finally, she offers a framework for mutual examining of the painting (lines 10-24). [7, 8]

The turn in line 1 initiates the talk about the paintings:

1 Airi: ensin puhu-taan to-sta?.hh
         first talk-3PL that-ELA
         first let's talk about that one?

2 Sisko: mm:.
         PCT
         mhm.

The formulation of the turn serves this purpose. The adverbial *ensin* ('first') is in the theme, by which I mean the position that in a clause internal syntactic structure precedes the verb, and is most often occupied by a subject in active transitive clauses (Vilkuna 1995). It is followed by the verb *puhutaan* ('talk') that denotes to the activity itself. The verb is in passive form, which in spoken Finnish can be used as a first person plural imperative. Hence, the the verb form makes the utterance a proposal. The painting is pointed to by the pronoun *tosta* (an elative form of the pronoun *toi*). It organizes the indexical ground as symmetric, and simultaneously points at the referent as open for further discussion. By symmetric ground I mean that both the participants have equal access to the referent, due to their mutual understanding of the on-going activity. The activity itself – "talking about the surrounding paintings" – is shared in a sense that it is what the participants are oriented to doing in this particular situation. This includes that they share the understanding of what the role of the referent is in the activity.

---

7   The dashed line (above lines 9–10 in the transcript) marks gaze. The object of gaze is written in the beginning of the line. For the sake of readability, I have only transcribed gaze where it is particularly relevant for this analysis.

8   In these data, there are sequences of talk that are organized around the co-developing of a topical line. However, it seems that constructing and assessing a referent in these sequences is an activity that the participants are oriented to; hence, the talk is not organized around topical development but around the activity (see Sacks 1992 [1968], April 17). The demonstratives place the referent primarily within the activity, and indicate how the utterance is related to the unfolding activity simultaneously as they function in organizing the activity itself. In addition, indexes seem to cumulate, and hence it would be an overstatement to claim that it is the demonstrative alone that marks the turn/utterance to do such and such a thing. E.g. in extract 1 line 5 there is 1) the utterance's position (after the pointing to a referent), 2) the demonstrative pronoun *se*, and 3) the particle *nyt*, that all together produce a particular interpretation of what the utterance is doing, and what its sequential implications are. There might even be grounds to ask, whether the demonstrative is actually doing anything else than expressing a relation of a referent to a particular kind of context, where the demonstrative would be chosen due to the context. However, there is a reflexive relation between an utterance and its context, i.e. the context is set through the utterance itself, and one cannot tear these apart or put them in a causal or temporal order.

There is no speaker change after the pointing. By a minimal response *mm.* (line 2), Sisko agrees to talk about the painting that Elvi points to, but withdraws from taking the next turn. Ochs Keenan & Schieffelin (1983 [1976]) have suggested that a discourse topic is a proposition rather than a single entity. In a way, their observation is evidenced in my data, where a pointing of a referent usually co-occurs with a proposition concerning the referent. The proposition provides for a mutual point of view to the referent: a framework, which provides grounds for understanding further talk. It is the pointing together with the proposition that composes a topic offer. The turn in line 1 only consists of a pointing. Therefore, I suggest that although there is a transition relevance place after line 1, there is also an implication that Airi will continue talking. I understand Sisko's minimal response that passes the turn as expressing her orientation to that implication. In lines 4–5 Airi takes a turn again:

```
4   Airi:   h::$(h)y(h)y k(h)yl   se on       aika kaamee.hh$.hhniin
                          PTC      it be+3SG   quite awfull           PTC
            h::$(h)i(h)i it(h) is quite awful indeed.hh$

5           totah (2.4) se nyt jatka-a        si-tä       lootustee°ma-a°?
            PTC         it now continue-3SG   that-PTV    lotus theme-PTV
            so:h (2.4) it now continues the lotus theme?
```

In line 4, she first produces a negative assessment about the painting. The assessment is signalled as a parenthetical comment in various ways. To begin with, the painting is being referred to by a pronoun *se* (see the analysis of *se* below). In addition, the assessment is framed with laughter that signals the utterance as non-serious.[9] Finally, after the assessment the speaker rushes on to an in breath and produces a particle chain *niin tota*, which indexes return to the main line, to an activity projected by the earlier talk (Heinonen 2002: 110–113).[10] In doing that it projects more talk by Airi. By producing the particle chain right after the in breath, the speaker passes a possible transition place following a grammatically and pragmatically complete utterance. That way she expresses that the previous utterance – although an assessment – was not initiating an assessment sequence (for assessments, see Pomerantz 1984: 57–101, Goodwin & Goodwin 1987, 1992).

After a pause that follows the particle chain, she begins to tell about the painting. However, by the pronoun *se* and the particle *nyt*, the new utterance (*se nyt jatkaa sitä lootusteemaa*) is indexed as delivering subsidiary information. The pronoun *se* refers to the painting first as a subject in the theme, and then as a part of an object-NP *sitä* being the partitive

---

9   What is being done with a laughter-framed, self-deprecating comment in this position would be a subject of larger analysis than what I offer here. However, the subject is not within the scope of this paper.
10 Heinonen (2002) discusses cases where *niin tota* is in a second pair part, indexing return to an activity projected by the first pair part.

case form of *se* (*sitä lootusteemaa*).[11] It designates its referent to be an entity that is adequately identified for the purposes at hand, and needs no further discussion (see Laury 1997: 58–128). Thus it expresses that the utterance does not offer the painting to be talked about within the framework of "lotus theme".

The particle *nyt* supports the interpretation of the information as subsidiary: *nyt* can mark that a clause is a part of the ongoing activity, but is not taking the main line of the talk forward (Hakulinen 1998). Together with the pronoun *se*, the particle marks the utterance as one that offers background information. Since the utterance follows a (mere) pointing of a referent, but the indexical expressions *se* and *nyt* mark it as expressing subsidiary information, there still is an implication that the speaker will continue talking. This is an implication that the participants orient to.

Contradictory to my claim, there is a pause (line 6), which ends only when Sisko takes the next turn (*mitä lootusteemaa*) in line 7:

6   (3.2)

7 Sisko: mitä lootusteema-a
            what lotus theme-PTV
            what lotus theme

However, her turn does not take the talk forward, but functions as a next turn repair initiator. The NP *sitä lootus teemaa* is used as a recognitional (Himmelman 1996: 230–239; for *se*, see Laury 1997: 102–103, 118), which makes either a confirmation or a repair initiation by the recipient a relevant next action (cp. also "try-marking", Sacks & Schegloff 1979). Himmelman (1996) describes recognitional use as such where "the referent is to be identified via specific, shared knowledge rather than through situational clues or reference to preceding segments of the ongoing discourse". He mentions three features that are attached to the recognitional use, all of which fit to the above example: 1) the identification of the referent may cause problems for the recipient, which is oriented to by the speaker, 2) the referent is often of only peripheral importance, and 3) additional information which makes the referent more accessible is often added in relative clauses or other modifiers of similar complexity. (Himmelmann 1996: 230.)

It must be noted that recognitional use can't be taken as an inherent property of the pronoun *se*, since other reference forms can be used as recognitionals, as well. Furthermore, *se* also has non-recognitional uses, for example tracking (the first *se* in line 5). However, Himmelmann's observations are useful in this analysis: the new referent (lotus theme)

---

11   Though the clause is a transitive clause, its function is rather to express a description of the subject-NP than an event where the subject-NP would be an agentive participant, and the object-NP a goal. The subject-NP functions as an object of description, and the verb together with the object-NP compose the description. Hence it is functionally close to predicate nominal clauses.

is introduced as identifiable, and it is offered a subsidiary role in further talk. In addition, the pause leaves space for the recipient to confirm that she recognises the referent in question. In this extract, the recipient initiates a repair sequence (line 7).

The trouble source for the repair initiator (line 7) is the "lotus theme". As soon as the initiator of the repair (Sisko) has confirmed (by nodding, line 11) that she has identified the referent, the speaker introduces a new aspect to the painting, and the repair sequence becomes a side sequence. The continuation (beginning by *mutta* 'but' in line 10) can be interpreted either as turn-internal or turn-initial, depending on whether Sisko's nod counts as a turn or not. On the one hand, it is a confirming response, and acting as a sequence closing third to the repair sequence. On the other hand, the response being only a nod – and not a verbal response – it can be seen as an orientation to the incompleteness of the on-going turn. The continuation (line 10, 12–14) introduces another angle to the painting:

```
                              |PAINTING................
10       loo[tus keskellä? (0.5)    (0.2) mut]ta: (.) se on
                                          but         it be-3SG
         lo[tus in the middle? (0.5)|(0.2) but] (.) it has

11 Sisko: [NODDS REPEATEDLY             ]

12 Airi:  (.) jostain  syy-stäh (.) ruven-nu  mu-a    kiinnosta-ma-an
              for some reason-ELA begin-PCP 1SG-PTV interest-3INF-INE
              (.) for some reason (.) begun to interest me

13        tää    (0.6) pelkän    tumma-n  ja  vaalee     (0.4) #niin#ku
          this         pure-GEN  dark-GEN and light-GEN        PTC
          this   (0.6) pure dark and light (0.4) #like#

14        vaihtelu?
          variation
          variating?
```

Sorjonen (1989: 174–176) has pointed out that *mutta* ('but') often initiates turns that do not continue "talking on topic", but continue "talking topically". Typically, they are used for introducing new sub-topics to the conversation (ibid). Talking topically refers to talk that merely involves attention to topical coherence, whereas talking on topic consists of "blocks of talk about 'a topic'" (Sacks 1992 [1968], April 24). In extract 1, the utterance (in lines 10, 12–14) continues topical talk about the painting, but does not continue on the topic of the previous utterance ("lotus theme").

In addition, the utterance is syntactically constructed to accomplish a transition in the course of the talk. There are two co-referential NPs in the utterance (lines 10, 12–14). The former (*se*) is an argument of the verb, and the latter (*tää pelkän tumman ja vaaleen niinku vaihtelu*) is structurally a right-dislocation.[12] In my data, constructions with a right-dislocated NP determined by the pronoun *tä(m)ä* are used for re-defining the topic.[13] If there is a pronoun *se* as the first NP (in the argument position), the utterance begins a new sub-sequence in an activity that is going on already. In extract 1, the participants are already talking about a particular painting. The pronoun *se* indexes the continuation of the overall activity, and points to its referent as sufficiently defined for the momentary purposes: a topical referent for the on-going talk. The right-dislocated NP specifies the reference by expressing a new category that the referent belongs to.

The pronoun *tää* in the dislocated NP designates the referent to be open for further discussion, which means that it offers the referent for further characterizations. The categorization functions as a framework that continues in the following characterizations of the painting. The pronoun also organizes the indexical ground as asymmetric. That way it indexes that there is a change in the activity, as well: the utterance shifts the talk from delivering subsidiary information about a topical referent to offering a framework ("variation of light and dark") for discussing on topic.

The turn in lines 20–26 continues discussing the painting in the "dark and light"-framework:

```
20 Airi: ja silleen että (.) toi  ei           niinku (.)tavallaan o-is
         and so+that that  that NEG+3SG PRT    in-a-way be-COND+3SG
         and so that (.) that would not like (.)in a way be

21       mitään ainet-ta         toi kukka. (4.8) et  et   sillon se ei
         any    material-PTV     that flower        that that then  it NEG+3SG
         any like material that flower. (4.8) that that then it

22       oo niinkun mikään esine. >tai se ei         oo< kuka-n
         be like   any    object  or  it NEG+3SG be      flower-GEN
         is not like any object. >or it is not< a picture of

23       kuva         oikeestaan vaan si-tä on         vaan
         picture      really     but  it-PTV be+3SG    merely
         a flower really but it has only been

24       si-tä      kukka-a     käyte-tty (1.2) niinku to-hon
         that-PTV   flower-PTV  use-PSS+PCP PTC        that-ILL
         that flower used (1.2) like for the purposes of that

25       (1.4)      sommittelu-unh
                    composition-ILL
         (1.4)      compositionh
```

---

12 The terms "co-referential" and "dislocation" are only used to clarify the syntactic construction in question, and to refer to particular elements in it. However, I find literal understandings of these terms highly questionable.

13 The data consist of video recorded face-to-face conversations (approximately 45 minute conversation between the two artists, and half an hour television talk show) and audio recorded everyday telephone conversations (approximately one and half hours).

The reference to the flower is first determined by the pronoun *toi*, in the utterance that explicates the abstractness of the motif by negating the "materiality" of the flower. In the continuation, the flower is referred to with the pronoun *se*, which marks it as sufficiently characterized. Instead, in the NP that refers to the composition (*tohon sommitteluun*) in the last utterance, is determined with the pronoun *toi* (*tohon* in the illative case). The pronoun *toi* designates that the referent is yet open for further characterizations. And it is the composition – consisting of the variation of dark and light – that the speaker offers to be commented on.

To sum up, the painting is first referred to by the pronoun *toi*, where both the participants know what the activity will be, and the referent is still to be discussed. When the speaker is talking about an aspect of the painting that is not offered for further discussion, she uses the pronoun *se* to refer to the painting. *Se* is also used adnominally in an NP that introduces a subsidiary aspect of the painting. If an NP introduces an aspect that is offered for the following talk, it is determined by the pronoun *tää*. The pronouns *tää* and *toi* maintain the referent under observation, and the pronoun *se* merely tracks a referent in the conversation. In addition, the pronoun *tää* makes identifying – in the meaning of 'knowing about' – the referent particularly salient in the act that is the turn is accomplishing. Therefore, I propose that the referential feature of *tä(m)ä* and *toi* is "open", and *se* is "closed". As has been implied already in this section, the pronoun *tää* does not only introduce a new topic framework, and offer it for further talk. It also indexes re-organizing of the activity. This is due to its indexical feature, which I will discuss in the next section.

Before turning to the indexical features, I will briefly compare my view of the pronoun *se* to the views of the other authors in this book, and discuss the notion of definiteness in the light of interaction. Tiainen-Duvallon (2002, in this volume) claims that the pronoun *se* is the most neutral reference form: there are no additional meanings or functions attached to its use besides reference.[14] Furthermore, she brings out that the use of the pronoun *se* is not constrained by a lexical mention or the presence of the referent, but the identification of the referent is guided by the host construction of the pronoun, and its position in a larger linguistic context (in this volume). Although for Tiainen-Duvallon, it is the syntactic construction that provides for the identifiability of the referent, her findings fit well with my views. In conversation, actions are accomplished in and through linguistic constructions. Hence, recognizing the activity and recognizing the construction are just two sides of the coin: using a

---

14 This comes close to what Schegloff (1996) writes about practices for referring to persons in talk-in-interaction. He asks: "How do speakers *do* reference to persons so as to accomplish, on the one hand, that nothing but referring is being done, and/or on the other hand that some thing else in addition to referring is being done by the talk practice which has been employed? Relatedly, how is talk *analyzed* by recipients so as to find that 'simple' reference to someone has been done, or that referring has carried with it other practices and outcomes as well?" Following Schegloff's line of thought, one could say that with the pronoun *se*, nothing but referring is being done.

construction that links to some previously used construction can be seen as a way of marking that the activity accomplished by the construction is a part of some previous activity. In addition, the pronoun *se* implies that the referent is sufficiently identified in relation to that activity.

Laury (1997) and Juvonen (2000) both discuss the adnominally used pronoun *se* as a marker of identifiability. They arrive at different conclusions. According to Laury, *se* is on its way to a definite article since it means "identified in general".[15] However, she notes that the use of *se* requires more exact kind of identifiability than other article languages, so that it is not fully grammaticalized. For example, in English it is possible to say *He threw his jacket in the corner*, when the speaker does not expect the addressee to be able to identify which one of the corners of the room is in question. In Finnish, *se* would not be used. (Laury 1997: 260–261). Juvonen (2000) puts an emphasis on the criterion of obligatoriness, and notes that there is no obligatory grammatical category of definite articles in Finnish. However, she proposes that there might be an optional category with at least two members, namely *tä(m)ä* and *se*, since they are both used adnominally in anaphoric references (2000: 191–197).

In conversational data, *tä(m)ä* and *se* are both used for referring to previously mentioned – and that way identifiable – entities. Yet, they do not convey the same meaning, since *tä(m)ä* designates that the identification of the referent is relevant in the on-going activity, and *se* designates that its referent is sufficiently identified for the purposes at hand. In addition, "identifiability" is not a static feature of a referent in interaction. Rather, referents in conversation can be re-identified, according to the situational purposes. (See Laury 1997: 34–51.) Hence, I propose that Finnish *se* could be understood as a marker of definiteness *in situ*, rather than definite in general. By that I mean that the *se* marks the referent to be sufficiently identified in relation to a shared interactional ground, at the moment of the referential act. (See also Laury, this volume.)

Indexical features

In the following two sections, the focus will be on the conversational activities, and the indexical dimension of reference. In the analysis, I will only deal with the pronouns that are in the theme. Initiations of new utterances, and particularly the initiations of turns, are indexically loaded, since they express how the utterance is connected to the previous context, and what kind of an activity it is building up (Schegloff 1996: 73–83). Hence, the indexical features become particularly prominent in the theme. It is important to note that turn beginnings do not necessarily coincide with sequential organization: speakers may initiate a new activity sequence

---

15 The class identified in general does not require previous mention in discourse. Thus it includes things known from context or general knowledge, and things identified because they are the only member of the class, such as *the sun* (Greenberg 1978: 61–62).

either in the beginning of a turn or in the middle of a turn (see e.g. extr. 1, l. 10,12, extr. 2, l. 15). Hence, what is said about turn beginning goes for utterance beginnings, as well.

I will discuss two utterances that accomplish assessments. Both of them include a demonstrative pronoun referring to the assessable, and the assessable is a situation that has been described in the talk preceding the assessment. In extract (2) (Birthday), the pronoun that refers to the assessable is *se*, and in extract (3) (The drought), it is *tää*:

(2) (Birthday)

```
10  Jussi:   → no: nii.       se[hän  on i]ha: ihan    hy[vä tapa] viettää
                 o:kay. Well  it[      is qu]ite quite a go[od way ] to celebrate

11  Salme:                       [(m:m)     ]            [(mm.) ]

12  Jussi:   → viettää päiviäh.=
                to celebrate (one's birth)dayh.=

13  Salme:    =mm.
```

(3) (The drought)

```
33  Sari:    ...ku-  kaikki tehtiin aaiiveeks ja.=ja
             ...since all was made to AIV and.=and

34          → tää on  sur:keeta elukoitten
               this is sa:d wen thinking the

35          → kannaltaki ajatel[len
               animals          [too

36  Eeva:                      [o:n kyllä juu. [.hhh
                               [it i:s yes right. [.hhh
```

In the extracts (2 and 3) the assessable has not been explicitly mentioned (by a noun) and hence constructed as a discourse referent, but the referent is identifiable via the on-going situation. The previous talk functions as an interpretation source for the pronoun: it construes a situation, which is referred to by the pronoun (Cornish 1996). Simultaneously, the reference shapes the situation as a discourse referent.

My suggestion is that the indexical feature for the pronoun *se* and *toi* is symmetric, and for *tä(m)ä* asymmetric. The feature "symmetric" designates the indexical ground, i.e. the activity from which the referent is to be identified, to be shared by the participants. Therefore, *se* and *toi* often mark that the utterance is continuing some previous activity. The feature "asymmetric" means that the participants do not share the activity at the moment that the reference is made. In addition, the origo is momentarily biased towards the speaker of the pronoun, since the referent is to be identified in relation to what she is doing by the on-going utterance. Hence, the use of the pronoun *tä(m)ä* is disruptive, and asks the recipient to be particularly attentive to what is being done. With the following analyses, I wish to show that the two assessments above differ from each other in how they stand in relation to their interactional contexts, and that they also accomplish distinct sequential tasks.

Birthday

In extract (2), Jussi has called Salme to inquire about her brother's upcoming birthday. The whole inquiry sequence begins several lines before the extract. The initial inquiry has gotten a rather reserved answer, and it turns out that Salme's brother intends to have a low profile party where only his closest relatives are invited. The answer is then followed by an accounting turn by Jussi, and a confirming (*joo.*) answer by Salme. The turn in line 1 initiates a post expansion of the inquiry sequence:

(2) (Birthday)

```
1  Jussi:  mp.h:: no j- (.) .hh joo ni hän viettää sitte.
           mp.h:: well r- (.) .hh right so she celebrates then.

2  (.)

3  Salme:  joo.
           yes.

4  Jussi:  mnt ihan  [siinäh
           mnt just  [thereh

5  Salme:  [(--)

6          (0.8)

7  Salme:  juu eih se on tonne:- (.) vaan kutsunuh (0.5) Ma- tonne
           yes no she has there- (.) only invited (0.5) to Ma- there

8          mikä: se on nyt. (0.8) >Majalan Kestituvalle meitin<
           what is it now. (0.8) >to Majala's Cottage us<

9          siskot ja veljet käskeny sinne vaan.
           sisters and brothers she has told (to go) just there.

10 Jussi: → no: nii.  se[-hän on i]ha:  ihan hy[vä tapa] viettää
           PTC PTC   it-CLT  is quite quite  good  way  celebrate+INF
           o:kay. Well it [is  qu]ite quite a  go[od way ] to celebrate

11 Salme:              [(m:m)   ]           [(mm.) ]

12 Jussi: → viettää       päiv-i-äh.=
           celebrate+INF day-PL-PTV
           to celebrate (one's birth)dayh.=
```

```
13  Salme:  =mm.

14          (0.5)

15  Jussi: → .hh tässä    vaiheess[ah. .hhhh ky:llä ja terveisiä
               .hh at this    stag [eh. .hhhh ye:s and greetings

16  Salme:                      [mm:.

17  Jussi: sitte tuolta    Topparistah:[:.
            then from that Topparih:[:.
```

It is a request for confirmation, and gets an agreeing response (line 3). However, in line 4 Jussi continues his turn with a syntactic increment (*ihan siinä* 'just there') of his own previous turn. The increment is taken up by Salme as an invitation to further elaborate her brother's birthday plan (lines 7–9).

The target turn (lines 10, 12 and 15) is an evaluation of the plan as "quite a good way to spend one's birthday". It consists of two units: a particle chain *no nii*, and an evaluating utterance.[16] *No nii* is used to mark a transition, and it marks specifically closings (Raevaara 1989). The following assessment then gets a minimal response *mm.* by Salme. The incremented *tässä vaiheessa* (line 15) somewhat modifies the previous assessment, and it gets another minimal response (line 16) in overlap with the end of the increment. Directly after the increment, Jussi produces an in-breath, a particle *kyllä* ('yes'), and introduces a new topic *ja terveisiä sitten tuolta Topparista* ('and greetings then from Toppari'). The new topic initiates a totally new sequence, and thus confirms the closure of the previous one.

The assessment offers a summary of the previous sequence: by evaluating the plan as a good one, the speaker also expresses his approval of the plan, and expresses that the participants are in agreement. Inquiring about another person's birthday could get an interpretation of an indirect means for getting an invitation to a birthday party, or imply that there should be a party.[17] However, Jussi is the pastor of the local congregation, and the call is apparently due to his profession. Particularly in small communities, it is customary that the pastor visits the people belonging in his congregation in their special days. Now Jussi needs to know whether to prepare himself for a visit or not. The assessment in this extract expresses that not giving a party is not a problem.

16   Strictly speaking the whole turn is actually in lines 10, 12, 15 ja 17. The utterance *tässä vaiheessa* is a syntactic increment to the previous assessment, and Jussi continues talking directly after that by introducing a new topic.
17   This interpretation is evidenced in the turn-initial particle chain *juu ei* (yes no) in Salme's answering turn in line 7. This particle chain seems to be in use when answering questions that have a negative implication. The particle *juu* confirms the negative implication in the previous turn, and *ei* negates the implicated state of affairs. In extract 2, there is no explicit negative claim in the previous turn hence the particles confirm an implicated negation.

The assessment initiates what Schegloff (1995) calls a sequence closing sequence, i.e. a short sequence that is used to close long sequences. The basic form of sequence closing sequence is composed of three turns: 1) the initial turn, 2) response turn by the recipient, and 3) turn consisting of final closing token or assessment, often followed an initiation of new sequence. Assessments are among the most common initiating turn types, other common types being e.g. summaries and idiomatic or aphoristic formulations of the outcome of the topic. (Schegloff 1995: 189–190). The response turns can be overt agreements with the action or stance displayed in the previous turn, but also they can be quite minimal, like small particles, laughs, even just sighs (Schegloff 1995: 192–193).

The particle *mm.* in line 13 is not agreeing, but rather it withdraws from taking a stance towards the previous assessment, and expresses mere acknowledgement. However, its speaker is in a situation of cross-cutting preferences: had it been agreeing, she would have confirmed that is good not to invite the Jussi to the party. Jussi's next turn is the final turn: the increment in its beginning might be due to the minimal response in line 12, since it does modify the assessment. The post-completion stance marker (Schegloff 1996: 90–92), the particle *kyllä*, is further doing away with doubts (Hakulinen 2001: 172, 190–194), and takes the TCU to its closure. The particle is then followed by an in-breath and an initiation of a new sequence, which confirms the closure of the whole previous sequence.

Assessments are often used to bring a sequence to its end: they provide for an overview, or a conclusion, of the previous talk. Whether they function as sequence closing thirds or initiate a sequence closing sequence, the pronoun referring to the assessable is usually *se*. It does not offer the assessable to be further discussed, but designates it to be sufficiently known for the mutual activity. In addition, it indexes the context to be symmetric: it shapes the assessment to be a part of the preceding sequence, and of an activity that is shared by the participants. That way it expresses that the participants share an understanding of the previous sequence, as well.

The drought

In extract 3, Sari is the caller, and the formal[18] reason for her call is to check that Eeva has found a bunch of flowers that Sari had brought Eeva while she was not home. After a series of other topics (all initiated by Sari) the call gradually turns into troubles-telling. Sari's talk is leading the topic through step-wise topic shifts: weather, drought, worrying about the drought, worrying in general, and finally the actual trouble: Sari's depressed brother. The transition from business as usual towards an attention to a trouble (see Jefferson 1988) is done during the extract. Because of the length of the extract, I discuss it in three parts: 1) the weather, 2) the drought, and 3) the trouble. In the first part (3.1), Sari initiates a topic about the warm weather:

---

18 The reason for the call is the one that the caller expresses as the reason, and to which she returns at the end of the call (see e.g. Schegloff & Sacks 1973).

(3.1) (The drought: the weather)

1 Sari: → [lämmint on vaa riittäny.
        [it has been warm for long.

2 Eeva: oh<u>on</u>: ollu j- niin. [.hh
        it h<u>a</u>:s yes.   [.hh

3 Sari: [kr kr krr

4 Eeva: [m:-

5 Sari: →[mut ei siällä kovin paljo eiks vaa
        [but it didn't very much it did

6   >eikö< <u>y</u>öllä satanu.
        rain last night didn't it

7   (0.8)

8 Eeva: kyllä <u>mei</u>llä sato täällä. <u>ai</u>ka <u>r</u>eippaa[stim.
        yes <u>we</u> did have rain here. quite a <u>hea</u>[vy one.

9 Sari: [<u>J</u>aa:
                                                     [<u>O</u>:h.

10 Eeva: .mhh me oltiin parilla <u>s</u>yntymäpäivillä
         .mhh we visited a couple of <u>b</u>irthday parties

11   J<u>u</u>ssin kans tuala <u>P</u>ellilässä päin <u>ei</u>lej ja-
         with <u>J</u>ussi there near <u>P</u>ellila yesterday and

12   (.) ja <u>s</u>iälä ei satanu <u>y</u>htään.
         (.) and <u>t</u>here it didn't rain at <u>a</u>ll.

13 Sari: <u>juu</u>. [(sitä)
         <u>yes</u>. [(it)

14 Eeva: [<u>s</u>it kun tultiin tänne niin täällä
         [<u>t</u>hen when we came backe here then here it had

15   oli tullu.>ja tuli viälä< <u>u</u>udestaanki
         rained.>and it rained yet< <u>a</u>gain too

16   sitte <u>ai</u>[ka reippaasti.]
         then <u>qui</u>[te heavily.   ]

17 Sari: [°<u>juu</u>. k<u>u</u>° se   ol]i niin <u>kau</u>:heesti
         [°<u>yes</u>. Because° it] was so <u>aw</u>:fully

18   >ku täsä ku< <u>mei</u>tillä tuli ihan semmonen (.)
         >since here since< by <u>us</u> it came really such (.)

```
19          .hh (.) että miten >se ny< päivällä tosa (.)
            .hh (.) that how >it now< during the day there (.)

20          viiden: #m# millin kuuri ihan- (.) ku- kuuro
            five mill showar all- (.) sho- shower

2           lihan yks kaks ja, .hh
            all of a sudden and .hh

22 Eeva:    mm:

23 Sari:    se on niinku .eheh Hakolassa oli jo
            it is like .eheh in Hakola already it hadn't

24          (.) yhtään tullu.
            (.) rained at all.

25 (.)

26 Eeva:    [ai jaaha.   ]
            [oh is that so.]
```

Retrospectively analysed, the topic about the weather turns out to be goal directional. First, the question about the rain (lines 5–6) is negatively formulated, and sets therefore a preference for a negative answer. Had the answer been negative, there would have been a place to introduce the issue of drought. However, the answer (l. 8) is positive. The response particle *jaa* (l. 9) implies that what was said above was news, and that way it confirms the preference implied in the question. Secondly, Sari initiates a turn (l. 13), as soon as Eeva has told that there was no rain in Pellilä. She withdraws at this point, since Eeva continues talking, but takes the turn at the first possible transition place (l. 17), or even a bit before it.[19]

In her turn in lines 17–21 an 23–24, Sari does not comment on what Eeva has previously said, but begins her own telling. She first tells about the rain around her house, and continues by telling that there had been no rain at all in Hakola (the place where the farm apparently is). This information is received as news with the particle *ai jaaha* (l. 26). The topic of no rain leads up to a longish telling about the drought and its consequence, the shortage of the cattle food (extract 3.2). Sari's orientation towards a trouble is first manifested in line 28, where she adds a stance expressing utterance *mää murehdin* ('I worry'):

---

19 The turn in lines 14–16 is composed of two TCUs. However, the second TCU is arrived at with a rush-through, therefore it doesn't provide for a speaker change. The rush-through might be the reason for the early start in line 17: usually the transition space begins at the last syllable of the last word.

(3.2) (The drought: the drought)

```
27  Sari:     [että (tota) tav]a:ttoman (.) rajattu ja meillä tuala
              [that (PTC)  ve]ry (.) restricted and by us there at

28            kotona kun .hh siälä kans mää #m-# (.) .hh murehdin
              home since .hh there also I #w# (.) .hh worried

29            (me: niinku) kauhee k:arja meill on kolkkytaviis päätä
              (we like) a big cattle we have thirty-five heads

30            ja- #uw-# l:oppuu iha jo se rehu mikä on (.)
              and- #uw# ends already that feed that there was (.)

31            .hhh mikä on kylvetty sillä tavalla se-
              .hhh that there was cropped that way to be cat-

32            seku:liks ja, .hh ei uutta (urehuva) nyt tuu
              cattle food and .hh no there won't be new (cattle food) now

33            ku- kaikki tehtiin aaiiveeks ja.=ja
              since all was made to AIV and.=and

34        → tää on sur:kee-ta eluko-i-tten
            this is sad-PTV    animal-PL-GEN
            this is sa:d when thinking the

35        → kanna-lta-ki ajatel[l-e-n
            side-ABL-CLT think-INF-INSTR
            animals            [too

36 Eeva:  →                     [o:n kyllä juu.  [.hhh
                                 is PTC   PTC
                                [it i:s yes right. [.hhh

37 Sari:  →                                      [ei  mikkään
                                                  NEG nothing
                                                 [no nothing

38        → kasva ma[a san     et
            grow 1SG   say+1SG that
            grows   [I say that

39 Eeva:  →         [kedo-t kuihtu.
                    field-PL wither+3PL
                    [Fields wither.

40 Sari:  → nii on kauhee-ta.=kyl mä(h)ä sano-n  kans > että.<
            so  is awful-PTV PTC  1SG    say-1SG PTC       that
            so it is awful.=Indeed I say too that.
```

The telling is interrupted when Sari produces an assessment (l. 34–35). It initiates a sequence in which the participants together moan about the drought (34–40). Referring to the assessable, the pronoun *tää* (l. 34) indexes that the utterance does not continue the previous activity, the telling, but disengages from it. The activity changes from telling to assessing, in which the recipient is invited to take part, as well. When indexing that the previous activity does not function as the ground for the reference, it organizes the indexical ground momentarily as asymmetric: at the moment the reference is made, it is only the past activity that is mutual for the speaker and the recipient. That way it directs the recipient to pay attention to the on-going turn in order to figure out what the activity is that forms the indexical ground.

The first assessment (l. 34–35) is looking forwards rather than backwards (cf. extract 2). The pronoun *tää* points at the assessable as open for further characterizations. That way it offers the referent to be commented on by the recipient, as well. In addition, when looking at the assessment in a larger sequential context, it can be seen as preparing the situation for troubles-telling by inviting the recipient to engage with the worrying.[20] During the telling that precedes the assessment (lines 27–33), Eeva produces no minimal responses. Hence she does not show alignment as a troubles-recipient.[21] In the assessment sequence, she engages herself with the worrying, and that way she becomes a more suitable troubles-recipient. As is shown in the continuation of the conversation, Sari is indeed leading the conversation to troubles-telling:

(3.3) (The drought: the trouble)

```
41  Sari:    .hhh mää olen tommonen kauhee suremaan #m:#
             .hhh I am that way awfully sorrowful #w:#

42           murehtimaan mää aina mitäs niistä mutta kun
             worrysome I always that so what about them but since

43           .hh tulee aina sillai ajateltua ja:. .hh
             .hh one always comes to that way to think and:. .hh

44           (.)
```

---

[20] Retrospectively, Sari's orientation towards a tellable trouble can be seen already earlier in the call. She is persistently initiating new topics at several places that are possible places for initiating closing section. In addition, her questions concerning Eeva's husband and work are interpretable as seeking troubles: that is, trouble telling is reciprocal in a way, that it is easier to talk about troubles if the participant has some troubles to tell too.

[21] The lack of responses might be due to the ambivalence of the talk. The previous talk has been chatting about holidays, Jussi's and Eeva's work, and weather. At this point there has not been an actual announcement of a trouble yet, although the verb *murehdin* (line 28) hints of an up-coming one. Anyway, Sari's talk functions as a lead-up to the trouble that is announced in lines 48–50.

45 Eeva: mm.

46 Sari: → mitä se mu ve- veljeniki kun se on niin taas
           what that b- brother of mine too since he has so been again

47   → ollu niin- (.) niin kauheen masentunu ja.
           so- (.) so awfully depressed and.

48   (.)

49 Eeva: → vai niih.
           oh he has.

The turn in lines 46–47 is a troubles announcement (Jefferson 1988: 424–428), for which *vai niih* (l. 49) is a go-ahead response. The response expresses Eeva's alignment as a troubles-recipient. The call continues with a lengthy telling of troubles. As Jefferson shows, troubles-telling is an activity where the participants have specific roles: a troubles-teller and a properly aligned recipient (Jefferson 1988; Jefferson & Lee 1981). Assessing, in turn, is an activity in which participants express and build up a mutual orientation and stance towards some state of affairs (Goodwin & Goodwin: 1992). Therefore the initiating of an assessment sequence (l. 34) is a means for appealing to the recipient, in order to proceed to the actual trouble.

In the troubles-announcement, Sari uses the pronoun *se* as an adnominal determinant in the NP that refers to the brother (*se mu veljeniki* 'that brother of mine'). Although the use of *se* indexes continuity, and simultaneously it seems to be in an utterance that is in an initial position, it is not in contradiction with my earlier claims. The troubles-announcement initiates troubles-telling, but it does not explicitly initiate a new sequence. Rather, the troubles approach (l. 41–43) and announcement (l. 46–47) are formulated as continuation of the previous talk. Jefferson (1988) describes troubles telling as talk that follows a certain trajectory, rather than a clearly defined sequence. In troubles telling, the participants balance between an engagement between business as usual and attention to the trouble. (Ibid.) This can be seen in the extract, where the transition to the trouble is made step-wise, embedded in the talk about worries in general, which was actually initiated already in line 28 by the verb *murehdin*. In lines 41–42, Sari describes herself as a person who worries a lot. In her description, she uses the word *murehtimaan* ('to worry'), which is a non-finite form of the verb *murehtia*, and links back to line 28. In addition, there is a pronoun *niistä* (a plural elative form of the pronoun *se*) in the next utterance (l. 42), which refers to an indeterminate group of people or things that Sari worries about, including her family and the farm. The reference to the actual trouble, the brother (*se mun veljeniki* 'that brother of mine'), is then made as an addition to the previously mentioned group of people. Embedding the troubles-announcement in the more general talk is a way of managing between the troubles-talk and the business as usual.

Summary

In extract (2) (Birthday), the assessment is taking the previous sequence to its end. The pronoun *se* that refers to the assessable organises its indexical ground, i.e. the context, to be symmetric in relation to the referent. In other words, it indexes that the utterance – as well as the act that is accomplished through the utterance – belongs to and continues an activity that is already going on. That way it outlines – supported by the utterance that accomplishes the reference – the previous activity as the indexical ground for the reference.

In extract (3), then, the assessable is referred to by the pronoun *tää*, and the assessment initiates a whole new sequence. Furthermore, the assessment does not continue the previous utterance or the sequence that the previous utterance is a part of, but rather disengages from it. Although it stands outside from the main line of talk, it is functional in what the talk is leading to, namely troubles-telling. It functions as a means to get the recipient to join in the worrying mode, and that way to prepare the situation for troubles-telling. Therefore, when looking at the assessment sequence in its context, it can be seen that it does become a part of a larger activity, but as an independent sequence.

In my analysis, I have followed Hanks (1990, 1992) in using the term indexical ground of reference. It is best understood as a bundle of different aspects of context that are made relevant by the referential expression itself and the utterance accomplishing the reference (Hanks 1996: 182). For example, 3rd person references (demonstratives or personal pronouns) to participants in a conversation activate the participation framework (see Seppänen 1998, in this volume). Even in demonstrative reference to either inanimate referents, or referents that are not present in the situation, the indexical ground is a set of coordinates, more abstract than the speaker's location (Hanks 1990: 39). The demonstratives may activate spatial context, when it is salient in the situation (cf. Agha 1996). The underlying, primary organization of indexical context lies, however, on interactional activities.

Epilogue

In my description of Finnish demonstrative pronouns, I have used the notion of referential indexicals, and suggested that it can be further developed with the tools and insights provided by the conversation analytical framework. As my conclusion, to tie my suggestion to a larger linguistic framework, I wish make a brief survey on the history of the notion. It was introduced by Silverstein (1976) to replace the classical notion of shifters. The term "shifter" was originally brought up by Jespersen (1922; 1992 [1924]) to refer to the class of referring expressions whose meaning shifts according to the situation of use. Jakobson (1971 [1957]) explicated the idea further. According to him, the meaning of shifters consists of conventional rules that express a relation between the signs themselves and their objects in a particular situation. Hence, shifters are indexical symbols. (Jakobson 1971 [1957]: 386–389; for *index* and *symbol*, see Peirce 1955 [1940]: 104–115).

Silverstein (1976) continues Jakobson's line of thought. He claims that reference is only one of the several functions of language, and by no means the primary one (Silverstein 1976). The other functions are included in an utterance as its pragmatic meaning, which Silverstein defines as "the meaning of a linguistic sign relative to its communicative functions". Thus, utterances convey referential, i.e. semantic, and pragmatic meanings, both of which are represented in the formal features of utterances. Building on this line of thought, he defines shifters as indexes, which convey some aspect of the context as their pragmatic value. He further separates two classes of indexes, namely referential and non-referential, where non-referential indexes convey such merely pragmatic values as i.e. social roles of the participants. Furthermore, he proposes that the indexical features need not be present in the situation a priori to the utterance, but indexicals may function creatively. This is due to the conventionalized contextual features that are conveyed by the indexicals.[22] (Ibid.)

In his study on Maya deixis, Hanks (1990, 1992) continues developing the notion of shifters as a functionally distinct class. However, rather than focusing on the automatic correspondences between linguistic forms and contextual variables, he focuses on what people actually do with language. For him, the context is dynamic and socio-centric, and deictics are tools for creating unique indexical contexts for reference in real-time. (Hanks 1990: 9–15.) I find it natural to complement Hanks' insights on deixis with the conversation analytic approach. In conversation analysis, the context is understood as dynamic, and co-constructed, which fits well with Hanks' line of thought. While Hanks offers a theoretical framework, conversation analysis provides tools for studying the micro-organization of social activities. Microanalysis of interaction, then, reveals new information for the semantic description. As I have shown in this article, also the Finnish demonstratives relate the referent to the ongoing context, simultaneously organizing the context. I have proposed that referent identification is related to the on-going interaction, which is then reflected on the semantics of reference forms.

---

22 Lea Laitinen (1992, 1995; also Rojola & Laitinen 1998) has done a considerable amount of work on indexicality in Finnish. She also has introduced the thoughts of Silverstein to Finnish linguistics. In addition, Eeva-Leena Seppänen (1998) and Marja-Leena Sorjonen (2001) have studied indexicals in Finnish interactions.

REFERENCES

Agha, Asif. 1996. Schema and superposition in spatial deixis. *Anthropological Linguistics* 38: 643–682.
Chafe, Wallace. 1994. *Discource, consciousness and time: the flow and displacement of conscious experience in speaking and writing.* Chicago: University of Chicago Press.
Cornish, Francis. 1996. Antecedentless' anaphors: deixis, anaphora, or what? Some evidence from English and French. *Journal of Linguistics* 32: 19–41.
Du Bois, John. 1980. Beyond definiteness: The trace of identity in discourse. In Wallace L. Chafe (ed.) *The pear stories: cognitive, cultural and linguistic aspects of narrative production.* Norwood, N. J.: Ablex.
Etelämäki, Marja. 1998. Kuva puheenalaisena. In Lea Laitinen and Lea Rojola (eds.) *Sanan voima. Keskusteluja performatiivisuudesta.* Helsinki: Finnish Literature Society.
Goodwin, Charles. 1996. Transparent vision. In Elinor Ochs, Emanuel A. Schegloff and Sandra A. Thompson (eds.) *Interaction and grammar.* Cambridge: Cambridge University Press.
Goodwin, Charles and Marjorie Harness Goodwin. 1987. Concurrent operations on talk: notes on the interactive organization of assessments. *IprA Papers in Pragmatics* 1, No. 1: 1–54.
Goodwin, Charles and Marjorie Harness Goodwin. 1992. Assessments and the construction of context. In Charles Goodwin and Alessandro Duranti (eds.) *Rethinking context. Language as an interactive phenomenon.* Cambridge: Cambridge University Press.
Goodwin, Charles and Naoki Ueno (eds.). 2000. Vision and inscription in practice. *Mind, culture, and activity: an International Journal.* Volume 7, Numer 1&2.
Hakulinen, Auli. 1998. The use of Finnish *nyt* as a discourse particle. In Andreas H. Jucker and Yael Ziv (eds.) *Discourse markers: descriptions and theory.* Amsterdam: John Benjamins.
Hakulinen, Auli. 2001. On some uses of the discourse particle *kyl(lä)* in Finnish conversation. In Margret Selting and Elisabeth Couper-Kuhlen (eds) *Interactional linguistics.* Amsterdam: John Benjamins.
Hanks, William. 1990. *Referential practice. Language and lived space among the Maya.* Chicago: Chicago University Press.
Hanks, William. 1992. The indexical ground of deictic reference. In Charles Goodwin and Alessandro Duranti (eds.) *Rethinking context. Language as an interactive phenomenon.* Cambridge: Cambridge University Press.
Hanks, William. 1996. *Language and Communicative Practices.* Oxford: Westview Press.
Heath, Christian and Jon Hindmarsh. 2000. Configuring action in objects: from mutual space to media space. In Goodwin & Ueno 2000.
Heinonen, Mari. 2002. *Ni(in), ni tota ja tota ni paluun merkkeinä puhelinkeskustelussa.* MA thesis. Department of Finnish, University of Helsinki.
Himmelmann, Nikolaus. 1996. Demonstratives in narrative discourse. A taxonomy of universal uses. In Barbara Fox (ed.) *Studies in anaphora.* Amsterdam: John Benjamins.
Heritage, John 1996 [1984]: Harold Garfinkel ja etnometodologia. Transl. Ilkka Arminen, Outi Paloposki, Anssi Peräkylä, Sanna Vehviläinen and Soile Veijola. Helsinki: Gaudeamus.
Jakobson, Roman. 1971 [1957]. *On language.*
Jefferson, Gail. 1988. On the sequential organization of troubles-talk in ordinary conversation. *Social problems* 35: 418–441.
Jefferson, Gail and John R. E. Lee. 1981. The rejection of advice: managing the problematic convergence of a 'troubles-telling' and a 'service encounter'. *Journal of Pragmatics* 5: 399–422.
Jespersen, Otto. 1922. *Language: its nature, development, and origin.*

Jespersen, Otto. 1992 [1924]. *The philosophy of grammar.*
Juvonen, Päivi. 2000. *Grammaticalizing the definite article. A study of definite adnominal determiners in a genre of spoken Finnish.* Department of linguistic, Stockholm University.
Laitinen, Lea. 1992. *Välttämättömyys ja persoona. Suomen murteiden nesessiivisten rakenteiden semantiikkaa ja kielioppia.* Helsinki: Finnish Literature Society.
Laitinen, Lea. 1995. Nollapersoona. *Virittäjä* 99: 337–358.
Laury, Ritva. 1997. *Demonstratives in interaction. The emergence of a definite article in Finnish.* Amsterdam: John Benjamins.
Lyons, John. 1977. *Semantics 2.* Cambridge: Cambridge University Press.
Ochs Keenan, Elinor and Bambi Schieffelin. 1983 [1976]. Topic as a discourse notion: a study of topic in the conversations of children and adults. In C. N. Li (ed.) *Subject and topic.* New York: Academic Press.
Peirce, Charles. 1955 [1940]. *Philosophical writings of Peirce.* Selected and edited with an introduction by Justus Buchler. New York: Dover Publications, Inc.
Pomerantz, Anita. 1984. Agreeing and disagreeing with assessments: some features of preferred/dispreferred turn shapes. In J. Maxwell Atkinson and John Heritage (eds.) *Structures of social action.* Cambridge: Cambridge University Press.
Raevaara, Liisa. 1989. *No* – vuoronalkuinen partikkeli. In Auli Hakulinen (ed.) *Kieli 4. Suomalaisen keskustelun keinoja I.* Department of Finnish, University of Helsinki.
Rojola, Lea and Lea Laitinen. 1998. Keskusteluja performatiivisuudesta. In Lea Laitinen and Lea Rojola (eds.) *Sanan voima. Keskusteluja performatiivisuudesta.* Helsinki: Finnish Literature Society.
Sacks, Harvey. 1991 [1968]. *Lectures on conversation.* Volumes I & II. Gail Jefferson (ed.). Oxford: Blackwell.
Sacks, Harvey and Emanuel A. Schegloff. 1979. Two preferences in the organization of reference to persons in conversation and their interaction. In George Psathas (ed.) *Everyday language. Studies in ethnomethodology.* New York: Irvington Publishers, Inc.
Schegloff, Emanuel 1995: *Sequence organization.* Manuscript. [To appear: *A Primer in Conversation Analysis: Sequence Organization.* Cambridge: Cambridge University Press.]
Schegloff, Emanuel. 1996. Turn organization: one intersection of grammar and interaction. In Elinor Ochs, Emanuel A. Schegloff and Sandra Thompson (eds.) *Interaction and grammar.* Cambridge: Cambridge University Press.
Schegloff, Emanuel A. and Harvey Sacks. 1973. Opening up closings. *Semiotica* VIII, 4: 289–327.
Seppänen, Eeva-Leena. 1998. *Läsnäolon pronominit. Tämä, tuo, se ja hän viittaamassa keskustelun osallistujaan.* Helsinki: Finnish Literature Society.
Silverstein, Michael. 1976. Shifters, verbal categories, and cultural description. In Keith H. Basso and Henry A. Selby (eds.) *Meaning in anthropology.* Albuquerque: University of New Mexico Press.
Sorjonen, Marja-Leena. 1989. Vuoronalkuiset konnektorit: *mutta.* In Auli Hakulinen (ed.) *Kieli 4. Suomalaisen keskustelun keinoja I.* Department of Finnish, University of Helsinki.
Sorjonen, Marja-Leena. 2001. *Responding in conversation. A study of response particles in Finnish.* Amsterdam: John Benjamins.
Tiainen-Duvallon, Outi. 2002. *Le pronom anaphorique et l'architecture de l'oral en finnois et en français.* Thése de doctorat. École pratique des hautes études, Sciences historiques et philologiques.
Vilkuna, Maria. 1992. *Referenssi ja määräisyys suomenkielisten tekstien tulkinnassa.* Helsinki: Finnish Literature Society.
Vilkuna, Maria. 1995. Discourse configurationality in Finnish. In K. É. Kiss (ed.) *Discourse configurational languages.* Oxford: Oxford University Press.

EEVA-LEENA SEPPÄNEN

Pronouns, gaze and reference
The Finnish demonstrative pronoun *tämä* as a device for modifying participation frameworks in conversation

Introduction

The Finnish demonstrative system, which is based on three different demonstrative roots and includes adjectives and adverbs as well as demonstrative pronouns, has been described from various angles during fennistic history (see Setälä 1981, Penttilä 1957, Itkonen 1979) and is still the object of lively theoretical debate (see, for instance, Larjavaara 1990, Etelämäki 1998 and this volume, Laury 1997, Seppänen 1998). In the past few years, an increasing number of studies have used approaches which assume that the meaning of pronouns as referential indexicals is best understood by analyzing them in their actual situations of use and, most importantly, as an element of spoken interaction (e.g. Laury 1997, Etelämäki 1998 and this volume, Duvallon this volume, Pajusalu 1999, 2004 and this volume). My own research represents this approach.

There is, however, one feature of Finnish demonstrative pronouns that has received comparatively little attention in the descriptions of their meaning and referential potential: the use of demonstratives for human referents. In contrast to languages like English, the Finnish demonstrative pronouns can be used without a nominal head in referring to human referents; and in fact one of them, the pronoun *se,* also has a position in the system of personal pronouns as a colloquial counterpart of the standard-language third person personal pronoun *hän* 'she/he'.[1] But what is most interesting in the use of Finnish demonstrative pronouns for human referents is that speakers frequently use them to refer to their co-participants in the speech situation, and they are thus used for modifying participant roles in conversation.

The aim of this paper is to take a close look at the use of one these pronouns, *tämä* 'this' as a device for referring to co-participants in conversational interaction. What makes such use of pronouns interesting is the

---

1 The variation between *se* and the pronoun *hän*, which is the only third-person personal pronoun in written standard Finnish, and the process during which the dichotomy between *hän* as human-referring and *se* as inanimate or nonhuman-referring was established, have also received quite a lot of scholarly interest, see Laitinen 1995: 40–41, Paunonen 1993: 83.

fact that since the referent is a participant in the conversation, the act of reference unavoidably changes the participant status of the person referred to: on the one hand, a topical referent is brought into the conversation, and on the other hand, the participant framework is modified through reference to one (or more) of the participants, thus directing attention to him or her (or them). The fact that the referent is not just any identifiable entity in the context, but a person who is capable of taking the turn herself, makes the choice of the referential form especially consequential. It is bound to reflect the participant status of the referent and the speaker's interpretation of the participant framework up to the moment of reference, and it also functions to modify it from the current turn onwards.

Pronouns and the category of person

Even when the form being used to refer to a co-participant is a demonstrative, on some level, the person it refers to is also being addressed. In such use of demonstratives, speech is directed to the participants in such a way that one of them has a recipient status different from the others. Seeing demonstratives as devices for referring to persons involves a rearrangement of the system of referential forms. Put to such uses, the demonstrative is parallel to forms such as *sinä* 'you', *hän* 's/he' and *se* 's/he, it', that is, the set of forms that can be used to refer to co-participants in spoken Finnish. Thus we are no longer dealing with a tripartite demonstrative paradigm (*tämä, tuo, se*), as one would do when considering, for example, the semantic features of the demonstratives, but rather with one of a set of forms capable of being used to introduce a human referent into the conversation or to address co-participants in conversation (*sinä, tämä, hän*).

In fact, introduction of human referents as topics of conversation and addressing co-participants have rarely been examined as part of the same continuum. Forms of address have, of course, been a focus of interest in linguistics, but they have mostly been examined from a structural point of view such as their historical development, or from a sociolinguistic perspective involving the relationship between the speaker and addressee (e.g. Brown and Gilman 1972). Forms of address and referential forms have been kept apart, since addressing has not been considered to be the same thing as referring. In conversation analysis, practices for referring to persons in everyday conversations have received some attention, but the main research focus has been on reference to persons who are not participants in the conversation (cf. Sacks and Schegloff 1979, Schegloff 1996, Ford and Fox 1996). Reference to co-participants has occasionally been included in the studies concerning participation in conversation (C. Goodwin 1981: 154, M. H.Goodwin 1990: 239–257, Lerner 1993), but even there, the main emphasis has been on other practices.

The linguistic distinction which is under reanalysis in this paper, then, is the distinction between the third person and the so-called speech-act persons. In the linguistic tradition, the category of speech-act persons includes the first and second persons only, whereas third-person reference is always seen as belonging outside the speech situation. Thus, when semanticians have studied the relationship between linguistic categories of person and participation roles in speech situation, the third person has been excluded because "it does not correspond to any specific participant role in the speech event" (Levinson 1983: 69; Lyons 1977: 638; see also Benveniste 1971). This amounts to a claim that the third person does not correspond to the role of speaker or addressee. However, third person pronouns and demonstrative pronouns are in fact used for referring to co-participants in the speech situation, and they contribute to the participant role the referent has. This could be seen as evidence that the distinction between second and third person is not as sharp as has been assumed. The distinctions in the linguistic category of person can be made in another way, too, as suggested by Lyons (1975: 277–278). He emphasizes the distinction between first person and second and third persons:

> "There may be good reason to suggest, therefore, that 'first' (ego) and 'second' (tu) are not of equal status in the category of person: that the primary distinction is between 'first' (+ego) and 'not first' (-ego) and that the distinction of 'second' and 'third' is secondary."

This paper thus raises the following questions: how does a demonstrative pronoun work when used to refer to participants in conversation? How does it achieve reference and how does it affect the role of the referent in the situation? How does it compare to other ways of referring to participants in the conversation?

If we think about referring to co-participants in terms of participation, reference done with a second-person pronoun carries with it the role of addressee, and the referent may thus be projected to take the next turn (cf. Sacks, Schegloff and Jefferson 1974: 717, see also Lerner 1993). In this case, the other participants are excluded from speaking. If the speaker wishes to avoid this situation, and instead leaves open the matter of who should talk next, s/he needs another form of reference (cf. Sacks 1992: 573). As Schegloff (1996: 448) notes:

> "One regular alternative to "you" is a third person reference form, where the underlying issue may not at all be one of selection among alternative reference forms, but rather the choice of action which the speaker will implement, and/or to whom the utterance will be addressed."

In other words, reference to one participant affects the discourse identities of all participants. This can be taken as a starting-point when analysing reference to co-participants and the pronouns used for that purpose.

Demonstratives and the speech situation

This paper concerns one pronoun only, the Finnish demonstrative pronoun *tämä*, which can be translated into English by *this*. As has been discussed above, the Finnish demonstratives can be used independently for human (as well as non-human) referents; in other words, they can be used for human reference in the same way as third-person pronouns. Thus, in the data used in this study, the person-referring device is the demonstrative pronoun itself; in English translations, by contrast, a nominal head must be added to make the expression grammatical (see Appendix for the data with glosses and English translation).

In the data analysed below, we find the plural partitive form of this pronoun (the plural stem *näi-* + partitive ending *-tä*):

(1)

```
23 Raija : ja  se o-n     niil         lähellä: n- näi-tä    [tässä.
          and it be-3SG  like that     near       these-PTV  here
          and it is so close to t- these ones here
```

In Example (1), the speaker, Raija, uses the form *näitä* to refer to two of her co-participants. The present data is taken from a coffee-table conversation on a Christmas eve involving 12 participants, one whom is a 2-year old child. This is a family gathering - the participants are the hosts' children, parents, aunts and cousins.

Among the earlier studies of Finnish demonstratives, Laury's (1997) "non-concrete view" gives a good basis for studying the function of demonstrative pronouns in regulating the participation framework, as it is based on the analysis of these pronouns in actual face-to-face interaction. What is most important in Laury's description is that the expression of the referent's concrete distance from the deictic origo is not taken as the basic semantic feature of the demonstratives; instead, the social and interactional factors are considered more important in determining the use of demonstratives. Laury also shows that these pronouns are not only used to refer to objects and spaces but that they function dynamically to create or constitute place and perspective.

This is an appropriate perspective on the structuring of the speech situation: language is not used to refer to pre-existent entities in a pre-existent context, but it is rather used for constantly reorganizing the situation. This is also an appropriate point of departure for the examination of pronouns used to refer to persons. The context shared by the speaker and addressee becomes all the more complex when the target of reference is one of the participants in the conversation. In such situations, every referential form has the potential of modifying the status of all the participants in the participation framework. In spoken Finnish, the three demonstratives together with the third person personal pronoun *hän* form a system in which each of them occurs in different sequential positions in conversation and performs different interactional functions (see Seppänen 1998).

There are two points which I wish to make through the analysis of these particular data. The first point concerns the way in which a demonstrative pronoun modifies the current participation framework. I will argue that *näitä* is used in this example as a device for keeping the participation framework open for more than one recipient to take the next turn, since no participant is selected as the addressed recipient. The second point concerns the interplay of the referential form with the participants' gazes. I will demonstrate that the balance between the recipients is not gained by reference alone, but by combining speech and gaze.

Many detailed studies have focused on the ways in which talk provides a participation framework that includes the recipients of talk as well as including the speaker (cf. eg. C. Goodwin 1981, 1984, 1987, M. H. Goodwin 1990, Goodwin and Goodwin 1990). According to the terminology used in these studies, already classics, participation frameworks of conversation consist of participants' different discourse identities. The speaker's orientation to recipients with different discourse identities affects the formulation of their turns, for example a story teller's orientation to both knowing and unknowing recipients. (See also Seppänen 1996.) On the other hand, the formulation of the turn provides for certain discourse identities relevant for the activity which is performed by it. (See C. Goodwin 1987.) The role of the participants' gazes has been shown to be of central importance in this process. (Goodwin 1981, 1984.)

The interactive use of the form näitä

Keeping the balance between recipients

Turning to the data, the first question which will be addressed is: what is the function of the demonstrative pronoun *tämä* 'this' as a device for referring to a co-participant and thus modifying the current participation framework? In other words, what kind of interactive work is this speaker performing by referring to a co-participant with a demonstrative pronoun?

Raija's *näitä* 'these (people)' occurs (line 23) in a context in which the discussion has concerned the recent move of three of the participants, Sini, Timo and their 2-year old daughter Marjut, back to the neighbourhood after having lived elsewhere for a while. Immediately before this extract, Sini has told Raija how they managed to find a good house for the family. Liisa, who is Sini's mother-in-law, is also interested in this topic, and she joins in on line 2 and explains how she helped the young couple find the house.

(2)

```
01 Sini:    sit   me men-tiin      [si-tä ↑ kat-
            then  we  go-PAST-PSS  it-PTV  look
            then we went to ↑look at it-

02 Liisa:                    [>niim me ol-tii<      Marken (.)
                             yes  we  be-PAST-PSS  1nameF-GEN
                             >yes we were< at Marke's (.)
```

```
03            lak[kiais-i-ssa          ja [mä rupe-si-n       siellä ä:
              graduation party-PL-INE and I  begin-PAST-1SG there
              graduation party and there I started to e:m

04  Sini:    [nii::?                  [↑nii  joo  Marke-n
              PTC                      PTC   PTC  1nameF-GEN
              yea::?                   ↓oh yes at Marke's

05  Liisa:   [puhu-ma-an   (>että kato<) tietää-ks  ↑kukaan,]
              speak-INF-ILL  that PTC    know-CLT   anyone
              talk about    (>that you see<) does anyone know

06  Sini:    [lakkiais-i-ssa      (- - -)        ol-la        ]
              graduation party-PL-INE            be-INF
              graduation party  (- - -) to be

07           (.)

08  Liisa:   mm [::.
              PTC
              uhum::.

09  Raija:      [joo joo
                 PTC PTC
                 oh yes

10  Sini:    niin-ku  mei-l   ol-i          siel[lä e-
              PTC PTC  we-ADE  be-PAST-3SG   there
              you see there we had a-

11  Raija:                                [nykyinen asunto nii?
                                           current  flat   PTC
                                           (your) current home eh?

12  Sini:    nii::?   nii::?
              PTC      PTC
              ye::s?   ye::s?

13           (.)

14  Sini:    et  tota
              PTC PTC
              so that

15           (.)

16  Liisa:   ja Marke sano          sii-he sit ↑joo:: Bekkie-m mökki,
              and 1nameF say-PAST-3SG it-ILL then yes  Lname-GEN cottage
              and then Marke said to that ↑o:h yes Beck's cottage,

17  Sini:    ↑joo::=
              yes
              ↑ye:s
```

18 (Raija):=[juu
              PTC
              =yes

19 Liisa: =[ja siinä.
              and there
              =and that was it.

20   (0.5)

21 Liisa: kerro-v   [vaa.
            tell-IMP-2SG only
            please go on.

22 Sini: [°joo°
                        yes
                        °yes°

23 Raija: ja se o-n   niil   lähellä: n- näi-tä [tässä.
            and it be-3SG like that near   these-PTV here
            and it is so close to th- these ones here.

24 Sini: [>se o-n   täs-<
                                                       it be-3SG here
                                                      >it is here-<

As can be seen in lines 1 through 19 (and in the longer extract in the appendix), Sini and Liisa are both telling the same story, each from her own point of view. While relating the story, they compete both for turns and for Raija's attention. Liisa recognizes this competition and attempts to withdraw from it (lines 19–21). Thus Liisa finishes her explanation with a concluding phrase (*ja siinä* 'and that was it'), and when Sini does not continue hers – there is a half second pause in line 20 – she asks her to go on, thus explicitly giving Sini the right to speak. But with the silent *joo* 'yes' (in line 22), Sini indicates that she also will not go on.

Raija's comment (in line 23), which we focus on, thus comes in a context where both Sini and Liisa have been describing the house and telling how they found it, and, while doing so, each yields her turn in favor of the other. Raija's choice of reference form can be seen as a reaction to the delicacy of this kind of a situation.

What Raija is saying is that the new house is very close to to Sini's parents-in-law, Liisa and Keijo, who are the hostess and host of the coffee-party. The pronoun form *näitä* 'these' is the plural partitive form of the demonstrative pronoun *tämä* 'this', and here Raija is using the form to refer to Liisa and Keijo. Although Raija refers to a couple, the husband Keijo is not attending to the conversation, but moving around serving coffee. For this reason, we can interpret the demonstrative as referring to

Liisa, but treating her as one of a couple.[2] *Tässä*, which means roughly 'here', refers to the area where both Liisa's and Keijo's house and Sini's new home are, thus underlining how near the houses are to each other. (Here we can say that by using the demonstrative adverb *tässä* 'here', Raija creates a common ground in such a way that all the participants of the conversation, the house where they are, as well as the house which they are talking about, all belong to it.)

We can see here a phenomenon which is by no means restricted to Finnish conversation. Raija is performing a certain kind of interactive work, work which in other languages requires other devices. As we have seen, the situation here is delicate, and Raija's choice of referential form manages the balance of it. Liisa and Sini have been competing for the right to tell, and Raija is very careful in her orientation towards the both of them. If, on the one hand, she had addressed Liisa by using a second person pronoun, saying something like "and it is so close to you here", she would have displayed orientation towards Liisa and excluded Sini. The second person pronoun would, in such a sequence, contribute to a participation framework where the discourse identity of addressed recipient would belong to Liisa alone, and thus her position as a teller would be supported by giving her the primacy to take the next turn. If, on the other hand, Raija had commented on Sini's house with a turn in which Liisa had no part, she would have ignored Liisa's part in telling about it, and thus supported Sini's discourse identity as a teller. But what Raija is in fact doing is that she mentions something which is important to both the mother and to the daughter-in-law, that is, how close they live to each other. Her comment is formulated in such a way as to display orientation towards both of them as focal participants in the situation.

The topic of conversation is Sini's house. Thus Sini is the most natural addressee of comments on this topic: if the addressee were not linguistically marked, Sini would most probably be considered to have that role. Raija's lack of an explicit address form referring to Liisa (line 23) can thus be seen as an orientation towards Sini. And indeed Sini reacts to this orientation: she takes the next turn and gives a lengthy description about the advantages of the flat (see lines 24–38 in the appendix). But Liisa's position in the participation framework needs more support than does Sini's, as Liisa has joined Sini's topic later, and also because she has tried to withdraw from it (in line 21). Thus Raija has to mark her orientation towards Liisa more explicitly than her orientation towards Sini.

Raija does not address Liisa with the second person pronoun, but instead uses a plural form the pronoun *tämä* 'this', which displays consideration towards her as a previous speaker. This happens through a typical feature

---

2   During the entire extract, Keijo does not sit at his place at the table, but moves between the table and the kitchen fetching fresh coffee, and goes around the table pouring the coffee into the guests' cups. Thus, although the pronoun is in the plural and refers to a couple (cf. Lerner 1993), we can take it as referring more to Liisa than to Keijo. Raija's orientation to Liisa (but not to Keijo) with her gaze will be demonstrated later in more detail.

of the pronoun *tämä* when used in referring to a co-participant in conversation. Namely, each of the three Finnish demonstrative pronouns occurs typically in different sequential position, referring to a participant who has occupied a certain discourse identity. Very roughly speaking, *tuo* 'that' is the only pronoun used to refer to an unexpected referent, to someone who has been a quiet listener. *Se* 'that, it, the' refers anaphorically to a person who has been previously mentioned, and *tämä* 'this' refers to a person who has not been mentioned before but who has been the speaker of the previous turn or of some other recent turn (see Seppänen 1998 for details). This agrees with Laury's description of the basic meaning of these pronouns. According to Laury (1997: 59), "the use *tämä* involves the speaker presenting a referent to his or her addressee(s), while the use of *tuo* involves pointing out a referent." The person-referring *tämä* can be used to draw the recipients' attention to someone who is already salient in the situation, in other words, who is included in the current sphere of both the speaker and the addressee(s), to say something new about him or her. On the contrary, *tuo* can be used to point out someone who is not salient.

It is mainly the contrast between *se* and *tämä* which is relevant here. If someone has been talking about herself, then this person is both the speaker of the previous turn and a person who is spoken about, and both the pronouns *tämä* and *se* can be used to refer to her. In those cases the choice between *tämä* and *se* marks which role the speaker considers the most salient one – whether the referent is considered more as a person who is talked about or as a participant in the conversation. Thus reference by the pronoun *tämä* also has the flavour of treating the referent as salient and paying attention to her as the previous speaker. In the example analysed here, this feature of *tämä* supports Liisa's previous discourse identity as a teller, without however necessarily projecting her to be the speaker of the next turn. Thus *tämä* is used here as a device for keeping the balance between the two recipients.

Näitä and gaze

What are the discourse identities of the two recipients of Raija's turn, Sini and Liisa? Are they addressees of the turn? In linguistic terminology, the referent of a third person form can hardly be called an addressee, yet Liisa is here a focal recipient of the turn. Sini, for her part, is not referred to in this turn, and yet the speaker's orientation towards her is quite clear.

By looking at the participants' gazes we can further clarify the analysis of their discourse identities connected to this turn. The role of the speaker's and the recipient's gazes in creating and re-creating participation frameworks is well known from the detailed analyses in the classic studies of Goodwin and Goodwin (see C. Goodwin 1981, 1984, 1987; Goodwin and Goodwin 1990). When a person-referring pronoun is claimed to have the effect of modifying the current participation framework in a certain way, it is relevant to study also how the use of the pronoun co-operates with the participants' gazes. And indeed Raija's orientation towards both

Sini and Liisa can also be shown by studying the gazes of these three participants.

In example (3) below, lines 21–25 contain Raija's, Liisa's and Sini's gazes.[3] For the sake of clarity, only the gazes of the three focal participants are included here. In addition it is important to note that there are nine other people present. In example (3) we can see that, during her turn on line 23, Raija turns her gaze from Liisa to Sini and back again to Liisa.

(3)

```
                    Sini  ,, . Keijo
   21  Liisa:       kerrov [vaa.
       Sini         Liisa , .Raija
       Raija        Sini , . . Liisa

   22  Sini:               [°joo°
                            yes
                            °yes°

                    Liisa          ,.xSini,.xLiisa
   23  Raija:       ja se on niil lähellä: n- näitä [tässä.
       Liisa        Keijo      ...Raija   x
       Sini         Raija          x

                                         Raija
   24  Sini:                        [>se on täs-<
       Raija                              Liisa
       Liisa                              Raija   ,

                    Raija    x
   25  Sini:        <todella hyvin> siis viih[dytää,
       Raija        Liisa , . xSini
       Liisa        . Sini
```

Before line 23, Raija's gaze has been moving back and forth between Liisa and Sini, as she has turned her gaze towards the current speaker. On line 23, when Raija begins her turn, she is gazing at Liisa, who has been the previous speaker. But Liisa does not meet her gaze, because at that moment her gaze is oriented towards Keijo. Raija then turns her gaze to Sini, and as Sini has been gazing at Raija from the beginning of the turn, Raija's and Sini's gazes meet each other before the last syllable of the word *lähellä* 'close to'. After the word *lähellä* Raija stammers a

---

3   The transcription of gaze direction is adopted from the system created by C. Goodwin (1981) with slight modifications. The speaker's name on each line is in italics, and the speaker's gaze is marked above the line. Each recipient has a line under the speaker's line. A continuing line indicates gaze towards the recipient whose name is marked above the line. Dots indicate turning the gaze towards someone, and commas indicate withdrawing of gaze. When the gazes of two participants meet, there is an X on both gaze-lines to highlight the eye-contact. See the map in appendix 2 for the participant's placements at the table. Keijo is not sitting at his place but moving around serving coffee.

little before the word *näitä* 'these (people)', and while she is stammering, she turns her gaze from Sini back to Liisa and keeps it fixed there until the end of her turn.

If we go back to the beginning of line 23 to see what Liisa was doing, we notice that Liisa, who at the beginning of line 23 had been watching how Keijo manages the pouring of fresh coffee, turns her gaze to Raija. Liisa's gaze reaches Raija precisely at the moment when Raija glances at Sini. But Liisa is ready when Raija's gaze turns back towards her, and their eyes meet at the beginning of the word *näitä* 'these (people)', which is the demonstrative that refers to Liisa herself and to her husband. And Sini gazes at Raija during the whole turn.

One plausible reason for Raija to first turn her gaze from Liisa to Sini could be simply that Liisa is not answering her gaze. When a speaker gazes at a recipient, that recipient should be gazing at her (see e.g. C. Goodwin 1984: 230). This rule is violated in the beginning of Raija's turn in line 23. Raija needs eye-contact to continue her turn, and seeks for it elsewhere when Liisa is not gazing towards her.

However, the same reason cannot explain why Raija turns her gaze back to Liisa in the middle of the turn, as Sini does give her eye-contact. On the contrary, the reason for this action can be in the pronoun *näitä* itself: it is typical for reference with *tämä* 'this' that the speaker looks at the referent (Seppänen 1998). Yet it also appears that Raija is not satisfied with having Sini's attention only: after achieving eye-contact with Sini, Raija looks again to Liisa, as if wanting to make sure that both Sini and Liisa give her their full attention and act as her recipients.

Thus the final result of this gaze-analysis is that during her turn, Raija maintains eye-contact with her two recipients, but Liisa is in the focus of gaze both in the beginning and at the end of the turn. During the delivery of the actual pronoun *näitä*, Raija has eye-contact with the referent, or more precisely, with one of them, as the other referent, Keijo, is engaged in activities other than speaking and listening.

All the above observations support the analysis made here of the use of the pronoun *näitä*, and its effect on the participation framework of the situation. Through the reference with *näitä* the participation framework is kept open for two participants to act as focal recipients of the turn. Reference to one is formulated in a way which does not exclude the other from the possible speakership of the next turn. Hence the speaker includes both recipients in her gaze, but gives slightly more attention to the one referred to. In this way the speaker supports the referent's position by her gaze while she is not addressing her with a straight second-person pronoun.

Conclusion

To briefly sum up the results of this case study under discussion, the analysis made in this paper has revealed the following features of referring to co-participants in conversation with the Finnish demonstrative pronoun *tämä* 'this' (in the data in plural partitive form *näitä*).

First, the reference form *näitä* seems to be designed for responding to the delicacy of a context where two former speakers have to be attended to. Raija is using this demonstrative pronoun to refer to co-participants in order to keep the participation framework equally open for two recipients simultaneously. By her choice of reference form, Raija avoids giving the discourse identity of addressed recipient exclusively to one participant but not the other. Secondly, during the utterances containing the form *näitä*, the balance between the two recipients (Liisa and Sini) is not gained by reference alone, but by the combined effect of speech and gaze. The speaker looks mainly at the pronoun's referent, but gives a glance to the other recipient as well, and during the utterance she attracts the gazes of both of her recipients. All this makes it equally possible for both recipients to take the next turn.

We can now return to the question posed in the introduction about the distinction between the categories of third person and the so-called speech act persons. In the case analysed here, reference with a second-person form instead of the demonstrative pronoun which was actually used would have meant giving the role of addressee to one of the focal recipients and excluding the other. The consequences which the use of the second person pronoun might have had for the arrangement of the current participation framework were avoided by the reference done with a demonstrative pronoun. This reveals that, in Finnish, the demonstrative pronouns are devices for negotiating the area in between the second and the third person: not addressing the referent, but paying attention to her role as a participant in the conversation. While demonstrative pronouns are third-person forms, they still can be used as if they were speech act pronouns. That is, demonstrative pronouns indicate the referent's role in the speech situation's participation framework. Linguistically, this means that the difference between the she second person and the third person may not be as sharp as it has been traditionally thought to be. The deepest distinction might indeed be between the first person and other persons, as Lyons (1975: 278) has suggested. It is possible to think that between the second and the third person in the speech situation there is a continuum, and different languages and cultures move along this continuum in a different way.

REFERENCES

Benveniste, Emile. 1971. *Problems in general linguistics.* Coral Gables: University of Miami Press.
Brown, R. and A. Gilman. 1972. The pronouns of power and solidarity. In Pier Paolo Giglioli (ed.) *Language and social context.* London: Penguin Books.
Etelämäki, Marja. 1998. Kuva puheenalaisena. In Lea Laitinen and Lea Rojola (eds.) *Sanan voima.* Helsinki: Suomalaisen Kirjallisuuden Seura. 34–80.
Ford, Cecilia and Barbara Fox. 1996. Interactional motivations for reference formulation: *He* had. *This guy* had, a beautiful, thirty-two O:lds. In Barbara Fox (ed.) *Studies in Anaphora.* Amsterdam: John Benjamins. 145–168.
Goodwin, Charles. 1981. *Conversational organization. Interaction between speakers and hearers.* New York: Academic Press.

Goodwin, Charles. 1984. Notes on stry structure and the organization of participation. In J. M. Atkinson and John Heritage (eds.) *Structures of social action*. Cambridge: Cambridge University Press. 225–246.
Goodwin, Charles. 1987. Forgetfulness as an interactive resource. *Social Psychology Quarterly* 50:2. 115–131.
Goodwin, Charles and Marjorie Harness Goodwin. 1990. Context, activity and participation. In P. Auer and A. di Luzo (eds.) *The conteztualization of language*. Amsterdam: Benjamins.
Goodwin, Marjorie Harness. 1990. *He-said-she-said: Talk as social organization among black children*. Bloomington: Indiana University Press.
Itkonen, Terho. 1979. Zur Semantik und Pragmatik der Finnischen Demonstrativa. In *Festschrift für Wolfgang Schlachter zum 70. Geburtstag*. Veröffentlichungen der Societas Uralo-Altaica 12. Wiesbaden: Societas Uralo-Altaica.
Laitinen, Lea. 1995. Persoonat ja subjektit. In Pirjo Lyytikäinen (ed.) *Subjekti. Minä. Itse. Kirjoituksia kielestä, kirjallisuudesta, filosofiasta*. Helsinki: Suomalaisen Kirjallisuuden Seura. 35–.
Larjavaara, Matti. 1990. *Suomen deiksis*. Helsinki: Suomalaisen Kirjallisuuden Seura.
Laury, Ritva. 1997. *Demonstratives in interaction: the emergence of a definite article in Finnish*. Amsterdam: John Benjamins.
Lerner, Gene. 1993. Collectivities in action: Establishing the relevance of conjoined participation in conversation. *Text* 13:2. 213–245.
Levinson, Stephen C. 1983. *Pragmatics*. Cambridge: Cambridge University Press.
Lyons, John. 1975. *Introduction to theoretical linguistics*. 7. edition. Cambridge: Cambridge University Press.
Lyons, John. 1977. *Semantics*. Vol. 1. Cambridge: Cambridge University Press.
Pajusalu, Renate. 1999. *Deiktikud eesti keeles. Dissertationes Philologiae Estonicae Universitatis Tartuensis*. Tartu: Tartu Ülikooli kirjastus
Pajusalu, Renate. 2004. Viron *üks* ja *kõik*. *Virittäjä* 108:2–23.
Paunonen, Heikki. 1993. Suomen mieli – oikea kieli. *Virittäjä* 97: 81–87.
Penttilä, Aarni. 1957. *Suomen kielioppi*. Helsinki: WSOY.
Sacks, Harvey. 1992 [1964–1968]. *Lectures on conversation*. Vol. 1. Ed. by Gail Jefferson. Oxford: Basil Blackwell.
Sacks, Harvey and Emanuel Schegloff. 1979. Two preferences in the organization of reference to persons in conversation and their interaction. In George Psathas (ed.) *Everyday language: Studies in ethnomethodology*. New York: Irvington.
Sacks, Harvey, Emanuel Schegloff and Gail Jefferson. 1974. A simplest systematics for the organization of turn-taking for conversation. *Language* 50: 696–735.
Schegloff, Emanuel. 1996. Some practices for referring to persons in talk-in-interaction: a partial sketch of a systematics. In Barbara Fox (ed.) *Studies in Anaphora*. Amsterdam: John Benjamins.
Seppänen, Eeva-Leena. 1996. Ways of referring to a knowing co-participant in Finnish conversation. In Timo Haukioja, Marja-Liisa Helasvuo and Elise Kärkkäinen (eds.) *SKY 1996. Suomen kielitieteellisen yhdistyksen vuosikirja*. Helsinki: Suomen kielitieteellinen yhdistys. 135–176.
Seppänen, Eeva-Leena. 1998. *Läsnäolon pronominit*. Helsinki: Suomalaisen Kirjallisuuden Seura.
Setälä, Emil Nestor. 1891. *Suomen kielen lauseoppi*. Helsinki: Otava.

APPENDIX

The data with glosses and translation

CHRISTMAS COFFEE: SINI'S NEW FLAT

```
01 Sini:     sit    me men-tiin      [si-tä ↑ kat-
             then   we go-PAST-PSS   it-PTV look
             then we went to ↑look at it-

02 Liisa:                            [>niim me ol-tii<         Marken (.)
                                     yes   we be-PAST-PSS    1nameF-GEN
                                     >yes we were< at Marke's (.)

03           lak[kiais-i-ssa          ja [mä rupe-si-n           siellä ä:
             graduation party-PL-INE and  I  begin-PAST-1SG      there
             graduation party and there I started to e:m

04 Sini:     [nii::?          [↑ nii  joo  Marke-n
              PTC               PTC  PTC  1nameF-GEN
              yea::?           ↑oh yes at Marke's

05 Liisa:    [puhu-ma-an (> että kato<) tietää-ks ↓kukaan,]
              speak-INF-ILL  that PTC   know-CLT   anyone
              talk about (>that you see<) does anyone know

06 Sini:     [lakkiais-i-ssa      ( - - - )       ol-la              ]
              graduation party-PL-INE             be-INF
              graduation party  ( - - - ) to be

07           (.)

08 Liisa:    mm[::.
              PTC
              uhum::.

09 Raija:    [joo joo
              PTC PTC
              oh yes

10 Sini:     niin-ku mei-l ol-i           siel[lä e-
             PTC PTC we-ADE be-PAST-3SG   there
             you see there we had a-

11 Raija:                                      [nykyinen asunto nii?
                                               current  flat    PTC
                                               (your) current home eh?

12 Sini:     nii::? nii::?
             PTC    PTC
             ye::s? ye::s?
```

51

13   (.)

14 Sini: et   tota
            PTC PTC
            so that

15   (.)

16 Liisa: ja Marke   sano   sii-he sit ↑ joo:: Bekkie-m mökki,
            and 1nameF   say-PAST-3SG   it-ILL   then yes Lname-GEN cottage
            and then Marke said to that ↑o:h yes Beck's cottage,

17 Sini: ↑joo::=
            ↑yes
            ↑ye:s

18 (Raija): =[juu
             PTC
             =yes

19 Liisa: =[ja siinä.
             and there
             =and that was it.

20   (0.5)

21 Liisa: kerro-v   [vaa.
            tell-IMP-2SG only
            please go on.

22 Sini: [°joo°
                           yes
                           °yes°

23 Raija: ja se o-n niil   lähellä: n- näi-tä   [tässä.
            and it be-SG3 like that near   these-PTC here
            and it is so close to th- these ones here.

24 Sini: [>se o-n   täs-<
                                                           it be-3SG here
                                                           >it is here-<

25 Sini: <todella hyvin>   siis viih[dy-tää, se o-n   niin-ku
            really well   PTC enjoy-PSS   it be-3SG PTC PTC
            and we <really> like it there, it is like

26 Tinska: [°no nii joo°
                                       PTC PTC PTC
                                       °oh yes really°

27   (.)

28 Sini: ensinnä-ki siis se että me-hä aatel-tii
firstly-CLT thus it that we-PTC think-PSS-PAST
youknow the first thing is that we thought of course

29 et ku Helsingi-s useimmat ihmise-t asu-u
that because PLACENAME-INE most person-PL live-3SG
that because in Helsinki most people are living in

30 aika ahtaasti et me aatel-tii? (0.3) sillee
quite tightly that we think-PSS-PAST like that
rather small rooms so we thought? (0.3) y'know

31 yritet-tii sopeutuu sii-he et muute-taa
try-PSS-PAST adapt-INF that-ILL that move-PSS
we tried to face it that we must move into

32 johonki [↓ yksiö-ö
some-ILL one room-ILL
a ↓one-room flat or something

33 Raija: [piene-mpä-ä nii,
small-COMP-ILL PTC
a smaller flat yea

34 Sini: nii.
PTC
yes.

35 (0.4)

36 Sini: ja sitte toi o-n aika i:so ja
and then that be-3SG quite big and
and then that flat is quite big and

37 (Tyyne):mm::.
PTC
uhum::.

38 Sini: ja sit siin o-n hirmu kaunii-t maisema-t.
and then there be-3SG awfully beautiful-PL landscape-PL
and the landscape around it is awfully pretty.

39 Tyyne: nii [siin o-n ihana luonto kyl,
PTC there be-3SG lovely nature PTC
yes the nature there is lovely indeed,

40 Raija: [<vo:i: miten kiva joo[::>
PTC how nice PTC
<o::h how nice re:ally>

41 Sini: [joo::,=
PTC
ye::s,=

42 Raija: =jo[o
          PTC
          =yes

43 Sini: [joo.=
          PTC
          yes.=

44 Tyyne: =min' oon   lapse-na hiihtä-nyp paljon nii-llä
          I   be-1SG child-ESS ski-PCP   a lot those-ADE
          =I often used to go skiing around there when I

45   seudu-i-lla.
          area-PL-ADE
          was a child

46 (Sini): joo::?
           PTC
           oh yeah?

47 Keijo: TE-HÄ   asu-i-tte   si[inä
          you-PL-CLT live-PAST-2PL there
          you lived there didn't you

48 Liisa: [o-n   s:auna-t   ala:kerra-ssa ja?
                             be-3SG sauna-bath-PL downstairs-INE and
                             it has a s:auna dow:nstairs and?

49 Keijo: Tyyne-hän   asu   siinä ylhää-llä,
          1nameF-CLT live-PAST-3SG there up-ADE
          youknow Tyyne used to live there,

50 Liisa: uusi-ttu < ↓ keit[t i ö j u s t i i n   o-n]
          renovate-PCP kitchen   right now   be-3SG
          the <↓kitchen was renovated just recently there is

51 Sini: [↑ nii::
                           PTC
                           ↑yes::

52 Tyyne: [juu siinä iso-lla   mäe-llä,]
                           PTC there great-ADE hill-ADE
                           yes there on the big hill

53 Liisa: [jääkaapi-t [pakastime-t>
          fridge-PL   freezer-PL
          a fridge and a freezer>

TRANSCRIPTION CONVENTIONS

.	falling final intonation
,	level final intonation
?	rising final intonation
↑	rise in pitch
↓	fall in pitch
here	emphasis
JOO	increased volume
:	lengthening of the sound
°oh°	silent talk
< >	talk inside is spoken at a slower pace than the surrounding talk
> <	talk inside is done at a faster pace than the surrounding talk
(.)	a micropause less than two tenths of a second
(0.3)	silences timed in tenths of a second
=	no silence between two adjacent utterances
[	utterances starting simultaneously
]	point where overlapping talk stops
(− −)	talk not discernible

RITVA LAURY

First and only
Single-mention pronouns in spoken Finnish

Introduction

Third-person pronouns are ordinarily thought of as anaphoric devices, and their use is thought to be connected to textual cohesion. However, the use of third-person pronouns is not limited to contexts where the referent has already been mentioned. This paper examines the use and interpretation of all three Finnish demonstratives, *se*, *tämä*, and *tuo*, in ordinary conversation for first mentions of referents which are not concretely present in the context, and are not rementioned in subsequent discourse.

The paper has three main parts. First, I examine the use of first-mention pronouns in view of what has been said about them in previous research. I show that although first-mention pronouns have been claimed to refer to generic referents only, they can, in fact, given the type of information shared by the participants, refer to particular, individually identifiable referents. Secondly, I examine first-mention uses of the Finnish demonstratives in light of recent proposals regarding the semantics and pragmatics of these pronouns in order to see how well these proposals account for such uses and, conversely, what such uses can reveal about the semantics and pragmatics of these pronouns. Finally, I propose a functionally motivated explanation for the phenomenon of first-mention pronouns.

Data

The data for this paper consist of conversations between friends and family members. Some of the data were tape recorded by the author in 1991 and subsequently transcribed using the transcription system described in Du Bois et al (1992). The rest were tape recorded for the Turku spoken language project in the 1970s. Transcripts exist for these data in archives located at the University of Turku, but the portions of the transcripts used here were transcribed from audiotapes using the Du Bois et al system by the present author. For transcription symbols, see the appendix.

Background

Research on first-mention pronouns

As can be seen from two other papers in this volume, Duvallon (this volume) and Seppänen (this volume), and from several others (Brown and Yule 1983, Fox 1987, Ward et al 1991, Gundel et al 1993, Ziv 1996), and contrary to claims about the impossibility of such uses (Sanford and Garrod 1981, Heim 1982, Roberts 1989), third-person pronouns can be and are used at first mention of their referents.

In cases where third-person pronouns are used for first mentions of referents present in the context, their use may seem easier to explain. In such uses, the interpretation of the pronoun relies on both contextual and interactional cues, although it does so in considerably more subtle and interesting ways than one might first suppose, as can be seen in the work by Seppänen (1998, this volume), who shows that the use of pronouns for participants in conversation is motivated by, and at the same time shapes, the participation framework in the current interactional context, and Etelämäki (1996, this volume), whose work shows that the actional structure of conversation is a crucial factor in determining the choice of referential form, and who also makes the crucial point that talk not only points to referents in context, but also, in significant ways, creates both the context and the referents themselves, which in turn rely on that context for their interpretation. And as Duvallon (this volume; see also Tiainen-Duvallon 2002) shows, first-mention pronouns can also rely for their interpretation on the current syntactic environment, such as the argument structure and the semantics of the predicate with which they appear, even when lexical mentions of the referent do not follow until later in the discourse. Duvallon shows that reference formulation is an extended process, and that the lexical representation for a referent may not even be available to the speaker at the point where the initial, pronominal mention is made.

In those cases where third-person pronouns are used for referents not present in the context, and when no lexical mention of the referent follows, several researchers have suggested that the use of the pronoun is licensed by various types of links to surrounding discourse, and the reference is resolved on that basis. Such uses were already discussed, based on invented data, by Brown and Yule (1983: 220), who suggested that the reference of first-mention pronouns was based on what was predicated on them, as Duvallon also proposes (this volume). Both Ward et al (1991) and Gundel et al (1993) present examples from written data which contain first-mention pronouns, and suggest that their interpretation relies on the discourse context. Ward et al discuss their example in terms of anaphoric islands and show that pronominal mentions which are based on so-called inbound anaphora and appear unacceptable in de-contextualized sentences are in fact interpretable and indeed do occur in discourse (1991: 467). They conclude that the interpretation of inbound anaphora is based, not solely on a paradigmatic or morphological relationship between the pronoun and its antecedent, but rather on pragmatic factors, so that, for example, the mention that a person is an *orphan* will license a pronominal reference to the deceased parents if the surrounding textual context is rich enough. Slightly differently, Gundel et al (1993) suggest that first-mention pronouns are interpretable if the antecedent is inferable (Prince 1981) from the discourse context; they suggest that "the mention of someone waving towards a boat is enough to create and bring into focus a representation of people on the boat (Gundel et al 1993: 282)," so that a reference with a pronoun to the inferred people is then possible. Both Ward et al and Gundel et al support their discussion with actual examples of first-mention pronouns from written texts.

However, neither Ward et al (1991) nor Gundel et al (1993) explain why all referents paradigmatically or morphologically related to a preceding lexical item in sufficiently rich contexts, or all inferable referents, are not referred to with pronouns. Ziv (1996) provides a partial explanation when she suggests that the interpretation of first-mention pronouns relies both on scripts activated by the preceding discourse and Grice's Relevance Principle. Ziv suggests that such pronouns have referents which play a stereotypical, contextually relevant role in the script activated by the preceding discourse (1996: 60–61), and that consequently, they cannot refer to entities familiar to the addressee, only to referents which are 'type identifiable' in the sense of Gundel et al (1993). Thus, when using a first-mention pronoun, it is even possible that "the speaker could in fact not have a particular person in mind upon uttering the sentence, nor would he expect the hearer to visualize anybody specific; rather the referent would be anybody who fits the description of the relevant prototypical role player in the script under discussion (Ziv 1996: 60)". According to this view, then, first-mention pronouns are used for referents which are not individually identifiable to the addressee but rather only the type or category the referent belongs to is evoked by the mention.

A very similar point was made by Fox (1987), based on English conversational data. Fox suggests that in her examples, the first-mention pronouns have referents that are frame-evoked (67) and are used to refer to members of a particular category: in each of her examples, "the pronoun in question could be replaced with a category label, such as clerk, doctor or teacher (1987: 69)". Like Ziv (1996), Fox also suggests that in first-mention uses of a pronoun, the exact identity of the referent "seems to be unimportant; in a somewhat paradoxical way, then, a pronoun is used when the recipient is incapable of identifying the specific referent, and is in fact not expected even to try to identify the referent (1987: 67)."

Although, as suggested by the previous research, surrounding discourse context and inferability are crucial for the interpretation of first-mention pronouns, this paper will show that their referents are not limited to prototypical role-players. I will show that first-mention pronouns can also be used for specific individuals, as long as shared information is specific enough. Further, I will propose a cognitively based discourse explanation for the use of first-mention pronouns: I will suggest that they are typically used when the referents are not going to be reactivated in the upcoming discourse. Further, I will suggest how, in their first-mention use, the features of the three Finnish demonstratives call on different aspects of the context in the interpretation of the pronoun, while at the same time functioning to actively organize the context in certain ways. The following section briefly summarizes the research on Finnish demonstratives.

Research on Finnish demonstratives

Traditionally, the meaning of the three Finnish demonstratives has been considered to be based on concrete, spatial factors. Thus *tämä* has been described as proximal, while *tuo* has been described as distal. The placement of *se* on the proximal-distal scale has been more problematic, and it has been noted that *se* has an important anaphoric function (Setälä 1891, Penttilä 1963; for a summary of research on Finnish demonstratives, see Laury 1997: 53–58; see also Etelämäki, Kaiser, and Seppänen, this volume). In later research, social factors have become more prominent, first in the work of Itkonen (1966, 1979), who proposed that distance is not relevant for the use of the Finnish demonstratives, but rather the roles of the speaker and hearer in the speech situation and what they were able to perceive were what determined the choice among the three pronouns. In his comprehensive description of Finnish pronouns, Larjavaara (1985, 1990) combined the traditional, distance-based view of the semantics of the demonstratives with Itkonen's insight into their connection with speech roles, suggesting that *tämä* and *tuo* are speaker-centered, while *se* is hearer-centered, and that *tuo* and *se* are distal to the speaker, while *tämä* is proximal.

Itkonen's and Larjavaara's work, like that of their predecessors, is based mostly on invented examples. In contrast, the most recent research on the Finnish demonstratives (Laury 1997, Seppänen 1998, this volume, Etelämäki 1996, this volume) is based on audiotaped and videotaped, actually occurring data. This research has rejected the distance-based view entirely. Instead, it is strongly influenced by the seminal work of Hanks (1990, 1992), and claims that the use of demonstratives is based on interactional features such as the roles of the participants in the speech situation (Goffman 1981) and on the conversational action currently underway. Further, all three of the theorists above see reference in conversation as a reflexive activity, in that the use of referential forms not only reflects, but also actively constructs the context.

However, the three descriptions differ in their details. Laury's (1997) view is that the use of the demonstratives is based on the participants' actionally and cognitively defined spheres, which are constantly in flux as conversation proceeds, and are also defined by the use of deictics themselves. She suggests that *tämä* places its referent in the speaker's sphere, while *tuo* places its referent outside the speaker's sphere (which may or may not include the addressee). Actionally, *tämä* involves presenting a referent, while *tuo* involves pointing one out. *Se* places its referent within the addressee's sphere (59). Seppänen (1998, this volume), whose work deals with the use of demonstratives to refer to participants in conversation, has shown that the use of *se* for participants treats them as discourse referents, while *tämä* treats them as active participants in the conversation, in contrast with *tuo*, which places its referents outside the current interaction. Etelämäki (1996, this volume), on the other hand, has suggested that *tämä* and *tuo* mark their referents as still open to further characterizations, while *se* presents its referent as adequately defined for the current purposes, or 'closed' for further characterizations. In addition, according to Etelämäki, the demonstratives also index the participants' understanding of the nature of the ongoing activity, presenting it either as symmetrical, that is, already shared by the participants, in the sense of continuing the current activity (*se* and *tuo*), or as asymmetrical, that is, not shared by the participants at the point that the reference is made (*tämä*). Thus *tuo* and *se* are often used at points where the current activity is continuing, while *tämä* often involves a change or a reinterpretation of the activity.

After this discussion of the features of the three demonstratives as described by Finnish linguists, I will focus on their use in first mentions of referents not present in the interaction. I will start with uses of *se* in such contexts, followed with uses of *tämä* and *tuo*.

Use and interpretation of first-mention pronouns

The use of unstressed pronouns for referents which have not been mentioned before is interesting because it goes counter to many proposals regarding the nature of referential forms and their appropriate use. Most theorists agree that unstressed pronouns are used for referents which are topical in discourse and in the forefront of attention for the speaker and addressee (Lyons 1977, Ariel 1990, Ward et al 1991, Gundel et al 1990, 1993, Chafe 1976, 1994). A typical statement is that of Gundel et al (1990), according to whom "the most highly activated entities are not only in the speaker's and hearer's awareness, but are also at the center of attention at the current point in discourse. This status, which we refer to as 'in focus', includes activated entities which are likely to be continued as topics of subsequent utterances. 'In focus' is a necessary condition for appropriate use of (...) unstressed pronominals (1990: 444)."

In contrast to what we might expect, though, the referents of first-mention pronouns in my data were typically neither topical, salient, nor at the center of attention at the current point in discourse. Thus it strongly appears that being in focus is not a necessary condition for the appropriate use of unstressed pronominals. Instead, their use and interpretation can best be explained through reliance on interactional and cognitive factors such as the context jointly created by the participants in conversation and the nature of the shared information they have about the current context.

In terms of focality, it appears that first-mention unstressed pronouns are used for referents not present in the context just when there is no reason to pay special attention to the referent, that is, when the referent is not focal and is not going to become topical in the upcoming talk. Consider example (1), taken from a conversation between four young women friends who are preparing to go out together for the evening. Speaker A has just told her friends that she has visited a doctor's office because she has a sore throat and a temperature and is losing her voice. There is some conversation about the location of the medical office A visited, and after the participants have together established that, there is a short exchange on cigarette brands, after which A continues her story.

(1)

   1 A: Joo ja,
             PTC and
             Yeah and,

   2   ... Se oli   ^hyvä   tota   noinni,
             3SG be-PAST good   PTC   PTC
             It was funny like,

   3   ... Sinne pääsi   ^ensinnäki,
               thereto get.in-PAST first-CLT
             First of all, you could get in there,

   4   ... ^suoraa,
               direct.ADV
             right away,

   5   vaikkei   siel ollu   mittän ^päivystävää,
             although-NEG there be-PAST.PCP any-PTV on-call-PTV
             Even though there was no-one on call,

   6 R: ... ^Joo vai.
               PTC PTC
             Really.

   7 A: .. Mmm.

→   ... Ens *se* sanos   et tota noin ni et,
             first 3SG say-PAST that PTC PTC PTC that
             First s/he said that uh that,

   9   ... et,
               that

  10   .. niiku,
             PTC
             Like,

  11   .. siihe ois   vissii   ollu   ^puol tunti aikaa   et,
             3SG-ILL be-COND probably be-PAST.PC half hour-PTV time-PTV that
             It might have been in a half hour that,

12   … et,
      that

13   ^lääkäri=,
      physician
      Dr.,

14   .. oliks   se joku … Sironen,
         be-PAST-Q 3SG some PN
      it might have been something like Sironen,

15   .. vai mikä se oli   ja,
         or what 3SG be-PAST and
      or what was it and,

16   et   'hän.
      That 3SG
      That him/her.

The pronoun mention in line 8 is the first and only mention of its referent in the discourse. Even though the referent is not present in the environment, and is otherwise in no way topical or focal for the addressees, neither we nor the participants in the conversation have any trouble identifying the referent. The pronoun clearly refers to the receptionist at the medical office A had just visited.

As noted above, in her study of English anaphora, Fox (1987) found several similar cases in her conversational data. She, like several other researchers (Ward et al 1991, Gundel et al 1993, Ziv 1996), suggests that pronouns can be used in this way provided that the referent can be identified based on the frame (or script, or cognitive schema[1]) evoked by the preceding context.

If we adopt this explanation, as it seems reasonable to do, the identifiability of the referent mentioned with the pronoun in line 8 in example (1) relies on the similarity of the medical office schema shared by the participants. They all know that medical offices employ receptionists who reserve appointments for patients in the fashion described by A, and are therefore able to resolve the referent of the minimal referential form in the absence of any lexical antecedent. And, as was suggested by Fox (1987) and Ziv (1996), the addressees are not expected to be able to identify the particular, individual referent. Only the type identifiability of the referent is relevant here, and the mention is thus similar to a category label, such as *the receptionist*. In that sense, first-mention pronouns seem like an extreme example of inferables (Prince 1981), referents that can be mentioned using a definite noun phrase on the first mention due to an already evoked schema.

---

1   I am using the terms frame, schema and script interchangeably here to stand for previously acquired, schematic information. Although there are certainly differences in the use and meaning of these terms, I am not going to make such distinctions here.

However, in my data, the use of first-mention pronouns is not limited to the stereotypical role-players or type-identifiable uses found by other researchers studying first-mention pronouns. Speakers in my data use first-mention pronouns also to refer to particular referents individually identifiable to the addressees. Consider the following example, in which relatives gathered together for a Boxing Day party are discussing the problems of removing dirt from the cracks between the planks in wooden floors typical in Finland.

(2)

1 L: Sithä ^tuol oli 'tuolla,
then-CLT there be.PAST there
Then there was um,

2 .. mm,

3 ... mm ^Vaskijärvellä,
    V.-ADE
At Vaskijärvi,

4 ku,
as
because,

5 'siel kun ei voi ^imuroida [koskaa],
there as NEG be.able vacuum.1INF ever
you never can vacuum there

6 E: [mm]

7 L: ku [ei o ..] ^sähköö,
as NEG be electricity-PTV
because there is no electricity

8 E: [Miksei.]
why.NEG
Why not

9 ^Jaa 'juu juu [juu].
PTC PTC PTC PTC
Oh, I see, I see.

10 M: [@] @ @ @ @
11 A: [@ @ @]

12 L: [^Nii,]
PTC
Yeah,

13 ja siel on kanssa ne [...] ^vetäny vähän tollee,
and there be also 3PL draw-PAST.PCP a.little thus
and there they've also developed little like,

14 X   [((GROANS))]

15 L: ..^raoille,
        crack-PL-ILL
        cracks,

16   .. ne .. ^lattialaudat.
        DET   floor-board-PL
        the floorboards.

17   Ni,
        PTC
        So,

→   .. 'kerran ku *ne* ^meni,
        once   as 3PL go-PAST
        Once when they went [there]

19   ni siel oli 'ilmeisesti ^hiiret   kato tonkinu,
        PTC there be-PAST apparently mouse-PL PTC dig-PAST.PCP
        Apparently mice had been digging there,

20 E: Nii.
        PTC
        I see.

21 L: 'ettiny   ^ruokaa,
        look.PAST.PCP   food-PTV
        looking for food,

22   .. ^ruoanmuruja,
        food-GEN-crum-PL-PTV
        crumbs of food,

The pronoun *ne* 'they' (a plural form of *se*) in line 18 is the first mention of the referents in this conversation, and the referents are in no way central or topical in the discourse. All the participants in the conversation, however, know which family has a summer cottage at Vaskijärvi. Therefore, the reference to the people who are said to have gone there is eminently individually identifiable to all of the participants, speaker and addressees alike.

The interpretation of first-mention pronouns in cases like example (2) cannot be explained on the basis of cognitive schemas, which are generic by definition. A better model for explaining such uses is the concept of the indexical ground developed by Hanks (1990, 1992). The indexical ground refers to aspects of the context developed together by the participants during a conversation (see also Etelämäki, this volume, for use of this concept slightly different from mine), which forms the basis for the interpretation of indexical elements such as pronouns. The indexical ground is profoundly social and dynamic in nature, and its symmetry (or asymmetry) is crucial for the formulation and interpretation of referential forms in context. The more information the participants share about the ground, the more symmetrical the ground is, and consequently, the more the individuated and exact the reference can be (Hanks 1990: 48). The concept of the indexical ground thus combines the insight about schemas as generic information that members of the same community may share and the more exact information that those who are part of the same family or other social group may share, rely on and create in communication. The emphasis this model puts on the dynamicity of communicative events is also an important part of it. Participants do not enter conversations with ready-made referents, but rather referents are created as a result of interaction (cf. Etelämäki, this volume, Seppänen, this volume). In other words, in this view, frames or scripts do not come already populated with referents, but rather they are filled in or created as discourse proceeds.

The concept of the indexical ground is helpful for explaining the different interpretation of the first-mention pronouns in examples (1) and (2). In both examples, the interpretation relied on a place that had already been mentioned, in example (1), the medical center A had said she had visited, and in example (2), the community of Vaskijärvi. The mention of the places and what was said about the activities of the referents (see Duvallon, this volume) formed the indexical ground which was the basis for constructing the referent. In example (1), the indexical ground was not symmetrical. Only A had visited the doctor's office, and in constructing the referent, the addressees had to rely on their generic knowledge about medical centers. Thus the interpretation of the reference was generic as well, although A was referring to a particular individual. In example (2), the situation is quite different. All the participants share similar, exact information about Vaskijärvi and its residents, and thus the indexical ground is highly symmetrical, and the referents are particular individuals.

The Finnish demonstratives in first mentions

In this section, I will consider the use of the three Finnish demonstratives in first mentions to see whether these uses are consistent with the previous descriptions of the semantic and pragmatic features of these pronouns as described above.

Examples (1) and (2) both involve the use of *se* in first mentions of their referents. As discussed, the feature of *se* which distinguishes it from the other two Finnish demonstratives, *tämä* and *tuo*, is its textual relevance: it is the main anaphoric pronoun of spoken Finnish. The use of *se* is of course not anaphoric in first-mention uses, since there is no antecedent, but it does rely on the previous discourse for its interpretation in terms of relying on the frame-related knowledge evoked by it. These uses are addressee-centered (Larjavaara 1985, 1990) in the sense that their interpretation is based on knowledge the addressee has both of the frame and of the preceding discourse. In that sense, *se* also places the referent in the addressee's sphere: it proposes that the referent is identifiable based on information the addressee already has (Laury 1997). Further, as has been suggested by Seppänen (1998) on the basis of the use of *se* for participants in the conversation, *se* treats its referent as a discourse referent – the previous discourse, and not the speech situation, is the basis for the identification of the referent.

The use of the pronoun *se* in first-mention contexts is also highly consistent with the description proposed by Etelämäki (1996, this volume). In her framework, the referential feature of *se* is that the referent is closed, or 'known enough for the on-going purposes'. Broadly, then, the use of *se* tells the participants in the conversation that, as Etelämäki puts it, "the referent is adequately identified for the purposes at hand, and needs no further discussion (this volume)." For the types of first-mention uses of *se* in my data, where the mention is done with an unstressed pronoun, this is an apt characterization, as the referents are not rementioned or characterized in any way subsequently. And, as Etelämäki also suggests, *se* is used here in contexts which are symmetrical in the actional sense,[2] as they continue the already ongoing activity: in both example (1) and example (2), *se* is used within a narrative told by one of the participants; they occur in open sequences, as also suggested by Seppänen (1998).

In my data, *tämä* is also used in first mentions of referents not concretely present in the context. However, in such uses, and differently from first-mention uses of *se*, it appears that the present conversational context, rather than the preceding discourse, is used in the interpretation of the pronoun. Consider the following example, taken from a conversation among several women friends. Just previous to this excerpt, there has been a brief exchange about where M picked the mushrooms she is serving, followed by a dialogue between M and speaker A about A's summer cottage and the mushroom harvest there. This leads speaker A to turn to the other participants (line 23) to tell about a recent visit of speaker M's family to her summer cottage.

(3)

17 A: .. kyllähän siellä voi   sitte,
        PTC-CLT   there be.able then
        Probably it's then possible,

18 M: Toivot[tavasti].
        hopeful-ADV
        Hopefully.

---

2   Note that Etelämäki (1996, to appear) has further developed the concept of the indexical ground and its symmetry or asymmetry. She uses it to refer to the structure of the interaction at the moment a reference is made, in terms of whether the action is currently shared by the participants or not. This differs from the way it is discussed in Hanks (1990: 48–49), and the way I have used it in the discussion of examples (1) and (2) above, where the symmetry or lack of it have to do with the nature of the information shared by the participants and called upon in verbal interaction. See Etelämäki (this volume) for a more extended discussion of how she defines the concept.

19 A: [sieniä <x   poi]mia x> ihan vieläki.
            mushroom-PL-PTV pick1INF   even still
            to still pick mushrooms there.

20 M: M[m=].

21 A: [M=]m.

22   ... (1.0)

→ A: .. Ku 'nää .. oli <P siel P>
            as   these be-PST there
           When these (people) were there,

24   .. siellä ^meillä   käymässä   ja.
              there 1PL-ADE   visit3INF-INE and.
           There at our place visiting and.

25   .. Marjatta löysi   'hirmu hyvät   ^suppilovahverot <WH sieltä WH>.
              M.   find-PST terribly good-PL   funnel.chanterelle-PL there
           Marjatta found terrific funnel chanterelles there.

26 M: ... (1.5) Noist   ^jäi   'pieniä.
                     those-ELA remain-PAST   small-PL-PTV
           There were small ones left behind from those.

27   ... Siel oli   'aika paljo ^tulossa.
               There be.PAST pretty much coming-INE
           There were quite a few coming up.

The use of *nää*, the plural form of *tämä*, in line 23, is a first mention of referents not concretely present in the situation only in the sense that it refers, in addition to speaker M, also to (unspecified) members of her family who are not participants in the interaction, or even at home at the point the reference is made. We could say that speaker M is acting as proxy for her absent family who form the rest of the group the demonstrative refers to. Given that, simple proximity coupled with speaker orientation could be considered to be the semantic features of *tämä* which are relevant for its use here (Larjavaara 1985, 1990.) However, this example blurs the distinction between what should and should not be considered presence in the situation or even proximity (see also Laury 1997: 67–68): although M is present, her family is not, and they are in no sense more concretely proximal than were the referents of the tokens of *se* in examples (1) and (2), since they also referred to residents of the same city where the reference was made.

It seems more reasonable to say that this mention functions to place the referents, M and her family, in the speaker's current sphere, which for the purposes of this reference also includes the addressees. For the purposes of this use of *tämä*, the current sphere is thus defined to include not only M, who is in the same room as the speaker, but also the other usual occupants of the apartment where the participants in the interaction currently are (Laury 1997).[3] In this way, the mention indexes not only the relation of inclusion the referents in the current speech situation, but also dynamically creates the situation, the current sphere in which the referents are placed. Thus, the interpretation of *tämä* as a first-mention pronoun seems to crucially involve the present context, and not the preceding discourse, as was the case with *se*.

The features proposed for *tämä* in recent studies discussed above are also quite useful for understanding its use here. As shown by Seppänen (1998: 59–71, this volume), *tämä*, when used for persons present in the current speech situation, indexes the referent's role as an active coparticipant, so that it is typically used for someone who has just taken a turn, and it also functions in a way similar to speech act pronouns and other terms of address, so that the referent of *tämä* is likely to take a turn at talk soon after the reference is made, as speaker M does here. The use of *tämä*, according to Seppänen, is also likely to involve a footing change, a reorientation by the speaker toward his or her addressees through a change of the participant framework, for example, the addition of new addressees. This is so in example (3). Just prior to this excerpt, speaker M and speaker A have been conducting a dialogue concerning their experience at A's summer cottage; in the turn in line 23, A expands the participation framework by directing her speech not only to M, but also to the other participants (see also Seppänen, this volume, for a detailed discussion of the use of a similar case where a participant uses a plural form of *tämä*).

Further, as suggested by Etelämäki (1996, this volume), *tämä* is also used here in a context which is asymmetric in the sense that the turn the mention is made in begins a new activity sequence in the conversation which is not yet shared by the other participants. This agrees with Seppänen's characterization of *tämä* as a demonstrative which is used for the introduction of new topics or new points of view (Seppänen 1998: 60–66). A's turn, which begins in line 23, initiates a short narrative about M's visit to A's family's summer cottage and her success as a mushroom picker. As also suggested by Etelämäki for *tämä*, the referent, unlike the referents of the tokens of *se* in examples (1) and (2), seems to be open for further description and characterization, as shown by the fact that in this case, the referent is further specified in line 25, where speaker M is mentioned by name. The reference is thus further narrowed down to include only M, and not the rest of her family, making it different from the first mentions done with *se*, although the referent of *nää*, M's whole family, is not mentioned again.

In contrast to *tämä*, as noted above, the pronoun *tuo* has traditionally been considered to be distal in terms of its semantics (Larjavaara 1985, 1990), while Laury (1997) suggests that *tuo* places the referent outside

---

3   Intuitively, such reference would seem possible for the inhabitants or usual occupants of any space: it seems correct to say that either *nämä* or its (rough) English equivalent, *these people,* could be used, for example, to speak of the occupants of a room, house, or even a town or a country, even if none of them were present at the moment the reference is made: imagine a tour guide discussing the former occupants of a historical site centuries after the referents actually were there: *These people worshipped the sun.*

the speaker's (and addressee's) current sphere. Seppänen (1998: 71–81) proposes that *tuo* is used to point to unexpected referents from outside the current conversational context, and that *tuo* may initiate new sequences, although it is not as likely as *tämä* to be used for changes in footing: it tends instead to maintain the current participant framework. Slightly differently, Etelämäki (1996: 48, 29; this volume) suggests that *tuo* is symmetrical in its indexical feature: it maintains the current activity rather than starting new activity sequences. Etelämäki also proposes that *tuo*, like *tämä*, but unlike *se*, marks its referent as open for further characterization, and also that recipients of *tuo* have independent access to the referent, which is identifiable from the situation (1996: 48).

Example (4) below is an example of a first-mention use of *tuo*. In this example, taken from a conversation among several young women, speaker A (not the same person as speaker A in the previous example) has been telling about a case of scarlet fever at the daycare center where she works. She has mentioned that the elder sister of two children who had just enrolled in the program had been diaganosed and quarantined the very day the two youngsters spent their first day at the center.

(4)

```
19  A:   <F ja=,
             and

20       jos ne  ois       päivä myähemi ne .. m=uksut tullu,
         if  3PL be-COND day   later    DET   kid-PL  come-PAST.PCP
         if they had come a day later those kids,

21       ni ei   ne ois       tullu         ollenka.
         So NEG  3SG be-COND  come-PAST.PCP at.all
         they wouldn't have come at all.

22       Mut nyt ne muksut  oli     päivän  meil    tartuttamas,
         but now DET kid-PL be-PAST day-ACC 1PL-ADE infect-3INF-INE
         but now the kids were there spreading it around for a day.

23       ja  sit  ne meni    karantteeni.
         and then 3PL go-PAST quarantine-ILL
         and then they were quarantined.

→        Noi     ihmetteliki       kui niitte   Nokat   valu     koko aja,
         tuo-PL  wonder-PAST-CLT  how 3PL-GEN  nose-PL drip.PST whole time-ACC
         Those (people) wondered why their noses were dripping all the time,

24       ja  niitten  kurkut  o  semmoset iha   merkilliset,
         and 3PL-GEN  throat-PL be such    quite strange
         and their throats were really strange,

25       .. ja  Punaset  ja.
            And red-PL   and.
            and red and.
```

26   ... (.9)Sillo o,
             then be
        There are,

27   tommosi alkuoirei,
        such-PTV beginning.symptom-PL-PTV
        early symptoms like that,

28   niinku vähä flunssa [alkuoirei,
        PTC   little flu-GEN beginning-symptom-PL-PTV
        a little like early symptoms of the flu,

29 E: [aijjaa.
                              PTC
                              I see.

30 A: ja sit   nousee korkke kuume.
        and then rise   high   fever
        And then you get a high fever.

31 R: ... Huih.
            PTC
            Gee.

32   .. jos sul   onki   [sellane].
           If 2SG-ADE be-CLT such
           I wonder if you have one of those.

33 A: [@ @]

34   mut mul   oli   ennen tätä   jo.
        But 1SG-ADE be-PAST before this-PTV already
        But I already had (those) before this

35 R: ... Oli   vai.
            be-PAST PTC
            I see.

After telling about the new children's case of scarlet fever, speaker A uses *noi* 'those (people)', a plural form of *tuo*, to refer to some persons who have not been mentioned previously. The predicate *ihmetteliki* 'wondered' makes it clear that the referents are human (Duvallon, this volume), and the preceding discourse leads us to conclude that the referents might be personnel at the daycare center, whose job it is to observe the children in their care and who would have noticed symptoms of disease. Thus it is the preceding discourse context which helps in the interpretation of the reference. In addition, the form points to referents outside the current speech situation (Laury 1997, Seppänen 1998); the reference is also unexpected (Seppänen 1998: 72–77). This use of *tuo*, as predicted by Etelämäki (1996, this volume) is done in a symmetrical context, and continues the current activity of telling about the incident; it also, unlike *tämä*, does not alter the participation framework (Seppänen 1998).

Why is *se* not used here, although the referent is interpretable from previous discourse? One obvious feature of this instance of reference is that in this context, *se* is not a possible choice, since it is already carrying reference to the new children. The strongly anaphoric nature of *se* would encourage it, in this context, to be interpreted as co-referential with the earlier mentions of the children. *Tämä,* on the other hand, would encourage interpretation on the basis of the current participation framework, and would also index a change in it. *Tuo*, in contrast with *se* and *tämä*, points to a referent that is unexpected (Seppänen 1998) and outside the current situation. Although it indexes continuity of the current activity and participation framework (Seppänen 1998, Etelämäki 1996, this volume), and is thus an appropriate choice in this situation, through its feature of pointing to unexpected referents from outside the current context (Seppänen 1998, Laury 1997), it also indexes discontinuity in reference. However, in contrast to the description of the nature of *tuo* by Etelämäki (1996), this use of *tuo* does not seem open to further characterization, or at least it is not further specified. Instead, it resembles the uses of *se* in examples (1) and (2) in that its referent is not rementioned.

In this section of the paper, we have seen that although all three Finnish demonstratives can be used for first mentions of referents not concretely present in the context, only *se* and *tuo*, at least in my data, are used as first mentions in contexts where none of the referents are participants in the speech event. *Tämä* seems to index inclusion in the present speech situation so strongly that it cannot be used, or at least is not used in my data, for referents that have neither been mentioned previously nor have any relevant connection to the present context such as a proxy person who is present. In these data, the interpretation of both *tuo* and *se* as first-mention pronouns relies on the context created in the preceding discourse, and both *se* and *tuo* can be used in contexts where the current activity is continuing and there is no change in the participation framework. Differently from *se*, *tuo* seems to be used as a first-mention pronoun in a context where there is a change in referential continuity. In that sense, it points out a referent from outside the current context. However, since my data only contained one instance of the use of *tuo* as a first-mention pronoun, it is not possible at this point to come to a definite conclusion about their use.

Why are first-mention pronouns used?

Finally, I would like to address the question of the referential form. Why do the speakers in the conversations from which the examples are taken use pronouns instead of lexical NPs for first mentions of referents entirely new to the discourse? It seems to me that the use of pronouns for referents which are not especially prominent or topical has to do with the phonetic and semantic weight of pronouns. According to Chafe (1976, 1987, 1994), the use of pronouns for given referents, referents which are already in the forefront of the addressee's attention, does not require much mental energy. Chafe discusses this phenomenon in terms of 'activation cost', by which he means, roughly, the amount of cognitive effort required to bring to awareness a particular referent; such cost is presumably higher for referents which have not yet been activated than ones which are already active. One could say that pronouns do not have much cognitive buying power. This is why they can be used to activate both 'cheap' referents which have already been evoked, as well as referents such as the ones in the two examples above, which it is not necessary to strongly activate, since they are not going to or meant to become topical or focal.[4]

From another perspective, the cognitive processing instructions (Givón 1990) that come with first-mention pronouns propose to the addressee that it is not necessary to strongly activate the referent, because it will not become important in the upcoming talk.

First-mention pronouns could be considered an example of the iconicity of language, in that the form of the pronoun reflects both its cognitive level of activation and its importance in and for the discourse. Semantically light third person pronouns are used for first mentions of referents which are not important in discourse and will not be rementioned, and therefore are not intended to be strongly activated.

In the data I have examined, such pronouns typically have an evidential function; they give the source of second-hand information. What is important or focal in such cases is the information that has been learned from someone else, and not so much the source of the information itself. This is so in example (1), where the focus is on the events that took place at the doctor's office, and how the receptionist handled making the appointment, not the receptionist as such. The same is true of example (2), where the focus was on the activities of the mice at the summer cottage. The mention of the residents of the cottage had to do with the fact that they were the original source of the information about the mouse incident. And in example (4), the first-mention pronoun also referred to persons whose thoughts and observations were discussed within the narrative. In this sense, it is interesting that Chafe (1998: 108) notes that although subjects are normally given, even new referents can occur in subject position when they have an evidential function. In Chafe's data, the new subjects were full, lexical noun phrases, but it is evident from these data that even new pronominal mentions can occur as evidentials.

Another interesting aspect of this kind of use of pronouns is that they may provide a pathway for the grammaticalization of third person pro-

---

4   In accounting for referential forms in discourse, appeal is often made to the number of times the referent has been mentioned and will be mentioned subsequently. In this context, it is important to keep in mind that discourse progresses in time, and at the point where a mention is made, the subsequent discourse has not yet happened. In that way, we are on shaky ground when making claims about the effect of subsequent discourse on present forms. However, it is, at least to me, reasonable to think that speakers do make plans and that they have an idea of how important a particular referent is in terms of what they intend to say. And at the same time, and more broadly, talk that is being formulated now does have a bearing on what can be expected to happen next in the interaction.

nouns into particles and formal subjects. If we posit that the condition for the use of pronouns is the topicality of the referent, it is difficult to understand why they tend to develop into functions that are semantically empty. As Bolinger (1977) noted, it is possible that semantically 'empty' pronouns still bear traces of referentiality. These traces may be a result of the use of pronouns in first-mention uses in contexts similar to the ones described above, where the use is more connected with evidentiality than reference per se.

Conclusion

I have proposed that the use of first-mention pronouns is not limited to the expression of type-identifiable referents, but that they can be used for mentions of particular referents as well. I have also suggested that the descriptions of recent studies of the use and interpretation of Finnish demonstratives have offered significant insights which help understand their first-mention uses. Finally, I have argued that the use of such pronouns is connected to the non-topical nature of the referents, so that the phonetic and semantic lightness of the first-mention pronouns is iconically related to their use in contexts where the referent is not intended to be strongly activated. I have also suggested that the use of first-mention pronouns is typically connected with evidentiality.

REFERENCES

Ariel, Mira. 1990. *Accessing Noun-Phrase Antecedents*. London: Routledge.
Bolinger, Dwight. 1977. *Meaning and form*. London: Longman.
Brown, George and George Yule. 1983. *Discourse analysis*. Cambridge: Cambridge University Press.
Chafe, Wallace. 1976. Givenness, Contrastiveness, Definiteness, Subjects, Topics and Point of View. In Charles N. Li (ed.) *Subject and Topic*. New York: Academic Press.
Chafe, Wallace. 1987. Cognitive Constraints on Information Flow. In Russell Tomlin (ed.) *Coherence and Grounding in Discourse*. Amsterdam: John Benjamins.
Chafe, Wallace. 1994. *Discourse, Consciousness, and Time: The Flow and Displacement of Conscious Experience in Speaking and Writing*. Chicago: University of Chicago Press.
Chafe, Wallace. 1998. Language and the Flow of Thought. In Michael Tomasello (ed.) *The New Psychology of Language. Cognitive and Functional Approaches to Language Structure*. Mahwah, N. J.: Lawrence Erlbaum.
Du Bois, John W., Susanna Cumming, Danae Paolino and Stephan Schuetze-Coburn. 1992. Outline of discourse transcription. In Jane A. Edwards and Martin D. Lampert (eds.) *Transcription and Coding Methods for Language Research*. Hillsdale, N. J.: Lawrence Erlbaum Associates.
Etelämäki, Marja. 1996. *Keskustelu tarkoitteesta kamerataiteen oppitunnilla – ja pronominit tuo, se, tämä*. Pro gradu thesis, Department of Finnish, University of Helsinki.
Fox, Barbara. 1987. *Discourse structure and anaphora. Written and conversational English*. Cambridge: Cambridge University Press.

Gundel, Jeanette, Nancy Hedberg and Ron Zacharski. 1990. Givenness, Implicature, and the Form of Referring Expressions in Discourse. In *Proceedings of the 16th Annual Meeting of the Berkeley Linguistics Society*. Berkeley: Berkeley Linguistics Society.

Gundel, Jeanette, Nancy Hedberg and Ron Zacharski. 1993. Cognitive status and the form of referring expressions in discourse. *Language* 69:274–307.

Hanks, William. 1990. *Referential practice: language and lived space among the Maya*. Chicago: University of Chicago Press.

Hanks, William. 1992. The indexical ground of deictic reference. In Charles Goodwin and Alessandro Duranti (eds.) *Rethinking context: language as an interactive phenomenon*. Cambridge: Cambridge University Press.

Heim, Irene. 1982. The Semantics of Definite and Indefinite Noun Phrases. Doctoral dissertation, University of Massachusetts, Amherst.

Lyons, John. 1977. Deixis and anaphora. In T. Myers (ed.) *The development of conversation and discourse*. Edinburgh: Edinburgh University Press.

Prince, Ellen. 1981. Toward a Taxonomy of Given-New Information. In P. Cole (ed.) *Radical Pragmatics*. New York: Academic Press.

Roberts, Craige. 1989. Modal subordination and pronominal anaphora in discourse. Linguistics and *Philosophy* 12:683–721.

Sanford, Anthony C. and Simon C. Garrod. 1981. *Understanding Written Language*. Chichester: John Wiley & Sons.

Seppänen, Eeva-Leena. 1998. *Läsnäolon pronominit. Tämä, tuo, se ja hän viittaamassa keskustelun osallistujiin*. Helsinki: Suomalaisen Kirjallisuuden Seura.

Tiainen-Duvallon, Outi. 2002. Le pronom anaphorique et l'architecture de l'oral en finnois et en français. Doctoral thesis, Ecole Pratique des Hautes Etudes.

Ward, Gregory, Richard Sproat and Gail McKoon. 1991. A pragmatic analysis of so-called anaphoric islands. *Language* 67:439–474.

Ziv, Yael. 1996. Pronominal Reference to Inferred Antecedents. In Walter De Mulder and Liliane Tasmowski (eds.) *Coherence & Anaphora*. Belgian Journal of Linguistics 10:55–68. Amsterdam: John Benjamins.

LEA LAITINEN

Hän, the third speech act pronoun in Finnish

This paper deals with the use of the third person pronoun *hän* in different varieties of Finnish, namely standard Finnish, as well as non-standard varieties of spoken Finnish, especially regional dialects and folktales. The differences between the varieties in the use of *hän* are due to dialectal, contact and language planning factors. In modern standard Finnish, *hän* is used exclusively for human referents, whereas in regional dialects it refers logophorically to the person whose speech or thoughts are being reported by the actual speaker. The logophoric system has developed further in two directions: on the one hand, the pronoun is used for protagonists in narratives, and on the other hand, it has grammaticalized to an evidential particle of ignorance.

Introduction

Due to its indeterminacy of gender, the Finnish pronoun *hän* 'he or she' has often been mentioned in folk-linguistic discussions as a peculiar exception among the third person pronouns in the languages of the world, even as a reflection of sexual equality in the Finnish society. The same kinds of opinions are sometimes also put forward by linguists. For instance, in his classic article on logophoric pronouns (1974), Hagège mentioned the Finnish *hän* and the Chinese *tā* as rare examples of the lack of gender distinctions in pronouns. He presented the following Finnish example (1), where the pronouns are referentially ambiguous:[1]

(1)

    Juhani kerto-i Marja-lle että *hän* tul-isi hän-en kanssa-an.
    Jean a dit à Marie que il/elle partait lui/elle avec
    John tell.3SG-PAST Maria-ALL that s/he come.3SG-CON s/he-GEN with-3SG.PX
    John told Maria that he/she was coming with him/her

1   The example was borrowed from Cantrall 1969. It contained an unknown verb form *hullei* (translated by Hagège in French 'partait'), which I have replaced here with *tulisi*. I have glossed the example in English.

In his article, Hagège emphasized how difficult it is for a linguist to avoid the influence of her mother tongue on the generalizations about formal distinctions in the pronominal systems of other languages, especially in expressions of the relations between speech act participants. In addition, his examples, such as (1) above, show how generalizations based on reference grammars or even on native informants' intuitions can be questionable as well, at least in the case of standardized languages. Actually, the history and use of *hän* in Finnish is a good illustration of this very issue.

Paradoxically, the pronoun *hän* is logophoric in non-standard Finnish. Thus, the referential distinctions Hagège needed could have been created, for instance simply by contrasting the logophoric *hän* with the demonstrative pronoun *se*, which functions in speech as a general third person pronoun for human referents (examples 2a and 2b).

(2a)

Juhani kerto(i)   Marja-lle että *hän* tu-lis(i)   *se-n*   kanssa
John tell.3SG.PAST Maria-ALL that s/he come-3SG.CON s/he-GEN with
John told Maria that he was coming with her

(2b)

Juhani kerto(i)   Marja-lle että *se* tul-is(i)   *häne-n*   kanssa-an
John tell.3SG.PAST Maria-ALL that s/he come-3SG.CON s/he-GEN. with-3SG.PX
John told Maria that she was coming with him

Logophoric pronouns refer to the speaker in his or her reported speech or thoughts. In many languages, they are used especially in indirect speech – as a sort of second-order speech-act pronouns (see Hagège 1974, Clements 1975, Hyman and Comrie 1981). This is the main function of the pronoun *hän* in Finnish regional dialects as well. However, in standard Finnish, *hän* is not logophoric. It refers exclusively to human beings, whereas the pronoun *se* is used only for non-humans (and is thus comparable to the English 'it'). Of course, different human referents can still be distinguished in standard Finnish as well, for instance by using the demonstrative pronoun *tämä* 'this' in contrast to *hän*, as in example 3. This system is used in writing, especially in translations into Finnish from European languages with nominal gender distinctions (see Varteva 1998; Kaiser, this volume).

(3a)

Juhani kerto-i   Marja-lle että *hän* tul-isi   *tämä-n* kanssa
John tell-3SG.PAST Maria-ALL that s/he come-3SG.CON this-GEN with
John told Maria that he was coming with her

Juhani kerto-i   Marja-lle että *tämä* tul-isi   *häne-n*   kanssa-an
John tell-3SG.PAST Maria-ALL that this come-3SG.CON s/he-GEN with-3SG.PX
John told Maria that she was coming with him

This paper deals with the logophoric use of the pronoun *hän* (and plural *he*)[2] and its extensions in Finnish. In the next section, I will first briefly introduce some grammatical properties that *hän* shares with speech act pronouns.

Shared grammatical features with speech-act pronouns

The third person singular pronoun *hän* shares several grammatical features with speech-act pronouns. The most obvious common feature is that *hän* is never used as a determiner (**hän tyttö* '*she girl'; cf. demonstratives *se tyttö* 'that girl', *tämä tyttö* 'this girl'). This is true both in standard and non-standard Finnish. Other commonalities that *hän* shares with speech-act pronouns are distributed in Finnish varieties differently, as I will show in the following sections.

Codings of person in standard Finnish

As already mentioned, the restriction of *hän* to solely human referents in standard Finnish parallels it semantically with speech-act pronouns. Grammatically, *hän* is grouped together with the 1st and 2nd person pronouns in standard Finnish in two ways. First, it has a separate accusative case form with the ending *-t* (example 4a), whereas other pronouns and all nouns as objects have the ending *-n*, identical to the genitive (example 4b). Actually, *-t* was adopted into the standard Finnish from the eastern dialects during the 19th century. By contrast, western dialects use accusative forms with the ending *-n* (*minun, hänen* etc.); thus, in those dialects the personal pronouns as objects do not differ from other nouns.[3]

(4a)

Opettaja näki *häne-t* (/ minu-t / sinu-t / meidä-t / teidä-t / heidä-t)
Teacher saw 3SG-ACC 1SG-ACC 2SG-ACC 1PL-ACC 2PL-ACC 3PL-ACC
The teacher saw her/him (me / you / us / you / them)

(4b)

Opettaja näki *se-n* (/ *tämä-n tytö-n*)
Teacher saw it-GEN this-GEN girl-GEN
The teacher saw it (this girl)

Secondly, when *hän* is used as a genitive modifier, a congruent possessive suffix must be added to its head in standard Finnish. This also holds true for all personal pronouns (example 5a), as opposed to other pronouns and nouns (5b).

---

2   The pronoun *he* 'they' has in speech the same logophoric properties as *hän*; it contrasts with the pronoun *ne* 'they'. In standard Finnish *he* refers to human entities, *ne* to non-humans. In this paper, I will concentrate on *hän*.

3   The specifically human interrogative pronoun (*kuka*) also has a separate accusative case with *-t* (*kenet*) in standard and eastern Finnish.

(5a)

minu-n poika-ni 'my son'
I-GEN son-1SG.PX

meidä-n poika-mme 'our son'
we-GEN son-1PL.PX

sinu-n poika-si 'your son'
you-GEN son-2SG.PX

teidä-n poika-nne 'your son'
you-GEN son-2PL.PX

häne-n poika-nsa 'his/her son'
s/he-GEN son-3SG.PX

heidä-n poika-nsa 'their son'
they-GEN son-3PL.PX

(5b)

tuo-n poika 'the son of that one'
that-GEN son

noide-n poika 'the son of those ones'
those-GEN son

se-n / tämä-n naise-n poja-t
the-GEN / this-GEN woman-GEN son-PL
the sons of the / this woman

niide-n / näide-n nais-ten poja-t
the-GEN / these-GEN women-PL.GEN son-PL
the sons of the / these women

In non-standard varieties of Finnish, the possessive suffixes are not used as regularly. In colloquial speech of today, they are disappearing in many positions; in dialects, the system is more complex than in the standard language (Paunonen 1995, Nuolijärvi 1986). As is usual in many languages, the standardization of Finnish directed the grammatical forms toward more simple, regular, and symmetrical systems (Laitinen 2004).

In any case, it is noteworthy that the 3rd person pronoun *hän* resembles the 1st and 2nd person pronouns in standard Finnish in some respects both semantically and morphosyntactically. This fact puts into doubt the classic descriptions of the third person as a non-person, opposed both in grammar and meaning to speech act persons, the genuine indexicals of speech (cf. Benveniste 1966: 251–257, Lyons 1977: 638). Actually, as shown in more recent studies, the indexicality of NPs should not be seen as a dichotomy but rather as a continuum, or as a potentiality for the speech act status (cf. Putnam 1975; for Finnish, see Seppänen 1996, Laitinen 1997, Laury 2001 and 2002, and Helasvuo 2001 i.a.). This becomes most evident when one analyzes data from ordinary speech. Next, we will look at the indexical nature of *hän* in light of certain modal constructions in spoken Finnish.

Constructions of necessity in dialects

One grammatical property connecting *hän* with 1st and 2nd person pronouns is its case marking in constructions of necessity, a very special morphosyntactic group of expressions in Finnish. These constructions have two features that make them stand out in the grammar of Finnish. First, while verbs normally agree in person and number with the nominative subject of the clause, the modal verbs of necessity (e.g. *täytyä* 'must, have to' and *pitää* 'ought to') are always used in the 3rd person singular form. Secondly, the case marking of subjects in these constructions is non-canonical as well: prototypical subjects are in the genitive case but nominative is also used in certain subject contexts.

In the modal contexts of necessity, the case marking system of subjects is different in standard and non-standard varieties. In standard Finnish, it is based purely on propositional meanings and does not have any connection to aspects of the speech event. The nominative marking is allowed only in the so-called existential constructions (see example 6a).[4] Otherwise, the case is genitive (see 6b). By contrast, in dialects, the case marking depends on the degree of the indexicality of the noun phrase, i.e. the speech act status of its referent. In brief, the genitive is used for the indexical NPs, most typically the speech act pronouns that have at least potential speech act participants as referents. Instead, the nominative case belongs to less indexical or even pure referential NPs – mostly to generic, inanimate and abstract subjects. If placed in the referential hierarchy of Noun Phrase types, arranged by Silverstein (1976) on the basis of case marking in a multilingual corpus, the NPs marked by genitive would find their place at the indexical end and the ones in nominative case at the pure referential end of the cline. (For the concept of referential indexicality and its metapragmatic interpretation, Silverstein 1981, 1987; in this volume, see Etelämäki.)

(6)

a. Minu-lla pitä-isi olla *morsian*
I-ADE shall-CON.3SG be-INF bride
I should have a bride

b. *Morsiame-n* pitä-isi ol-la kaunis
bride-GEN shall-CON.3SG be-INF beautiful
The bride should be beautiful
It's necessary for the bride to be beautiful

c. *Morsian* pitä-isi ol-la kaunis
bride.NOM shall-CON.3SG be-INF beautiful
A bride should be beautiful
It's necessary that the bride is beautiful

However, as illustrated in examples 6b and 6c,[5] animate NPs in the middle of the hierarchy can be conceptualized either as speech act persons, or as 'non-persons' without any participant role in a speech act. This happens by means of case marking, and the two options create crucial

---

4   This system is a somewhat failed result from an effort to standardize the case marking in the 19th century. – For the term existential sentence, Jespersen 1992 [1924]: 154–156; for its use in Finnish, Vilkuna 1989: 155–160, Helasvuo 2001: 7, 61–63, 97–103. For case marking in constructions of necessity in Finnish, Laitinen and Vilkuna 1993, Laitinen 1995 and 1997, Sands and Campbell 2001.
5   The examples in this section are fabricated and modified from an extensive corpus of regional dialects used in Laitinen 1992; for authentic examples, see Laitinen 1995 and 1997.

differences in meaning. First, in example 6b (genitive), the bride is treated as an intentional, personal being, whereas in example 6c (nominative), it is perceived as a generic and non-personal entity. At the same time, there is a difference in the modal function of the verb, as the translations above indicate. In 6b, the modality must be interpreted as an agent-oriented, internal obligation: either a deontic duty of the bride or her dynamic compulsion. In 6c instead, the necessity of a beautiful bride is external, based on epistemic or practical inferences of the speaker (cf. von Wright 1963, 1971). Thirdly, and most importantly, the modal scope also results in differences in the speech-act status of the NPs. In 6b, the obligation can be verbally directed to or uttered by the referent of the NP (marked by genitive). Thus, she is at least a potential speech act participant. In 6c, even the faculty of speech of the subject (marked by nominative) is irrelevant; for instance, the speaker could be seeking himself a bride from a group of several beautiful candidates.

This possibility to manipulate the indexicality of a referent is not open to 1st and 2nd person pronouns. Nominative, the case for non-speaking referents, is naturally an excluded option for speech-act persons. This restriction applies to *hän* as well; unlike for instance the 3rd person pronoun *se* 's/he' in speech, it is always marked by genitive (7).

(7)

Häne-n pitä-isi olla kaunis.
S/he-GEN shall-CON.3SG be-INF beautiful
S/he must be beautiful

We have seen that in standard Finnish, the pronoun *hän* bears a close resemblance to speech act pronouns grammatically. It does not function as a determiner, it has its own accusative form as a patient, and it receives a congruent possessive suffix on its head when functioning as a genitive modifier. In regional dialects as well, case marking in constructions of necessity shows that *hän* finds its place beside speech act pronouns in referential hierarchy. In the spoken language, the indexicality of *hän* is even more evident than in standard Finnish. Next we will consider the metapragmatic status of logophoric pronouns and verbs used with them.

Logophoric hän *in the spoken language*

In this section, I will discuss the logophoric functions of *hän* in Finnish dialects. First I will consider the referential potential of the logophoric *hän* compared to the third person pronoun *se* and, on the other hand, speech act pronouns. Then I will consider the metapragmatic contexts of logophoric use with respect to the verbs used in the main clause. The discussion of the use of logophoric pronouns with expressions of thought, perception, motives, and intentions will lead into a discussion of non-human referents of *hän*, such as animals.

Logophoric pronoun and speech-act persons

The logophoricity of the 3rd person pronouns *hän* 's/he' and *he* 'they' in Finnish dialects was discovered and empirically studied almost a hundred years before Hagège's article, referred to in the Introduction, was published, even though the present term was not used yet in Finnish linguistics. During the last decades of the 19th century, Finnish researchers published comprehensive syntactic studies based on the data they obtained on their field trips in different parts of Finland. Among other things, the logophoricity of *hän* was thoroughly described in several studies. The next example (8) is from Setälä (1883: 85).[6] Setälä's translation shows that *hän* is most typically used in an indirect reported speech context, co-referentially with the subject of the reporting clause (*se* in example 8):

(8)

> *Se* sano, että kyllä *hän* tiätää mitä se tekee
> s/he said that AFF LOG knows what.PTV s/he does
> S/he said that surely s/he knows what s/he (another person) is doing

Today, several logophoric phenomena are known in different European languages, especially as functions of long-distance and non-anaphoric reflexives (see e.g. Reuland and Koster 1991, Brinton 1995). The logophoricity of *hän* in Finnish dialects is, however, not a secondary function of the pronoun. It behaves similarly to the real logophoric pronouns in Western African languages, and it is morphologically distinct from both the 3rd person pronoun (*se*) in spoken Finnish and from the reflexive pronoun (*itse*) in all Finnish varieties. In many cases, its antecedent is the matrix subject, but a non-subject may also serve as antecedent. *Hän* may be separated from the antecedent by several clauses and even extend across utterance boundaries; as with logophoric pronouns in general, semantic or discourse factors seem to control its use more than syntactic conditions.

The logophoric pronouns closest to the area where Finnish is spoken can be found in the Saami languages. The third person singular pronoun (*son/sun* 's/he', as well as the 3. person *sij* 'they'), which has been thought to be even etymologically related to the Finnish *hän*, is syntactically, semantically and in terms of its grammaticalized functions completely parallel to the Finnish *hän* (see Laitinen 2002; SAS: 208). In contrast, in the close relatives of Finnish, Estonian, Votic and Livonian, the pronouns corresponding to *hän* (e.g. the Estonian *en-*) function as reflexive pronouns (see. SAS mp., EKG: 201–202). This is not surprising, since in both cases we are dealing with self-reference.[7]

---

6 See also Cannelin 1888, Latvala 1894, 1899, Sirelius 1894, Kannisto 1897, 1902.
7 Already E. N. Setälä (1883: 84–) paralleled Finnish logophoric pronouns with reflexive pronouns in Latin.

Because the oldest documentation of spoken Finnish dates from the 19th century, it is not easy to define the age of the logophoric function of *hän*. One piece of evidence is that the logophoric pronouns *hän* and *he* were used by Finnish-speaking people in Central Scandinavia, the so-called forest Finns, whose ancestors had emigrated from Eastern Finland during the 16th and 17th centuries. Because Swedish has no logophoric pronouns, *hän* must thus have been used logophorically in eastern varieties of Finnish at least for four or five hundred years ago. Example 9, which was recorded by Mägiste (1960: 51) from the last forest Finns, shows that the logophorics survived until the fall of the language:

(9)

    Se toimitti ihe tuo-n, jotta *hän* käv ja varast.
    S/he told   REFL that-ACC that LOG went and stole
    S/he told it her/himself that it was s/he who went and stole it

Today, the same pronouns are used in Northern Sweden by speakers of Tornedal Finnish, called Meänkieli ('Our Language') by natives. They have been accepted into the standard language as well. The next example is presented in the reference (and normative) grammar of Meänkieli (Kenttä & Pohjanen 1996: 88).[8]

(10)

    Se kehu,   ette *hään* se oon friski mies.
    s/he boasted that LOG CL is   strong man
    He boasted that he is a real strong man

In Finland proper, *hän*, as has been noted, is logophoric only in regional dialects, not in the standard. *Hän* is also losing ground in urban spoken language, as humans are mostly referred to with *se* (see Paunonen 1995: 165–177; Nuolijärvi 1986: 178–188). However, the logophoric *hän* is still used even in the spoken language, as can be seen from the following example (Tiainen 1998: 521). In this example, *se* refers to two singers, both Tapani Kansa (in lines 3, 4 ja 6) and Sting (in line 5). In contrast, *hän* refers unambiguously to Tapani Kansa, whose words are being quoted in lines 4–5.

(11)

    1 no joka tapaukse-s ni, kuul-tiin sit juttu-u
         well any case-INE so hear-PASS then story-PTV
    2 et Tapani Kansa ol-i
         that forename surname be-3SG.PAST

---

[8] In 1990's, Meänkieli received the satus of an official minority language in European Union, which, in addition to the revitalization of the language, also promoted its standardization. Probably, the 3rd person logophoric pronouns in the neighbouring Saami languages (Laitinen 2002) also support the longevity of these expressions in Meänkieli.

> 3 ku   *se* on   levyttä-ny nyt Stingi-n   piisi-n,
>   when s/he be.3SG record-PTC now Sting-GEN piece-ACC
> 4 ni *se*   ol-i   sano-nu et Stingi on saatana-n huono laulaja nii et,
>   so s/he be-PAST say-PTC that Sting is Satan-GEN bad   singer so that
> 5 *hän* laula-a   paljo paremmin *se-n* piise-j-ä
>   LOG sing-3SG.PRS much better s/he-GEN piece-PL-PTV
> 6 ku   *se* on nyt jonku   tämmöse-n   kevätlaulu-n   sieltä, ploka-nnu.
>   When s/he has now some-ACC this.kind.of-ACC spring.song-ACC there cull-PTC

Well, anyway, we heard then a story (2) that Tapani Kansa had, (3) because he has now recorded Sting's piece, (4) he had said that Sting is a damn bad singer. (5) He sings much better Sting's pieces himself (6) as he has now picked this spring song there.

In this example, *hän* refers canonically as a logophoric third-person pronoun to the speaker of the quoted utterance and corresponds to the first person in the direct quote. However, the logophoric pronoun *hän* can also refer to the addressee of the quoted dialogue in spoken Finnish, corresponding to the second person in the direct quote. In these cases, the main clause will usually have a directive speech verb of asking or requesting. In the next two examples (12 and 13) the verbs are *esittää* 'propose' and *kysyä* 'ask'; the recipient of the quoted directive is referred to with *hän*.

(12)

> minä *esit-i-n*   tä-lle   lääkäri-lle että jos *hän* tarkasta-is minu-wa vähäse.
> I propose-PAST-1SG this-ALL doctor-ALL that if LOG examine-CON me-PTV a.bit
> I proposed to this doctor that s/he could examine me a little

(13)

> se *kysy-i*   isä-lt   sit   osaa-k *hän* ruatti-i.
> s/he ask-PAST father-ELA then can-Q LOG Swedish-PTV
> S/he asked the father if he was able to speak Swedish

As can be seen, then, *hän* will elevate the status of the recipient of a request or question into that of a speech act participant. It should also be noted that in these examples, the main clause antecedents of *hän* are *lääkäri* 'doctor' in (12) and *isä* 'father' in (13). In regional dialects, *hän* is commonly used to refer to familiar persons who have higher status or are otherwise worthy of respect, such as parents, clergy, or officials, even when their speech is not being quoted. This has been considered a politeness function of *hän* (e.g. Vilppula 1989). In the next examples from 1970's, the dialect speaker being interviewed asks questions of the linguist using *hän* as a polite form of address:[9]

---

9 The use of third person as a deference form is not frequent today, because standardizers of Finnish in the 19th century preferred second person plural forms for polite address (see e.g. Suomalainen 1885).

(14)

    Gyl mar mä saa *häne-l* kaffe   keittä?
    Surely I may LOG-ALL   coffee.PTV boil-INF
    May I make some coffee for him/her ['for you']?

    Oli-ks *hän* äitiempäiväl   koto?
    was-Q LOG Mother's.Day-ADE at.home
    Was s/he [the interviewer] at home on Mother's Day?

Politeness can also be shown to derive from logophoricity. As we have seen, *hän* refers to potential addressees in interactive situations that are likely to arise in the speech community. These persons will often be second person addressees of questions or requests due to their position. Occasionally, in regional dialects, *hän* will refer to participants in the speech event in an even more general fashion:

(15)

    Vissii-kii-hä *se* jo   iltapäivä-st tul-loo,
    certainly-CL-CL s/he already afternoon-ELA come-PAST
    S/he is coming certainly already in the afternoon
    ku   *hää* jo   aamupäivä-st käsk   marj-oi   poimi-maa.
    because LOG already before.noon-ELA order.PAST berry-PL.PTV pick-INF.ILL
    because s/he ordered (us) to pick berries already before noon.

(16)

    me sano-ttiim   päivä-ä *hä-llej* ja *häv* vasta-s
    we say-PASS.PAST day-PTV LOG-ALL and LOG answer-PAST
    We said her/him Good Day and s/he ₗₒG answered

In example (15), the subject of the verb of movement *tulla* 'come' is the non-logophoric, anaphoric *se*. The coreferential subject of the speech act verb *käskeä* 'order', however, is *hän*. In example (16), *hän* refers to the same person, first as a recipient of talk and then as a speaker.

As we have seen, the logophoric pronoun used in narration can stand for both participants in a dialog: the one speaking and the one being spoken to. In the following narrative (17), the referent of *hän* remains constant even though the referent's participant role changes from the addressee (in line 3) to the speaker (in lines 4 and 7). The coreferential *se* is used non-logophorically (in lines 1, 2, 4 and 6).

(17)

   1 No sitten *si-tä*   tuota tervehti-mä-än ja ei kun totia   kaatamaan,
      well then s/he-PTV well greet-INF-ILL and no but toddy-PTV pour-IN-ILL
   2 ja anta-neet *si-lle-kin* ja kysy-neet että
      and give-PTC.PL s/he-ALL-CL and ask-PTC.PL that
→3 mistä   on *hän* ja kuka *hän* on.
      where from is LOG and who LOG is
→4 No *se*, että ei   *hän* etäältä ole, että kyllä *hän* täältä kirkolta on.
      well s/he that NEG.3SG LOG far.off be   that sure LOG here.from church-ELA is
   5 *Se* ei   selittä-nyt nii-lle   olosuhde-tta-an   se-n paremmin.
      s/he NEG.3 explain-PTC they-ALL circumstance-PTV-PX it-GEN better
   6 No *se*   sitten teh-nyt seura-a   nii-den kanssa, joi toti-a tunnin ajan – –
      well s/he then do-PTC company-PTV they-GEN with drank toddy-PTV hour time
→7 Ja sitten teki lähtö-nsä poikkeen, että nyt *hän* lähtee poikkeen.
      And then did leaving-PX away that now LOG goes away

Well, then (they went) to greet (him) and (started) to pour toddy, (2) and they gave him too and asked that (3) where he came from and who he$_{\text{LOG}}$ was. (4) Well, he (said) that he doesn't come from far away, that he comes from the same village. (5) He did not explain them his situation that better. (6) So, then he kept company with them, he drank toddy one hour – –. (7) And then he was about to leave, like: now he is going away.

Example (17) also provides evidence for the well-known fact that Finnish dialects make no clear syntactic distinction between direct and indirect quotes (Kuiri 1984).[10] In this example, the expressions of time and place (*nyt* 'now' in line 7 and *täältä* 'here from' in line 4) represent the deictics of the actual speech situation as they would in a direct quote. The past tense of narration also changes to present tense in these contexts. The particle *että* 'that' marks the beginning of the quoted speech in lines 2, 4 ja 7; this is typical of spoken Finnish in direct as well as indirect quotes (cf. Laury and Seppänen to appear).[11] With the exception of the third-person *hän* (in lines 3, 4 and 7), the syntax of the utterances quoted in (17) corresponds exactly to that of a direct quote.

Next I will discuss the interaction of *hän* with non-coreferential speech act pronouns in the same context.

(18)

      Se meina-s   jott-ei *hän* voi *te-itä*   seura-ta.
      s/he suppose-PAST that-NEG LOG can you-PL.PTV follow-INF
      S/he said that s/he can't follow you

---

10 Probably, this observation holds true for other languages too, in their non-standard varieties. I am grateful for this comment to Ritva Laury.
11 The speech act verb before the particle *että* is not compulsory. For instance, see line 4 in example 17: *no se että ei hän etäältä ole* 'well s/he that s/he doesn't come from far away'.

In example (18), the dialog being quoted involves an exclusive use of a second person (*te*): it does not refer to the addressees in the actual speech situation. The norms of standard Finnish would require choosing either a third-person form ('S/he can't follow them') instead of the second person form, as in an indirect quote, or first person ('I can't follow you') instead of *hän*, as in a direct quote. In logophoric syntax, referential forms from the direct and indirect mode are freely combined, as in (18).

(19)

1 Ko   yks-kin isäntä sano   *minu-lle* että, *älä*   ny   *lährem* mene-mää
   when one-CL farmer say.PAST me-ALL that NEG.2SG.IMP now leave go-INF.ILL
2 ennenku *häl* lähte-e ku   *häne-l*   on   nyv vähä viäl voi-ta   myytävä-nä.
   Before LOG leave-3SG because LOG-ADE be.3SG now a.bit still butter-PTV sell.INF-ESS
3 *Miä* sano-i si-lle   että jos *minu-n* tiällä nää-t
   I say-PAST s/he-ALL that if me-GEN here see-2SG
4 ni *miä* tule-n *sinu-n*   kärry-i-lle-*s*
   so I come-1SG you-SG.GEN wagon-PL-ALL-2PX

One farmer said to me that don't go now (2) before he leaves, because he has still some butter to sell. (3) I said to him that if you see me here (4) then I'll come on your wagon.

In example (19), the other participant in the narrated dialogue is the current speaker, who has first person privileges (*miä* in lines 3 and 4; *minulle* in line 1). The other quoted speaker, *isäntä* ('the farmer' in line 1), is referred to with *hän* (in line 2). As recipients, both are referred to in the second person singular forms: the speaker in the imperative form in line 1 (*älä lähre* 'don't go'), the farmer with the pronoun *sinun* ('your') and the singular possessive suffix (-*s*) in line 4.

In dramatic dialogue, turn taking can be indexed purely through alternation of person marking. Main clauses are not necessary:[12]

(20)

1 No kyssy-y ni ette on-ko   su-lla$_i$ se-m   mallinel luokka
   well ask-3SG so that be.3SG-Q you.2SG-ADE it-GEN shaped harness.bow
2 ette kestä-ä   tavalis-ie   kotiajo-ij   ajjaa.
   That stand-3SG ordinary-PL.PAR home.driving-PL.PTV drive-INF
3 Mie$_i$ hano   ett oov   varmasti, se vain tavalis-i aj-oi.
   I   say.1SG.PAST that be.1SG certainly it only ordinary-PL drive-PAST
→4 No *hän*$_j$ sitte vaihetta-a, *häl*$_i$ laina-a, ko sie$_i$ jätä-t *hä- lle*$_j$
   well LOG then change-3SG LOG borrow-3SG when you leave-2SG LOG-ALL
5 se-noma-l luoka-n.
   it-GEN own-ACC harness.bow-ACC
6 No mie$_i$ hano   ette no   see vain käy-pi laihim mutta kun-kas sitte ko *si*$_j$
   well I say.1SG.PAST that well it only suit-3SG kind-ILL but how-CL then when you
7 eh   myym milhäär raha-lla joh   mu-lla$_i$, särky-y se luokka
   NEG.2SG sell-INF any.ADE money-ADE if me-ADE break-3SG that harness.bow

---

12   Cf. example 17, line 4.

8   no e-m *mi*ᵢ   pääse sinu-stⱼ erinäh.
    Well NEG-1SG I get you-ELA rif-of
→9 Jaa s-oo *häne-v*ⱼ vahinko jos se katke-e, joo ei   se ole *sinuv*ᵢ vahinko.
    oh, it-is LOG-GEN damage if it break-3SG yes NEG.3SG it be you-GEN damage
10 *Häj*ⱼ jo   räknä-h   n-ette se on   semmonel luokka   jok ei   katkee.
    LOG already count-PAST so-that it be.3SG such harness.BOW that NEG.3SG break

Now, (s/he) asks that do you have a harness bow of the shape (2) that it will do for ordinary home driving. (3) I say that surely, it (will do for) only ordinary driving. (4) Well, s/he changes it then, s/he borrows it, if you leave her/him (5) that harness bow. (6) Well, I say that it suits me well but how (is it) then if you (7) don't sell (it) for any price, if I break that harness bow into pieces, (8) then I don't get rid of you ever. (9) Oh, it's her/his loss if it breaks, it isn't your loss (10) S/he already estimated that it is such a harness bow that doesn't break into pieces.

In example (20), the narrated conversation relies on the contrast between the pronouns *minä* 'I' and *hän*. The turns containing the logophoric pronoun (in lines 4 and 9) lack main clauses, and the only indication of speaker change is carried by *hän*.[13]

In this section we have seen that even though *hän* is a typical logophoric pronoun whose function in Finnish dialects is to refer to the speaker of quoted speech, it can also refer to the recipient of the quoted speech and also functions more generally as the pronoun of participancy in the interaction. It is possible that it is this function which has given rise to its use as a pronoun of politeness which refers to persons worthy of respect and also functions as a form of address. We have also seen that even though logophoric pronouns are typically used in indirect quotes (cf. Hagège 1974), the distinction between direct and indirect quotes is not firm in Finnish. The logophoric *hän* is also used in direct quotes alongside with speech act pronouns.

Next I will discuss the metapragmatic functions of *hän* through an examination of main clause verbs which transparently express the contexts typical of logophoric pronouns. At the same time, I will move to an examination of quotation of thoughts, perceptions, intensions and motives. This provides a pathway for an extension of the referential domain of *hän* to children, animals and other participants of interaction who lack the capacity of speech but not the capacity of expression of meaning nor the opportunity of making themselves understood and interpreted as rationally acting intentional beings.

---

13   Note that the dialogue particles (*no* in line 4 and *jaa* in line 9) of direct speech do not index turn transition unambiguously here, because they also appear initially in main clauses preceding the turns (*no* in lines 1 and 6) and once even in the middle of one of the turns (*no* in line 8).

Logophoric contexts

Similarly to other logophoric pronouns (cf. Hagège 1974: 299), *hän* refers back to an individual whose words, thoughts, feelings, states of knowledge, or awareness are transmitted in the reported clause. Thus, in addition to narrated speech or conversation, contexts of logophoric pronouns (and also 'logophoric reflexives', see Brinton 1995: 175) in different languages also include thoughts, feelings, and perceptions. These processes are often explicitly referred to in the main clause. The predicate will often be a mental verb such as *ajatella* 'think', *pohdiskella* 'speculate', *käsittää* 'understand', *uskoa* 'believe', and so on. The syntax of utterances of quoted thought can also conform to direct (21 a) or indirect (21 b) speech:

(21)

    a. Se *aattel'*   Nyt *hän* otta-a   kala-n.
       s/he think.PAST now LOG take-3SG fish-ACC
       S/he thought: now s/he will take the fish.

    b. Ei-hään net oikhein saatta-nhee *käsittää*   ette se oli tosi-khaan
       NEG-CL they really can-PAST.PL understand-INF that it was true-CL
       kaikki tämä mi-tä *het*   nyt sa-i-t   koke-a.
       all this what-PTV LOG.PL now can-PAST-3PL undergo-INF
       They couldn't really understand that it was really true, all what they now had to undergo

In the next examples (22), the main clause has a verb of perception and the quote has a logophoric pronoun.

(22)

    a. ja nii-tä   on   paljon ruottalais-ia,   jokka alka-vat oppi-mhaan suome-a,
       and they-PAR be.3SG much Swede-3PL.PAR that start-3PL learn-INF.ILL Finnish-PAR
       ko   net *näke-vät*, ette *he-i-le*   oon sii-tä   paljon hyöty-ä.
       when they see-3PL that LOG-PL-ALL be.3SG it-ELA much payback-PTV
       And there are many Swedes that start to learn Finnish when they see that they benefit from it.

    b. Niin äiti sa-i   *kuu-lla* missä *häne-n* poika-nsa o-vat
       so mother can-PAST hear-INF where LOG-GEN son-3PX be-3PL
       So the mother heard where her sons were

The perceiver is referred to in a way similar to a speaker or hearer, whose internal epistemic state is being discussed. Quotation of visual perception often also involves understanding or inference (22 a). A verb of hearing (22 b) in expressions of recipiency of speech is a context in which logophoric pronouns are also found in many other languages (e.g. Hyman ja Comrie 1981: 21–22).

In quoted speech, the main clause verb may actually be any expression of perceptible change of state or audible vocalization which may also imply meaningful communication (such as *innostua* 'get excited' in example (23), *itkeä* 'cry, mourn, lament' in example (24), etc.).

(23)

    Eino-han   *innostu*   kokonhan että kyllä   *hän* [vie].
    forename-CL get.excited.PAST totally   that surely LOG take.3SG
    Eino got totally excited: yes, he'll do it

(24)

  1 Ja se isäntä pan-i   lapse-t   hake-han   nii-tä   lehem-iä
      and the master put-PAST children-PL look-INF.ILL those-PTV cow-PL.PTV
  2 ja   sano   että s-on sitte kumma jos-etta   mee.
      And say.PAST that it-is then odd   f- NEG. 2PL go
→3 Ja *ne* *itk-i*   kovin ne lapse-t   ett-ei *het*   tohi mennä.
      And they cry-PAST lot the children-PL that-NEG LOG dare go-INF
→4 *Hek* koitti   käyrä, mutta siel-oli niih suuri elukka,
      they try-PAST go   but there-was so big animal
→5 että *het* täyty   palatat   takasin.
      that they must.PAST return-INF back
  6 *Net* tul-I   itke-in koti-a.
      they come-PAST cry-INF home-PAR

And the master of the house made the children look after the cows (2) and said that it's your hard luck if you don't go. (3) And the children cried that they dare not go. (4) They tried to go but there was such a big animal (5) that they had to return. (6) They came home crying.

In example (24), the plural *he* (*hek* / *het* 'they' in lines 3-5) refers logophorically to the crying children inside their story. Otherwise the coreferential personal pronoun *ne* (*ne(t) itki* 'they cried' in lines 3 and 6) is used.

The main clause may also contain a verb of movement such as the verb *lähteä* 'depart' in the next example, which implies purposeful action.[14] In such cases it is followed by the particle *että* and a change to present tense.[15] The logophoric pronoun indicates that what is being discussed are its referent's own goals, interpreted by the teller from his speech or from his behavior.

(25)

    ja, *se*-ol – –   sitte sii-tä   soare-sta *lähte-nä että häm männö-ö*
    and s/he be.PAST then that-ELA island-ELA go-PTC   that LOG go-3SG.PRS

---

14 See also line 7 in example 17: 'And then he was about to leave, like: now he is going away.'
15 The present tense also expresses the future in Finnish.

Selärranna-lep poikki.
PLACE.NAME-ALL across
And then – – he had left the island that he will go across (the lake) to
Selänranta

The logophoric *hän* is also typically used in causal subordinate clauses beginning with the conjunction *kun* 'because' which justify reactions, actions, or causes of behavior of the antecedent referred to.[16] The *kun*-clause will have past tense (examples 26 and 27):

(26)

ja näytteli raha-a-nsa ste oli rehvakas *ku* *hä-llä* rahha-a oli
and show-PAST money-PTV-3PX then was boastful because LOG-ADE money-PTV was
And (s/he) showed her/his money then, (s/he) was boastful because s/he$_{LOG}$ had money

(27)

Kana-t peläästy siittä kovasti, *kun* keske-llä yä-tä
chicken-PL scare-PAST that-ELA badly because middle-ADE night-PTV
tul-tiin *hei-tä* häirit-teen
come-PASS.PAST LOG.PL-PTV disturb-INF
ja *ne* rupes kova-sti kaakot-taan ja kotkot-taan.
And they start-PAST loud-ly cackle-INF and cluck-INF
The chicken were badly frightened about that because they were disturbed in the middle of the night, and they started to cackle loudly

Example 27 interprets animal behavior. Logophoric pronouns are used in all dialects of Finnish for animals whose actions are intentional or can be understood as such. In written standard Finnish *hän* was limited to human referents only at the very end of the 19th century. For example, in the linguistic journal *Virittäjä* (see 1898: 68; 86–87, 1899: 44) the use of the pronoun *se* to refer to an intentionally acting animal in a news story was considered a mistake due to Swedish influence. The author of the first Finnish novel, the national author Aleksis Kivi (1834–1872) consistently used only *hän* in reference to animals in his writing. The dialect data gathered by linguists at the end of the 19th century also contained many references to animals using *hän* (28–30).[17]

(28)

Mutt viimeselt opp-i se sorsa miu nii tunte-maa,
But finally learn.PAST that duck me so know-INF.ILL
jott-ei *hää* minnu-u ensikää pelännt, *hää* sen-ku ui omm-i-i aiko-j-aa.
that-NEG LOG me-PTV at.all fear-PAST LOG only swom own-PL-PTV time-PL-PTV.PX
But finally the duck got to know me so well that he didn't fear me at all, he swam at leisure

---

16 About causal and explanatory *kun* in Finnish, Herlin 1998.
17 Sirelius 1894: 97, Latvala 1894: 43, Kannisto 1902: 147–160.

(29)

Kärpäse-t on niiv vihas-i-a, että *he* vallal läpittes syä.
fly-PL be.SG3 so angry-PL-PTV that LOG quite through eat.SG3
The flies are so angry that they bite through (the shirt)

(30)

Totta *han* se-m paika-n katto, mistä *häm* pääsi tule-en kotio.
right LOG that-ACC place-ACC look.PAST where LOG got come-INF.ILL home
'Of course he [the horse] looked for the place where he came home'

Such examples are easy to come by today as well, even though prescriptive norms regarding the use of *hän* date back a hundred years. Present-day speakers often interpret it as secondary personification of pets in the urban society. In the light of dialectal data, however, the system is older. Especially domestic and game animals (cows, horses, dogs, sheep, reindeer; bears, foxes, wolves, often birds and fish as well) are marked through the use of logophoric pronouns as intentional beings whose behavior in interaction can be interpreted and should also be understood. Animals are treated as thinking beings with a will, and often as speech act persons with whom a human being or another animal is in communication with. The main clause will usually contain a a verb of perception (*nähdä* 'to see', *huomata* 'to discover', *katsoa* 'to look at'), or a mental verb (*tietää* 'to know', *aikoa* 'to want'; *luulla* 'to believe' like in 31a, *ymmärtää* 'to understand' like in 31b), but dialogic speech act verbs are also used (*puhua* 'talk', or *huutaa* 'shout', like in example 31c).

(31)

a. lehmä vissiil *luu-li* et *hän* tape-taa.
cow probably think-PAST that LOG kill-PASS
The cow probably thought that she will be killed

b. ei se *ymmärrä* et sää *hän-t* hyväil-et.
NEG it understand that 2SG LOG-PTV pet-2SG
It [the musquash] doesn't understand that you are petting him.

c. lehmä tul' takasih *huuta-maa* että, lypsee *häne-t*.
cow come.PAST back shout-INF.IL that milk.INF LOG-ACC
The cow came back to shout that she (should) be milked

d. välil mää puhu-i-m paha-a ett-ei *hän* saa otta-a jäneks-i-i.
Sometimes 1SG talk-PAST-1SG bad-PTV that-NEG LOG may take-INF hare-PL-PTV
Sometimes I talked badly [to the cat] that s/he must not catch hares

As is shown in example (31d), animals can also be referred to with *hän* as a recipient of human speech. This participant is often represented by a second person form as well, even when interaction between animals is discussed:

(32)

    Jos toinen hävis   ni sittem me-ni peräsä viälä ja prököttel-i si-tä
    if other lose.PAST so then go-PAST after yet and buck-PAST that-PTV
    ja oli   kommeeta   että nyt *häv* voitt-i   *su-n* kumminki.
    and be.PAST proud-PTV that now LOG win-PAST 2SG-ACC anyway

    If one [of the goats] got lost, [it] went after and bucked against the other and boasted that now she won you anyway

(33)

    – – minä siinä, minä pukka-si sukse-t ylö-, tuota sinne alas ja.
        I   there, I   push-PAST ski-PL up- well there down and
    no se-hä heti   oli *hän-ki* päällä, lume-m päällä ja karju.
    well it-CL immediately was LOG-CL on   snow-GEN on   and bark.PAST
    ääne-ssä että vaen, *sinä*   tule-t   miehe-m   peällEt tUOtA.
    sound-INE that I see 2.SG   come-2SG man-GEN onto oh

    – – and me, well, I pushed my skis up-, down there, and so, s/he [the bear] was immediately on the snow too and bawled loudly that uh huh, are you indeed jumping on the man!

In the examples above, the first one (32) concerns a dialogue between two goats after a fight, and the second one (33) represents a bear as addressing the hunter in the second person. The protagonist narrator in 33 observes and describes the movements of the bear as meaningful action: in the hunting context, the ability to interpret the other and identify with the other's thoughts is a question of life and death for both parties.

Seppänen (1998: 203–204) has shown that *hän*, as well as speech act pronouns, is used in the same fashion when interpreting the behavior preverbal infants. Sometimes *hän* is even used to refer to equipment such as computers or radios, as in example (34 a). In example (34 b), from 1894, the referent of *hän* is a clock:

(34)

    a. *hän* elää   *hän-en* oma-a elämä-ä-*s* vaa.
       LOG live.3SG LOG-GEN own-PTV life-PTV-PX3 only
       S/he$_{LOG}$ just lives her/his own life

    b. Nyt *hän* lö-i   kuus.
       now LOG strike-PAST six
       Now s/he struck six

As we have seen, the Finnish logophoric pronouns *hän* and *he* can be used to refer to all beings the speaker is in meaningful interaction with, or whose movements, changes of state, mental or physical states or other processes can be considered meaning-producing actions. In this respect, dialects and modern spoken language differ from standard Finnish, where the corresponding pronouns are restricted to anaphoric reference to humans. In the dialects, the logophoric pronoun has spread from expression of the status of speech act participation to a pronoun of politeness indexing higher social status. In addition, it has also developed into the pronoun of the protagonist in narratives, and in evidential contexts, into an index of uncertainty. The next section will deal with these two functions.

Extensions of logophoricity

We saw above that the logophoric pronoun is suitable for situations where matters are discussed from the point of view of its referent, as interpretations of his, her, or its perceptions, conclusions and goals. For that reason, it is not surprising that *hän* has become conventionalized as the pronoun referring to the protagonist in narratives and literary fiction. On the other hand, *hän* has also extended to certain contexts of uncertainty, in which it can refer to any entity, even to inanimate or abstract ones, in addition to animate beings. From this evidential function, it has further developed into an non-referential discourse particle. In this section, I will introduce these extensions of logophoricity.

The protagonist in narratives and fiction

Since the 1950s, Finnish literary fiction has utilized grammatical divergence from the standard spoken language in many different ways. One example is the focalizing system built on the contrast between the logophoric pronoun *hän* and the anaphoric pronoun *se*, which makes it possible to effect a transition from the consciousness of the protagonist to an observation of a minor character (Saukkonen 1969, Hakulinen 1988; Ylikahri 1996). *Hän* refers to the protagonist or some other character to be identified with, while *se* functions as the pronoun referring to a minor character who is only being observed. A similar system was actually used in the oral narrative tradition, and can be found in the old folk stories which were collected as data in the 1800s.

Finnish folk narratives naturally follow the logophoric principle. In most fairytales, *hän* also occasionally refers to the protagonist. The border between the protagonist and other characters is, however, not firm in folk stories. Many important characters can, in different episodes, gain prominence through marking with *hän*, while in less important roles, the same characters can be referred to with *se*. *Hän* is usually established as the pronoun referring to the protagonist only gradually as the story progresses.

(35)

1 Niitä   yks mies ol' niin väkevä, jot *se*   ku   män' ongitta-moa,
   they.PTV one man was so   strong   that s/he when went angle-INF.ILL
2 ni *si-ll*   ol' tukkipuu   ongen.vapa-na ja   maholehmä-n   roato
   so s/he-ADE was sawtimber.tree rod-ESS   and barren.cow-GEN carcass

3   onge-n sättö-nä. Sit *se* läks mu-ita   väkev-ii   mieh-ii ehti-meä,
    bait-ESS   then s/he went other-PL.PTV strong-PL-PTV men-PTV search-INF.ILL
4   ja ol' eräs mies vuore-n   kappale-ita loukuttama-ssa,
    and was one man mountain-GEN piece-PL.GEN clapping-INE
→5 ja si-lle   *heä* sano: sie-pä väkevä oou-t, ku vuore-n   kappale-ita loukutat.
    And s/he-ALL LOG said   2sg-CL strong be-2SG as mountain-GEN piece-PL-PTV clap2SG
6   *Se* vastas'   jot e-hä   mie väkevä oo, va Mikko Meikäläine on väkevä.
    s/he answered that NEG.1SG-CL I   strong be but FORENAME SURNAME is strong
7   No *hyö* män'-vät yhössä Mikko Meikäläis-en   luo.
    so log.pl went-3pl together FORENAME SURNAME-GEN to
8   Sitte se M. M. ol' niin tottelematon, jot *se* ei   totel-t   ket-eä,
    then that M. M. was so disobedient that s/he NEG3 obey-PAST anybody-PTV
9   *se* ol' niin mainio-n   väkevä.
    s/he was so splendid-GEN strong
→10 *Heä* män' kun'inkoa-lta pyytä-meä iseä-se   vanho-a velko-a – –
    LOG went king-ABL   ask-INF.ILL father-GEN.3PX old-PTV debt-PTV

There was a man who was so strong that when he went fishing (2) he had a sawtimber tree as a rod and a carcass of a barren cow (3) as a bait. Then he went to look for other strong men. (4) And there was a man clapping pieces of mountain, (5) and he said to him: why, you are really strong because you are clapping pieces of mountain. (6) The man answered that I'm not so strong, but Mikko Meikäläinen is strong. (7) Well, they went together to Mikko Meikäläinen. (8) That M. M. was so disobedient that he did not obey anybody, (9) he was so awful strong. (10) He went to ask the king the old debt of his father – –

Example (35) was recorded in 1886; the excerpt comes from the beginning of the fairytale. The pronoun *hän* (in the form *heä*) is not used for the protagonist until line 5; up until that point, *se* is used. Initially, *se* (line 6) is also used for his companion, the other strong man. When the men start on their journey together (line 7), they are referred to with the logophoric pronoun *he* 'they', in the form *hyö*. When they encounter a third man, he is again introduced with *se*, but subsequently receives a mention with *heä* (in line 10).

(36)

1   Ol ennen   uko-lla   kolome poikoo. *Se* sitten laitto   *ne*   palavelukse-e
    was formerly old.man-ADE three son-PTV. S/he then ordered they service-ILL
2   ja miäräs ku-lle-hii   palaka-n: nuorimma-lle rupla-n, keskimäise-lle kaks
    and named each-ALL-CL pay-ACC youngest-ALL ruble-ACC middle-ALL   two
3   ja   vanahimma-lle kolome. No sitte *ne*   läksi-vät yh-tä   tie-tä   kuluke-maa.
    And oldest-ALL   three   well then they started3PL one-PTV road-PTV walk-INF.ILL
4   Sitte tienhuara-ssa ei otta-nu vanahemma-t si-tä   nuorin-ta yhte-e matka-a.
    Then crossroads-INE NEG take-PAST older-PL   that-PTV youngest-PTV one same-ILL way-ILL
5   *Sen*   täyty   lähte-e eri   tie-tä   yksin kuluke-maa.
    S/he-GEN must.PAST start-INF separate way-PTV alone walk-INF.ILL
→6 Sitte tul   ensimäinen talo   *häne-lle*, ja män sii-hen tallo-o.
    Then came first   house LOG-ALL   and went that-ILL house-ILL

94

7 Kysy-ttii: Mistä   poika ja minnek-kä   matka?
     ask-PASS.PAST where.FROM   son   and whereabouts-CL way
→ 8 *Hiän* sano, *hiän* on   työ-tä   ja palaveluspaikko-o ehti-mä-ssä.
     LOG said   LOG is   work-PTV and service.place-PTV look-INF-INE

> Once upon a time there was an old man who had three sons. He ordered them to (look for a) place of work (2) and named a pay for each: a ruble for the youngest son, two rubles for the middle son (3) and three rubles for the oldest son. Well, then they started to walk together. (4) Then at crossroads the older sons did not take the youngest son along. (5) He had to go his way alone. (6) Then he met the first house and went in that house. (7) They asked: Where are you from, son, and whereabouts are you going? (8) He said that he is looking for work and service place.

In example (36) (from a fairytale recorded in 1895), there are three candidates for protagonists. Each one has been initially introduced with *se*. Only the youngest brother is the protagonist, who is only occasionally referred to with *hän* from line 6. *Hän* effects a temporary transition to the perspective of its referent. In line 6, the pronoun is in the allative case (*häne-lle*). This is typical of fairytales: when *hän* is first used as a pronoun, the protagonist is presented as an experiencer or a recipient and also usually in an oblique case. After that, in line 8, the pronoun *hän* is used logophorically in an interactional context.

Fairytales in which *hän* consistently functions as the pronoun referring to the protagonist are rare. The following example, which is here only roughly translated, comes from 1889:

(37)

> Kun plikka meni seuraavana aamuna kattoon puutansa, niin se oli jo hyvin suuri, ja plikka maisteli sen lehtiä, ja ne oli nin ernomasen hyviä – *hänen* vanhempansa oli sanonee, että *hän* söis lehtiä, nin kauvan kun tulis herelmiä, ja että *hän* lepäis sen oksilla yänsä, ja että siälä olis yhtä hauskaa kun ennen piänenä *heijän* keskellänsä. Plikka sano: Laula minun lintuni ja helise minun puuni! Ja puu laulo niin ihmeen kauniisti, ette plikka ollu koskaan ennen semmosta kuullu eikä nähny. Sitte plikka meni taas karjaan ja oli ilonen eikä surru enää ollenkan elämästänsä. Kun *hän* ehtoolla tuli kotio, nin *hän* sano taas puulle: Laula minun lintuni ja helise minun puuni!

> When the girl went next morning to look at her garden, so it was already very big, and the girl tasted its leaves and they were very good – her (LOG's) parents had said that she (LOG) should eat leaves so far the tree would come to fruition, and that she (LOG) should rest on the branches by night, and that (she) would have there as a good time as (she had) in the past with the parents (LOGs). The girl said: Sing, my bird, and tinkle, my tree! And the tree sang so beautifully that the girl had not heard or seen anything like that before in her life. Then the girl went again to herd and was happy and not saddened any more. When she (LOG) came home in the evening, she (LOG) said again to the tree: Sing my bird and tinkle my tree!

The story of the protagonist is more commonly carried forward even for long stretches with the anaphoric *se* or with an anaphoric zero subject. The logophoric *hän* is used when there is a transition to viewing the plot from the protagonist's perspective, as his or her own perceptions and experiences. However, each storyteller makes his or her own decisions, which is one of the principles of the poetic signification. The same is true for the focalization system of modern literature, which utilizes the expressive potential of the logophoric *hän* of the spoken language.

Next, I will discuss the other expansion of the logophoric pronoun in Finnish dialects, which has led in the opposite direction from the path taken by fiction: reference to inanimates and impersonal entities, even to the expression of non-referential meanings.

Evidential contexts of ignorance

As mentioned above, the personal pronoun *hän* does not refer to inanimate antecedents in standard Finnish of today. Actually, this is quite a new phenomenon, because from the 16th until the 19th century, *hän* sometimes had inanimate referents in written Finnish as well. However, this usage was probably not firmly rooted in the spoken language. Old written Finnish was mainly based on translations, and thereby the use of *hän* in writing was heavily influenced by other languages, especially by Swedish, the official language in Finland for four centuries. Its use for inanimates in writing can be at least partly explained by the influence of an earlier gender system in Swedish grammar (cf. Davidson 1990, Sandström 2000; see Laitinen, in preparation).[18] Herein, I will leave this issue aside. Instead, I will now concentrate on the use of *hän* for inanimate referents which is frequent in all regional dialects of Finnish.

Only two archaic, crystallized phrases in which *hän* refers to an inanimate, abstract entity have been accepted into spoken standard Finnish from the system of the dialects, *tiedä häntä* ('who knows') ja *hällä väliä* ('it doesn't matter'). These crystallized phrases express that the speaker either does not know something (cf. 38a) or does not consider something important (cf. 38b). The following examples were recorded from modern dialects.

(38)

    a. tiijäh *hän-tä*.
       know hän-PTV[19]

    Who knows [Literally: ('I/You don't) know it']

---

18 Accidentally, *hän* (dialectally pronounced sometimes even as *han*) bears a striking resemblance in its shape to the third person pronouns *han* 'he' and *hon* 'she' of Swedish. This can have influenced the choices in writing.

19 In this section, I will gloss *hän* ja *he* with capital letters: HÄN; HE. They will refer to both animates and inanimates, and the dividing line between referential and nonreferential use is not distinct.

b. *hä-llä* välj-ä!
   HÄN-ADE importance-PTV
   No matter what'; 'It doesn't matter [Literally: 'It (has no) importance']

(39)

    mikä-pä *hän-et* tietää.
    what-CL hän-ACC know.3SG'
    Who knows (it)

A matter the speaker does not know well or passes lightly is referred to with *hän* here. Examples (38a) and (38b) are negative in terms of meaning and partly also in terms of form.[20] Example (39), a paraphrase of (38), is, in contrast, a (rhetorical) question. Negatives and interrogatives are the contexts where the pronoun *hän* is chiefly found in Finnish dialects. In dialects, however, such usages are not only a matter of crystallized phrases, but rather productive. *Hän* can be freely used to refer not only to abstract antecedents, as in examples (38–39), but also to places (example 40 below), containers (41), substances (42), and concrete entities (43). In other words, its antecedents can belong to the referential NP types which are the least indexical in Silverstein's hierarchy (see above.)

(40)

    E-m mie tiijä liek *hän-nee* ke-tä hukku-nt.
    NEG-1SG I know be-POT.3SG HÄN -ILL anybody-PTV drown-PAST
    I don't know if anybody has drowned in it [i.e. in the lake]

(41)

    1 puuro-o oli nätti vatillinen semmonen e-m minä tiäk
       porridge-PTV was pretty basin such NEG-1SG I know
→ 2 kuijja paljo *häv* vet-i mutta ainakin semmonen
       how much HÄN take-PAST but at.least such
    3 että minu-n kotona-ni sa-i koko väki sii-ttä syä-rä.
       That I-GEN at.home-1PX may-PAST whole folk it-ELA eat-INF

There was a pretty basin of porridge, I don't know (2) how much it [i.e. the basin] took but at least so much (3) that at my home all the people could eat from it.

(42)

    1 Eei, se kunno-n kahve-tta ol-lum mutta ol-i *hän* si-llä nime-llä,
       no it real-GEN coffee be-PAST but be-PAST HÄN that-ADE name-ADE
    2 jottair ruiskahve-tta mi-tä *hän* ol-i.
       some rye.coffee-PTV what-PTV hän be-PAST

---

20   In Finnish, the negation element is a verb which agrees with the subject in person and number. It would be possible to add the negation verb in either first person singular (*en*) or third person singular (*ei*) to example 38. However, the negation is expressed by the partitive *häntä*. Example 38b also lacks the connective *ole* ('be').

No, it was no real coffee but it was anyway called by that name, rye coffee or something, what(ever) it was.

(43)

1 minkälaine *hääl* lie ol-lus se jala-lla pole-tta-va viikatej
what.kind.of HÄN be.POT be-PAST that foot-ADE treadle-PASS-PTC scythe
2 jo-lla o-l haka-nneet sileppu-u
which-ADE be-PAST hack-PAST.3PL chaff-PTV
3 vam mie e-n si-tä muistan näh-nein.
but I NEG-1SG it-PTV remember see-INF.1PX

(I wonder) what was it like, the pedal scythe (2) they used to hack the chaff with (3) but I don't remember having seen it.

In all of the examples above, *hän* is part of an interrogative clause: either a polar question (40 *liekö hukkunut* 'if it has drowned') or an information-seeking (wh-) question (41 *kuinka paljon* 'how much'; 42 *mitä* 'what', 42 *minkälainen* 'what kind of'). Most of the time, it is also preceded or followed by a negated clause expressing the speaker's lack of knowledge (40, 41: *en minä tiedä* 'I don't know', 43: *en muista* 'I don't remember').

This use of *hän* can also be interpreted as an expansion of logophoricity, as one of the layers of the grammaticalized functions of *hän*. The referential-indexical *hän* would, during its process of grammaticalization, in its logophoric-evidential use, have referred to inanimates and abstract entities in addition to animate referents. This would have formed the basis in certain contexts for a developmental stage in which *hän* would have lost its referentiality and started functioning also as a discourse particle, as a pure index. The starting point for this development would have been the following contexts, in which *hän* has an animate antecedent (44–46):

(44)

em minä tiäs sitte mitä *hä* höpis-i
NEG-1SG I know then what.PTV LOG waffle-PAST
I don't know what he waffled on

(45)

1 *Se* ol se valas! No e-n-hä mie mi-st tietä-nt!
it be-PAST that whale. Well NEG-1SG-CL I anything-ELA know-PAST
→2 En-hä mie *hän-t* osant pelätä. Sit *se* män tuoho, sii-he emäsaare-n – –
NEG-1SG I LOG-PTV can-PAST fear-INF then it went there that-ILL main.island-GEN
3 Sinne *se* jä-i paika-llee katso-maa sinne syvä-lle ranna-lle.
Thither it stay-PAST place-ALL.3PX look-INF.ILL thither deep-ALL shore-ALL
→4 Ja siit *se* taas ol si-ll aikaa mihi *hää* lie uint.
and then it again was that-ADE time-PTV where LOG be.POT swim-PAST

It was the whale! After all, I didn't know anything (about it)! (2) So, I couldn't fear it. Then it went there to that main island – – (3) And there it stayed on that deep bank watching (me). (4) And then again, meanwhile it had swum somewhere (wherever).

(46)

1 mon-ta *hei-tä* liem männy 'yhte-em matka-an (nin) *ne* kalastello-o ja
many-PTV LOG.PL-PTV be.POT3 go.PAST one-ILL way-ILL so they fish-3SG and
2 mi-tä *hyö häne-ssä* puuha-nno-o aina huvi-kse-e
what-PTV LOG.PL HÄN-INE busy-POT-3SG always pleasure-TRAN-3PX

Probably they were many of them who went together, and so they are fishing and whatever they are busying themselves with there, for fun

In examples (44–46), logophoric *hän* and *he* refer to a person or animal whose actions are reported or quoted in an interactive context. At the same time, the coreferential pronouns *se* and *ne* are also used (lines 1 and 3–4 in example 45, and line 1 of 46), but they refer to an actor under observation: the speaker or someone else has seen the movements of the whale (45) or people fishing (46). *Hän* and *he* are used by the speaker for expressing that she or he does not have a clear impression or clear knowledge of the details of the action. Even the person's identity, origin or gender can be left unspecified, as in the following examples:

(47)

a. 1 ja siinä kävi sittej joku semmonem miäs, tuli siältä Mouhijärveltä päin sitte,
and there came then some such man came there from Mouhijärvi from then
→ 2 mistä saakka *häl* liäsi ol-la (en) minä tiäj ja mikä miäs *hän* oli
where from LOG be.POT-PAST be-INF (NEG.1SG) I know and what man LOG was

And there came then some man from ther vicinity of Mouhijärvi then, (2) I don't really know whereabouts he came from and who(ever) he was.

b. Ja se tul-i semmonem miäs siähen sittet taikka nainem mikä *hän* ol-i
and it come-PAST such man there then or woman what LOG be-PAST
And some man came there then, or a woman, whatever s/he was

The following examples illustrate how several non-coreferential tokens of *hän* (and *he*), referring to both animates and inanimates, accumulate in contexts of uncertainty. In example 48, the first *he* (nom. *hyö*) in line 3 refers to berry pickers, the second to berries, and in example 49, the first *hän* (nom. *heän*) to the speaker's husband, the second to a photograph.[21]

(48)

1 Mutsiit rupes jo käy-mää marjaostaja koton, loppu-i lopu-ks.
but then started already come-INF.ILL berry.buyer at.home, end-PL.GEN end-TRAN

---

21 See also example 46 line 2. It contains another feature typical to expressions of lack of knowledge containing *hän*: the verb is in the potential mood. This is also true of examples 40, 43, 45, 47, and 49.

2   Siit ei huoli-nt   ennää   Viipuri-i   lähte-e vie-mää...
    then NEG bother-PAST anymore Vyborg-ILL go-INF transport-INF.ILL
→3 ko   laitto-it   ulos Saksa-a   ja mihi *hyö h-eit* laitto-it
    because send-PAST.PL out Germany-ILL and where HE HE-PTV send-PAST.PL

But then finally, the berry buyers started to come home [for buying berries]. (2) Then it was not worthwhile to transport [the berries] to Vyborg ... because they sent [them] to Germany, and wherever they sent them.

(49)

    liek-kö-hän   *heän-nih hän-essä*?
    be.POT3SG-Q-CL HÄN-CL HÄN-INE
    Is he possibly there as well?

The first two sections discussed the grammatical and semantic similarity of Finnish logophoric pronouns and speech act pronouns: as meaningfully behaving participants in interaction, *hän* and *he* are parallel to the 1. and 2. person. This section presents the other side of their metapragmatic nature, the epistemic distinction from speech act persons. The speaker may well take the point of view of the third person referent, he may interpret the referent's thoughts and identify its consciousness, as we saw in the discussion of *hän* in the interpretation of children and animals or in reference to the protagonist of a story. But the speaker still lacks access to thoughts or knowledge in the mind of the referent of *hän*. Most of the time, the referent is someone not present, whose earlier utterances are being quoted, or someone who lacks the capacity of speech, or a fictive character. Details which are less important for the story or have even been forgotten often receive less attention in speech, and it is at those points when *hän* is used.

According to Finnish linguists (e.g. Kannisto 1902, Vilppula 1989), the expression of dismissiveness is a function of these types *hän*. However, the implication of this kind of attitude is likely to arise in a particular syntactic context, namely with *hän* used in questions. A clear manifestation of this is the other possible, 'universal' interpretation of the wh-pronouns in the translations of our examples: for instance, *mitä* ('what') meaning 'whatever' in examples (42), (46) and (47), or *mihin* ('where') meaning 'wherever' in example (45). The translations show how uncertainty about circumstances can lead to insignificance, and lack of knowledge to the implication of lack of interest. (For universal concessive conditionals, cf. Leuschner 2004.)

Interrogatives are the most important context of the evidential use of *hän* in my data, and in such contexts, the referent can easily be inanimate. Another common context is concessive statements, as in examples 50 a–c below. In such examples, *hän* is likely to refer to inanimates – here to a body part, vegetative matter, and a substance:

(50)

    a. sa-is-hah   *hän-neen* nyt vaikka minkälais-ta rät't'-ii.
       get-CON3SG-CL HÄN-ILL   now though any.kind-PTV cloth-PTV
       Of course, one could get any kind of clothes for it [for the foot]

    b. antaa *hän-e,* *heijä-n* siinä kuivaantu-an ni, kyllä sit, kuiv-i-vat.
       let.SG3 HÄN-GEN HE-GEN there dry-INF   so surely then dry-PAST-PL3
       Let it, let them [the hay] dry there [on the frame], and indeed they dried

    c. pan-tiim   poika voi-ta   hake-ma-an:
       put-PASS.PAST boy   butter-PTV get-INF-ILL
       siinä *hän-tä* sitten on, ettei   *hän* aina   keskel   lopu.
       there HÄN-PTV then is   that-NEG HÄN always unfinished cease
       The boy was put to get butter: there you have it, that it won't run always out

Concessivity is expressed through verb initial word order (examples 50 a and b), verb final word order (50 c) and several particles (*nyt, kyllä, -han* and *sitten* in examples 50 a ja b). *Hän* has been interpreted as an index of the the speaker's lack of interest and dismissive attitude in these contexts as well. The tone of these utterances is often more likely to be light and calming, especially when the processes in question are ones with a positive and desirable outcome, as in example (50). A semantic link to the logophoric function of *hän* can only be felt on a very abstract level. While questions are likely to express that the matter of the lack of knowledge being dependent only on the referent of *hän* is not a problem in the situation of telling, the concessive clause, in contrast, expresses that the state or process of the referent of *hän* will not cause any special problems.[22]

As mentioned, *hän* has also been grammaticized into a particle in Finnish dialects. Examples 51 a–e illustrate the development toward a non-referential particle of the partitive *häntä* referring to an inanimate:

(51)

    a. minäkääh *hän-tä*   ymmärtä-nnä
       1SG-CL   HÄN-PTV understand-PAST
       I don't understand it either [that the floor of the house was weak]

    b. e-m   muistah *hän-tä* ennee   *se-n nimme-e.*
       NEG-1SG remember HÄN-PTV anymore it-GEN name-PTV
       I don't remember it anymore, the name of it

    c. e-n-kä-häm   minä *hän-tä* ennee   muistak-kaas
       NEG-1SG-CL-CL I   HÄN-PTV anymore remember-CL

---

22   This interpretation could be supported by investigating whether topics marked with *hän* are easily passed over in conversational discourse. Unfortunately, Finnish dialect data have so far consisted mostly of interviews.

satavuotis-ii   asij-oeta.
   hundred.year.old-PL.PTV thing-PL.PTV
   And I don't even remember it anymore, those hundred year old things

d. jotta ei   tiijäm miten-kä *häntä*   elä-siv
   that NEG know how-CL   HÄN-PTV live-CON.3SG
   vas eläsik-kö   *häntä*   miten-kää.
   or live-CON.3SG-Q HÄN-PTV somehow-cl
   Thus, [the child] doesn't know how to live, or should one live at all

e. em   mutta om-pa   *hän-tä*   laiska-na.
   NEG-1SG but   be.3SG-CL HÄN-PTV lazy-ESS
   No [I don't have a job] but why, one is lazy

In example (51 a), *häntä* is a referential pronoun which refers to a certain state of affairs, namely the flimsiness of the floor. (51 b) is a cleft, in which both the pronoun (*häntä*) and the "right dislocated" full NP (*sen nimmee*) refer to an abstract entity, the forgotten name; even here, *häntä* could perhaps be considered a referential pronoun. In example (51 c), the partitive object is a plural NP (*satavuotisii asijoeta* 'hundred-year-old things'). The singular *häntä* cannot be coreferential with it, and it is not possible to assign a clear referent to it at all.

In examples (51 d) and (51 e), *häntä* is even more clearly a particle, in other words, a pure index of the speaker's attitude. Differently from examples a–c, in which *häntä* could be parsed as the partitive object of a transitive verb (*ymmärtää* 'understand'; *muistaa* 'remember'), examples d and e are intransitive (the verbs are *elää* 'live' and *olla* 'be'). *Häntä* is clearly nonreferential. The pronoun *se* ('it') has undergone the same kind of particleization: its partitive form (*sitä*) has been grammaticized as a discourse particle (see Hakulinen 1987, Vilkuna 1989: 143–146). Just like the particle *sitä,* the particle *häntä* is especially likely to be found in existentials, passives, and in the so-called zero person constructions (examples 51 d and e). Similarly to *sitä,* the particle *häntä* also expresses the speaker's affective (ironical, boasting etc.) stance toward the matter under discussion.[23] A more exact analysis of its functions is, however, outside the scope of this article.

It bears mentioning, however, that in addition to the partitive, the nominative form of *hän* has also been grammaticized into non-referential functions as a particle clitic with the form *-han* or *-hän*, which is used in standard Finnish as well as the dialects. I have examined the development of the particle clitic *-hAn* in a different context (see Laitinen 2002).

---

23 These contexts are all subjectless, and the particle *sitä* has been considered to take the place of the subject (or speaker) in the utterance. The unexpressed agents of the Finnish passive and zero person are always human: the zero person corresponds semantically to the English second person generic *you* (see. Hakulinen 1987, Laitinen to appear).

Conclusion

The Finnish third-person pronoun *hän* has many grammatical and semantic features in common with the first and second person pronouns. In standard Finnish, it is used only as a personal pronoun for human referents. In contrast, in Finnish dialects, *hän* comes closer to the metapragmatic nature of speech act pronouns, because it always refers to a participant in a speech event. *Hän* is a typical logophoric pronoun in spoken Finnish. It differs morphologically from both the third-person pronoun (*se*) and the reflexive pronoun (*itse*). It refers to a human or an animal whose speech, thoughts, feelings, or other states of consciousness the actual speaker is quoting. In this article, on the basis of a large dialect corpus, I have presented the logophoric functions of *hän*, as well as its contexts of use and its expanded functions in both fictive contexts and in evidential contexts of uncertainty.

The logophoric *hän* (and its plural form *he*) is used alongside with speech act persons in quoted dialogue, and will be an alternative to the first and second person in those contexts. It refers not only to the speaker, but also to the addressee or the recipient. In addition, *hän* also refers to animates lacking the capacity for speech, such as children and animals, when their meaningful actions in interaction, thoughts, feelings, goals and motives are being quoted. Identification with the point of view of the referent of *hän* is the basis for its use in fictive contexts such as, for example, in references to characters in folk tales. *Hän* refers to inanimates in narratives at points where the exact content has been forgotten or has gone unheard by the teller, or is not especially important in the context. It is in contexts like this that *hän* has developed into a non-referential particle, a pure index with various discourse functions.

The referential scope of *hän* and its functions have become specialized, to a certain extent, according to syntactic contexts. In its basic logophoric function, when it refers only to animates, it can freely occur in any context. When the speech, feelings or thoughts of its referent are being discussed, the beginning of the quoted segment is often marked with the particle *että*. When the intentions of the referent of *hän* are being reported and the main clause contains a verb of movement, *hän* will most often occur in *että*-initial subordinate clauses expressing purpose; when reasons for actions are discussed after the fact, it will occur in *kun*-initial causal subordinate clauses. In expressions of lack of knowledge, the referential scope of *hän* is at its widest and the context is the most restricted. It is most likely to be found in question clauses within the scope of negative expressions of uncertainty. Another context which also allows inanimate referents of *hän* is concessive clauses, which share in common with question clauses the implication that the matter is not all that relevant for what is being discussed.

In this article, I have considered logophoricity the basic function of *hän*. I have approached the analysis of its other functions from that perspective, especially from non-normative spoken language data. From this perspective, *hän* represents, together with the speech act pronouns, the most indexical types of NPs. *Hän*, much more so than the first and second person pronouns, has widened its referential scope into non-human, even inanimate and abstract entities, and has also been grammaticalized into purely indexical functions. This side of it arises from its nature as a 'second degree speech act pronoun', whose primary context of use is the narrating of earlier speech events and interaction.

Data

This article is based on the study of a large dialect corpus collected from 1875 to 2000. The main corpus has been the Morphology Archives of the University of Helsinki. Additional data come from the series *Suomen kielen näytteitä* (parts 1–50) from the Institute for the Study of the Languages of Finland, the series *Kotiseudun murrekirjoja* (osat 1–18) from Suomalaisen Kirjallisuuden Seura, as well as from dialect samples and research published in the *Suomi* series approximately 1875–1910.

REFERENCES

Benveniste, Émile. 1966. *Problèmes de linguistique générale* 1. Collection tel, Éditions Gallimard.
Brinton, Laurel J. 1995. Non-anaphoric reflexives in free indirect style: expressing the subjectivity of the non-speaker. In Dieter Stein and Jenny Cheshire (eds.) *Subjectivity and subjectivisation*. Cambridge: Cambridge University Press.
Cantrall, William R. 1969. Pitch, stress and grammatical relations. *Papers from the fifth regional meeting of the Chicago Linguistic Society*, Chicago.
Cannelin, Knut. 1888. Tutkimus Kemin kielimurteesta. *Suomi III: 2*. Helsinki: SKS.
Clements, G. N. 1975.The logophoric pronoun in Ewe: its role in discourse. *Journal of West African Languages* 2: 141–177.
Davison, Herbert. 1990. *Han hon den. Genusutvecklingen i svenskan under nysvensk tid*. [Dissertation.] Lundastudier i nordisk språkvetenskap A 45. Lund University Press.
EKG = Eesti keele grammatika II. Syntaks. Keele ja Kirjaduse Instituut. Tallinn 1993.
Hagège, Claude. 1974. Les pronoms logophoriques. *Bulletin de la Société de Linguistique de Paris* 287–310.
Hakulinen, Auli. 1987. Avoiding personal reference in Finnish. In Jef Verschueren and Marcella Bertucelli-Papi (ed.) *The pragmatic perspective. Selected papers from the 1985 International Pragmatics Conference*. 140–153. Amsterdam: John Benjamins.
Hakulinen, Auli. 1988. Miten nainen liikkuu Veijo Meren romaaneissa [A woman moving in the novels by Veijo Meri]. In L. Laitinen (ed.) *Isosuinen nainen*: 56–70. Helsinki: Yliopistopaino.
Helasvuo, Marja-Liisa. 2001. *Syntax in the Making. The emergence of syntactic units in Finnish conversation*. Studies in Discourse and Grammar. Amsterdam: John Benjamins.
Herlin, Ilona. 1998. *Suomen kun*. [Dissertation: Finnish *kun*]. Helsinki: SKS.
Hyman, L. M. and B. Comrie 1981. Logophoric reference in Gokana. *Journal of African Languages and Linguistics* 3: 19–37.
Kannisto, Artturi. 1902. Lauseopillisia havaintoja läntisen Etelä-Hämeen kielimurteesta. *Suomi III: 20* s. 1–283. Helsinki: SKS.
Kenttä, Matti and Bengt Pohjanen. 1996. Meänkielen kramatiikki. Luleå: Kaamos.
Koster, J. and E. Reuland, eds. 1991. *Long-Distance Anaphora*. Cambridge: Cambridge University Press.

Kuiri, Kaija. 1984. *Referointi Kainuun ja Pohjois-Karjalan murteissa*. Helsinki: SKS.
Laitinen, Lea. 1992. *Välttämättömyys ja persoona. Suomen murteiden murteiden nesessiivisten rakenteiden semantiikkaa ja kielioppia*. [Dissertation: Necessity and Person. The Semantics and Grammar of Necessitative Constructions in Finnish Dialects.] Helsinki: SKS.
Laitinen, Lea. 1995. Metonymy and the grammaticalization of necessity in Finnish. *SKY 1995. Yearbook of the Linguistic Association of Finland*, 79–102. Helsinki.
Laitinen, Lea. 1997. Norms made easy: case marking with modal verbs in Finnish. In Jenny Cheshire and Dieter Stein (eds.) *Taming the vernacular: from dialect to written standard language*, 110–124. London: Longman.
Laitinen, Lea. 2002. From logophoric pronoun to discourse particle: A case study of Finnish and Saami. In Ilse Wischer and Gabriele Diewald (eds.) *New reflections on Grammaticalization*, 327–344. Amsterdam & Philadelphia: John Benjamins.
Laitinen, Lea. 2004. Grammaticalization and Standardization. Olga Fischer, Muriel Norde and Harry Perridon (eds.): *Up and Down the Cline – the Nature of Grammaticalization*. Amsterdam & Philadelphia: John Benjamins.
Laitinen, Lea. (Forthcoming). Zero person in Finnish: a grammatical resource for construing human reference. Lyle Campbell and Marja-Liisa Helasvuo (eds.) *Case and person: The human perspective*. Volume in review for publication.
Laitinen, Lea. (In preparation.) Assuming gender through translations? The third person pronoun in old written Finnish.
Laitinen, Lea and Maria Vilkuna. 1993. Case-marking in necessive constructions and split intransitivity. In Anders Holmberg and Urpo Nikanne (eds.) *Case and other Functional Categories in Finnish Syntax*, 23–48. Berlin – New York: Mouton de Gruyer.
Latvala, Salu. 1894. Lauseopillisia havaintoja Luoteis-Satakunnan kansankielestä. *Suomi III: 12*. Helsinki: SKS.
Laury, Ritva. 2001. Definiteness and reflexivity: Indexing socially shared experience. *Pragmatics* 11.4: 401–420.
Laury, Ritva. 2002. Interaction, grounding and third-person referential forms. In Frank Brisard (Ed.) *Grounding: The epistemic footing of deixis and reference*. (Cognitive Linguistics Research 21.) Berlin: Mouton de Gruyter. 83–115.
Laury, Ritva and Eeva-Leena Seppänen. (forthcoming). Complement clauses as turn continuations: Syntax, prosody and interactional functions of the Finnish *et(tä)*-clause. To appear in a special volume of *Pragmatics*. Elizabeth Couper-Kuhlen and Tsuyoshi Ono (eds.).
Leuschner, Torsten. 2004. At the boundaries of grammaticalization. What interrogatives are doing in concessive conditionals. In Anna Giacalone Ramat and Paul J. Hopper (eds.) *The Limits of Grammaticalization*. Typological Studies in Language 37. Amsterdam & Philadelphia: John Benjamins.
Lyons, John. 1977. *Semantics*. Volume 2. Cambridge, London, New York, Melbourne: Cambridge University Press.
Nuolijärvi, Pirkko. 1986. *"Ota minut sinun uniin". Nykysuomalaisen omistusmuotojärjestelmä*. Kieli 1. Helsinki: Department of Finnish Language, University of Helsinki.
Mägiste, Julius. 1960. *Vermlannin sammuvaa savoa. Kielennäytteitä vuosilta 1947–1951*. Helsinki: SKS.
Nuolijärvi, Pirkko.1996. Kielellisen variaation ja sosiaalisen muutoksen suhteesta. Artjärven murteen omistusmuotojärjestelmä. *Virittäjä 100: 2–*.
Paunonen, Heikki. 1995. *Suomen kieli Helsingissä: huomioita Helsingin puhekielen historiallisesta taustasta ja nykyvariaatiosta*. Helsinki: Department of Finnish Language, University of Helsinki.
Putnam, Hilary. 1975. The Meaning of Meaning. In *Mind. Language and Reality: philosophical papers*. Cambridge: Cambridge University Press. 215–271.
Rausmaa, Pirkko-Liisa (ed.). 1971. *Suomalaiset kansansadut I. Ihmesadut*. Helsinki: SKS.
Sands, Kristina and Lyle Campbell 2001. Non-canonical subjects and objects in Finnish. In Alexandra Y. Aikhenvald, R. M. W. Dixon and Masayuki Onishi (eds.) *Non-canonical marking of subjects and objects*. Amsterdam/Philadelphia: John Benjamins.

Sandström, Caroline. 2000. The changing system of grammatical gender in the Swedish dialects of Nyland, Finland. Barbara Unterbeck and Matti Rissanen (eds.), *Gender in Grammar and Cognition 2. Manifestations of gender.* Trends in Linguistics. Studies and Monographs 124. Berlin: Mouton de Gruyter

SAS = *Suomen sanojen alkuperä. Etymologinen sanakirja.* A–K. Helsinki: SKS 2001.

Saukkonen, Pauli. 1967. Persoonapronominien *hän : se, he : ne* distinktiivi oppositio. *Virittäjä 71*: 286–.

Seppänen, Eeva-Leena. 1996. Ways of referring to a knowing co-participant in Finnish conversation. *SKY 1996. Yearbook of the Linguistic Association of Finland*, 135–176.

Seppänen, Eeva-Leena. 1998. *Läsnäolon pronominit: tämä, tuo, se ja hän viittaamassa keskustelun osallistujaan.* [Pronouns of participation. The Finnish pronouns tämä, tuo, se and hän as devices for referring to co-participants in conversation. A published PhD thesis.] Helsinki: SKS.

Setälä, E. N. 1883. Lauseopillisia havaintoja Koillis-Satakunnan kansankielestä. *Suomi II: 16.* Helsinki: SKS

Silverstein, Michael. 1976. Shifters, Linguistic Categories, and Cultural Description. In Keith H. Basso and Henry A. Selby (eds.) *Meaning in Anthropology*, 11–55. Albuquerque: University of New Mexico Press.

Silverstein, Michael. 1981. Case marking and the nature of language. – *Australian Journal of Linguistics* 1/1981: 227–247.

Silverstein, Michael. 1987. Cognitive implications of referential hierarchy. In Maya Hickmann (ed.) *Social and Functional Approaches to Language and Thought.* Orlando: Academic Press, 125–164.

Sirelius, U. 1894. Lauseopillinen tutkimus Jääsken ja Kirvun kielimurteesta. *Suomi III: 10.* Helsinki: SKS.

Suomalainen, K. 1884. *Suomalaisia keskusteluja. Ajan ratoksi suomenkieltä suosiville Suomen naisille.* I. Sortavala. Published by the author.

Tiainen, Outi. 1998. Referenttien kuljettaminen diskurssissa [Résumé: La conduite des référents dans le discours.] *Virittäjä 102*: 498

Varteva, Annukka. 1998. Pronominit *hän* ja *tämä* tekstissä. [Summary: Die Pronomen *hän* 'er sie' und *tämä* 'diese(r/s)' im Textzusammenhang]. *Virittäjä 102*: 202–223.

Vilppula, Matti. 1989. Havaintoja *hän-* ja *he-*pronominien käytöstä suomen murteissa. [Summary: On the use of the 3rd person pronouns in Finnish dialects.] *Virittäjä 93*: 389–400.

Wright, Georg Henrik von. 1963. *Norm and Action: a logical enquiry.* London: Routledge & Kegan.

Wright, Georg Henrik von. 1971. *Explanation and Understanding.* London: Routledge & Kegan.

Vilkuna, Maria. 1989. *Free word order in Finnish. Its syntax and discourse functions.* Helsinki: SKS.

Ylikahri, Kristiina. 1996. *Hän-, he-* ja *se-, ne-* pronominien käytöstä Siikaisten murteessa. [Summary: The use of hän, he and se, ne pronouns in extensions of reported discourse in the Siikainen dialect.] *Virittäjä 100*: 182–203.

RENATE PAJUSALU

Anaphoric pronouns in Spoken Estonian
Crossing the paradigms[1]

Introduction

Every language has its own tracking devices, such as anaphoric demonstratives, personal pronouns, definite articles and zero anaphors. In their anaphoric use third person pronouns and demonstratives are particularly close in meaning, and the difference between them is usually connected above all with the context. It has generally been found that, in comparison with third person pronouns, anaphoric demonstratives are "stronger" indicators, i.e. anaphoric demonstratives are often used to indicate a referent that is somewhat unexpected and not currently at the centre of attention (Gundel et al. 1993, Himmelmann 1996, Diessel 1999, see also discussion in Kaiser, this volume).

Several investigations have been performed in the area of Finnish anaphoric demonstratives (see, for instance, Larjavaara 1990, Laury 1997, Seppänen 1998 and this volume, Etelämäki 1998 and this volume). Despite their linguistic proximity, pronoun use in Finnish and Estonian is nevertheless very different. To date, little research has been done into Estonian tracking devices. In the latest Estonian academic grammar (Erelt et al. 1993: 208–210), the most important principles on which basis personal pronouns and demonstratives are used as substitutes for nouns have been summarised, although these conclusions are not based on the empirical investigation of spoken language.

This article will attempt to ascertain the most important principles that influence the selection of anaphoric devices in spoken Estonian. Under examination are the demonstratives *see, seal* and *sealt* and the third person pronouns *tema* and *ta*. The data consist of exerpts from 51 everyday conversations from a spoken language corpus collected at Tartu University. The length of the excerpts varies from 1–6 pages, their average length being 5 minutes. The conversations have been gathered and transcribed by students of the Estonian language at Tartu University. The great majority of the participants in the conversations are university students, although there are also older speakers. In some conversations, the speakers' dia-

---

[1] This work was supported by the Estonian Science Foundation, Grant No.: 5813.

lectal background can be distinguished, although the speakers generally use the version of the Estonian language that is conditionally referred to as the common spoken language (*ühiskeel*): this is a spontaneous, almost standard everyday spoken language.

In addition to the above data, the results of previously published research based on radio interviews (Pajusalu 1995) and to a certain degree also on written language (Pajusalu 1997a) are also used in this article.

Anaphoric pro-forms in everyday conversation in the Estonian language

In Estonian written language, there are two demonstrative pronouns, *see* and *too*, the first referring to that which is nearby, and the second that which is distant, from the point of view of spatial opposition. However, there are dialects of Estonian (above all the western and island dialects), in which *too* does not exist, so there is idiolectal variation in its use. Thus the pronoun *see* is predominant in contemporary Estonian written language and the standard spoken language (Pajusalu 1996).

However, spatial opposition is productive in demonstrative adverbs (1), of which series (1a) refers to that which is close to the speaker, and (1b) to that which is distant from him.

(1a)	*siin*	static 'here'
	siia	direction of movement 'to here'
	siit	direction of movement 'from here'
(1b)	*seal*	static 'there'
	sinna	direction of movement 'to there'
	siit	direction of movement 'from there'

In accordance with the traditional definition, the third person pronoun possesses two forms: the short form *ta* and the long form *tema*. In Estonian all other personal pronouns also have short and long forms (for instance *mina* and *ma* 'I', *sina* and *sa* 'you'), which are, in contrast to Finnish, completely accepted in standard language. The difference between the short and the long form is not incidental or purely stylistical (i.e. is not connected with register), but is connected with various pragmatic factors, above all emphasis (see Pool 1999). In this article I will attempt to demonstrate that, in contrast to other personal pronouns, the two forms of the third person pronoun also have a referential difference. The demonstrative pronoun *see* also permits short forms in certain cases (for instance the inessive *selles* ~ *ses*), although these are not particularly common in spoken language. Short forms of *see* are used mainly in literary high style.

In the plural, the paradigms of the third person pronoun and demonstrative pronoun melt into one. Although there are three parallel forms in the nominative, in the other cases there is only one. In many plural cases there is also a shorter form, although this is not connected with different roots, but instead with different ways of forming the plural, and possesses no referential or pragmatic difference. Shorter and longer plural forms (e.g. the illative *nendesse~neisse*) function instead as stylistic variants. The entire paradigm can be seen in Table 1.

Table 1 presents the number of occurrences of the most common forms in the data under investigation. Since pronouns are very rare in some cases, and it is impossible to make any generalisations about them, numbers are

Table 1. Paradigms of the demonstrative see and the third person pronouns in the Estonian common language and the absolute number of occurrences thereof in the data under examination, excluding occurrences of the pronoun see as an agreeing component of an NP.

	Demonstrative pronoun	Long form of 3rd person pronoun	Short form of 3rd person pronoun
Nominative	**see (240)**	**tema (33)**	**ta (375)**
Genitive	**selle (23)**	**tema (16)**	**ta (4)**
Partitive	seda (67)		teda (25)
Illative	sellesse	temasse	tasse
Inessive	selles	temas	tas
Elative	sellest	temast	tast
Allative	**sellele (3)**	**temale (1)**	**talle (33)**
Adessive	**sellel (1)**	**temal (7)**	**tal (62)**
Ablative	sellelt	temalt	talt
Translative	selleks	temaks	
Terminative	selleni	temani	
Essive	sellena	temana	
Abessive	selleta	temata	
Comitative	sellega (12)	temaga (1)	taga (3)
Pl. nominative	**need (33)**	**nemad (13)**	**nad (64)**
Pl. genitive	nende		
Pl. partitive	neid (32)		
Pl. illative	nendesse~neisse		
Pl. inessive	nendes~neis		
Pl. elative	nendest~neist		
Pl. allative	nendele~neile		
Pl. adessive	nendel~neil		
Pl. ablative	nendelt~neilt		
Pl. translative	nendeks~neiks		
Pl. terminative	nendeni		
Pl. essive	nendena		
Pl. abessive	nendeta		
Pl. comitative	nendega		

presented only about those grammatical cases for which the number of occurrences exceeded 10. In the case of the pronoun *see*, I have not been taken into consideration the (particularly frequent) instances in which it is an agreeing component of an NP, which are examples of the use of *see* with the function of a definite article (Pajusalu 1997b, 2001).

Thus a different number of pro-forms can be used as anaphoric minimal NPs in different cases in Estonian. The maximal selection is in singular locatives in which, in addition to the three pronouns, there is also the distal pro-adverb (1b), and thus we have a total of four different anaphoric forms. The minimal number is 1, which is actually predominant in all plurals from the genitive onwards, since the parallel forms of the plural are variants of the plural and not of the root.

In Table (1) the forms examined in this article are emphasised in italics. Thus an attempt is made below to answer the question of what determines the selection of the anaphoric pronoun in the singular nominative, genitive, allative and adessive and in the plural nominative, where at least three different forms are possible. A much greater corpus of spoken language would be required in order to examine the other cases. The relation between proadverb *seal* and other pro-forms is also examined. The analysis is qualitative, and numerical data are presented only as background.

First, the main principles of entity tracking are examined, then the differences between the forms in different cases, and finally an attempt is made to present a coherent picture of the whole.

Animate/inanimate

An Estonian's linguistic intuition tells him that an animate entity is referred to with a personal pronoun, and an inanimate entity with a demonstrative pronoun. Thus, while the pronominal system of standard Finnish is sensitive to the feature of humanness (see, for example Laitinen, this volume), this is not the case with Estonian, where animacy is the determining semantic feature. Estonian academic grammar does, however, admit that there are certain instances in which the demonstrative *see* may refer to an animate entity and personal pronoun *tema/ta* to an inanimate entity (Erelt et al. 1993: 208–209).

The pronoun referents in all of the data were divided on the basis of the category animate/inanimate in the manner presented in Table 2. Adverbs *sinna, seal* and *sealt* belonging to this paradigm (see below) are added to occurrences of the pronoun *see*. One can see that all three may have either an animate or an inanimate referent, although *see* nevertheless largely refers to an inanimate referent, whereas *tema* and *ta* refer to animate referents. *Ta* nevertheless functions relatively more frequently as the pronoun of an inanimate entity than does *tema*; these are generally Lyons (1977) first-level entities, i.e. physical objects.

This article indeed focuses on these non-typical cases, i.e. the question of when *see* refers to an animate entity and *tema* or *ta* to an inanimate entity.

Table 2. The grouping of referential anaphoric pronouns on the basis of the category animate/inanimate.

	animate	inanimate
see	6 (1%)	346+98 adverbs=444 (99%)
tema	**71 (95%)**	4 (5%)
ta	**478 (84%)**	88 (16%)

Entity tracking

See generally refers to an inanimate entity, and the more abstract the entity, the smaller the possibility that it is referred to with the pronouns *tema* or *ta*. Everyday conversation usually involves abstract entities that are referred to once and do not become referents in discourse. These are non-material entities like noise in (1) or situations and events like customers being quiet in (2). The latter instance especially frequently involves such indeterminate entities that neither the speaker nor the listener may necessarily be able to identify them precisely (see also example (8), in which *see* stands for an important deed with which one leaves one's mark in history). This kind of reference is usually called discourse deixis and according to Himmelmann (1996: 224-226) demonstrative pronouns are typically used in this context in great majority of languages.

(1)

ära	kolista *see*	jääb	maru	vastikult	peale
NEG+IMP+2SG	clatter this	stay-3SG	very	disgustingly	on

siit   millegipärast
from-here   for-some-reason
don't clatter, for some reason *it* [*see*] is getting onto the tape from here (*see*=noise)

(2)

aga	inimesed	küsivad	nii	vähe.	*see*	on	lihtsalt
but	man-PL	ask-3 PL	so	little.	this	be-3SG	simply

õudne.
terrible.
but people ask so little. *that's* [*see*] simply terrible (*see* = the situation that people do not ask very often)

ta typically refers to an animate entity (3).

(3)

[a salesperson at a bookstore is describing how she behaves with customers in the store]

inimene	noh	hea	küll	ma	ei	lähe	*teda*	segama
man	oh	good	PTC	1SG	NEG	go	3SG-PTV	bother-INF

the person, well you know, I'm not going to go and bother *him* [*teda*]

sis	kui	*ta*	juba	loeb	ega	ma	ei	saa	*teda*
then	when	3SG-SH	already	read-3SG	NEG	1SG	NEG	can	3SG

when *he*'s [*ta*] already reading, I can't

aidata	lugeda	eks.	aga	noh	nii	alguses
help-INF	read-INF	PTC	but	oh	so	beginning-INE

help him read, right? But well, in the beginning

kui	*ta*	nagu	otsib	või (.)	*ta*	on	ise
when	3SG-SH	like	seek-3SG	or	3SG-SH	be-3SG	self

when *he*'s [*ta*], like, seeking, right (.) *he*'s [*ta*]

segaduses alles	*ta*	ei	tea	ka	täpselt	mida
confusion still	3SG-SH	NEG	know	too	exactly	what-PTV

still confused himself, he doesn't know exactly what

ta	nagu	tahab.	ja	*ta*	tahab	alles	pilti
3SG-SH	like	want-3SG.	and	3SG-SH	want-3SG	still	picture-PTV

luua.
create-INF

he [*ta*], like, wants. And *he* [*ta*] just wants to get an overall idea.

Tema refers emphatically to an animate entity, especially when that person is opposed to another person. In example (4), the speaker has spoken of his telephone bill and now is talking about Viivi's telephone bill, in contrast to his own.

(4)

Viivi	käest	küsisin	eile	et	palju *tema*	maksab
V.	from	ask-PAST-SG1	yesterday	that	much 3SG-LG	pay-3SG

Yesterday I asked Viivi how much *she* [*tema*] pays

When multiple entities are referred to in a conversation, one pronoun may attach to one entity and the second to the other. This is simple when one is in the singular and the second is in the plural, for instance when a left-handed person and her scissors were referred to in a conversation, the scissors were naturally plural. When one is animate and the other inanimate, it is also clear that *tema* or *ta* refers to the animate and *see* to the inanimate. In the case of two similar entities, however, it is more difficult to maintain comprehensibility. The general tendency is for the main (and therefore more salient) character in a conversation to be referred to with the pronoun *ta*, while secondary characters either with the pronoun *tema*

(5) or *see* (6). In written language, I have found that in these instances the demonstrative pronoun *too* has also been used to refer to persons (Pajusalu 1997a). It has been argued earlier that the order of mention is crucial, i.e. if two referents equal in terms of animacy (both animate or inanimate) are mentioned, the first pronominal mention refers to the first mentioned referent (Erelt et al. 1993: 209)[2]. In spoken discourse the order in which entities are mentioned does not play an important role, and this is, in my opinion, a rather doubtful criterion for written language too (for a discussion about "competing referents" and sensitiveness of personal pronouns to different criteria in Finnish see Kaiser, this volume). The significance of the entity in the framework of the discourse is of greater consequence.

In example (5) the discussion involves an active man who constantly devises odd business ideas. He is referred to with the pronoun *ta*. In the humorous description of the implementation of one business idea, however, another character enters onto the scene: a foreigner who wishes to come and shoot bears. He is referred to with the pronoun *tema*.

(5)

kui=   ta   käinud   siis   korra   Rootsis   turismireisil. (0.5)
when   3SG-SH   go-PCP   then   once   Sweden-INE   trip-ADE
when=*he* [*ta*] ((man1)) visited Sweden once on a tourist trip. (0.5)

tal   õnnestunud   isiklike   kontaktide   baasil.
3SG.ADE-SH   succeed-PCP   personal-PL.GEN   contact- PL.GEN   basis-ADE
he [*tal*] ((man1)) succeeded on the basis of personal contacts.

(1.5)   sõlmida   paljude   edukate   rootslastega (.)
         conclude-INF   many- PL.GEN   successful-PL.GEN   Swede-PL.COM.
to conclude with many successful Swedes (.)

leping. (0.5)   et ee   tulgu   nemad aga   Eestisse   jahile.
agreement   that   come-IMP.3PL   3PL-LG PTC   Estonia-ILL   hunting-ALL
an agreement. (0.5) that they come to Estonia to, uh, hunt.

enamus   lepinguid   läinud vett   vedama (.)   aga   üks
most   agreement-PL.PTV.   go-PCP water-PTV   pull-INF   but   one
Most of the agreements bore no fruit (.) but one

mees   saatnud   kirja=   et   vot   väga   hea=   et (0.5)   *tema*
man   send-PCP   letter   that   PTC   very   good   that   he3SG-LG
man sent a letter=that OK great=that (0.5) *he* [*tema*] ((man2))

2   Example from (Erelt et al. 1993: 209), in which choice between *ta* and *see* depends on the order of previous mention. I am not convinced that this is the only way to interpret it.
    Tüdruk   vilksas   poisi   poole;   <u>ta</u>   oli kahvatu.
    Girl   look-PAST.3SG   boy-GEN   towards   3SG   be-PAST.3SG pale
    A/the girl looked at a/the boy, <u>she</u> was pale.

saadab	nüüd	tšeki	ära (1.0)	kahe	nädala		pärast
send-3SG	now	cheque	PTC	two-GEN	week-GEN		after

will send a cheque now (1.0) in two weeks

on	Eestis.	et	olgu	karu	olemas (.)	*tema*
be-3SG	Estonia-INE	that	be- IMP.3PL	bear	be-INF	3SG-LG

he will be in Estonia. that the bear had better be ready (.) *he* [*tema*] ((man2))

tuleb	ee	laskma.
come-3SG	uh	shoot-INF

will come and, uh, shoot it.

In example (6) the main character is a ram that is reputed to have a very bad temper. In the same narrative another character, aunt Liisa, is introduced. Since *ta* has been reserved for the ram, aunt Liisa is assigned the demonstrative *see*. Later, when the talk is no longer of aunt Liisa, the ram is also referred to with the demonstrative *see*, but more in the sense of 'that ram's meat' than 'that ram'. The pronoun *ta* continues to be used to refer to the ram as a living creature.

(6)

Liisa-tädi, *see*	ei	tohtind	üldse	liikuda	niigu
Liisa-aunt this	NEG	allow-PCP	ever	move-INF	as

Aunt Liisa, *this* [*see*] ((aunt)) was not allowed to move at all and as soon as she

kummardas	nii	oinas	pani	plaksti,	ja	*ta*
bent-PAST.3SG	so	ram	put- PAST.3SG	slap	and	3SG-SH

bent down the ram butted, and *he* [*ta*] ((the ram))

käis	lahtiselt	ka	ja	siis	pärast	panime küll (0.5)
walk- PAST.3SG	loose	too	and	then	after	put- PAST.1PL

walked around loose too, and then after that we indeed tied (0.5) it

köide	*see*	läks	ükskord	põllu	pääle	*teda*
rope-ILL	this	go- PAST.3SG	once	field-GEN	on	3SG.PTV

up *she* [*see*] ((aunt)) went into the field one day to hit *him* [*teda*] ((the ram))

edasi	lööma näed	niiviisi	/.../
forward	bit-INF see-2SG	so	/.../

that's the way it was   /.../

ei	poisid	noh	nemad	ei	söö	*seda* (0.5)	ee	seda
NEG	boy-PL	uh	3PL	NEG	eat	this- PTV	uh	this- PTV

no the boys, eh, they don't eat *that* [*seda*] ((meat)) (0.5) ee that

just	see	ma=i	mäleta	mis	*ta*	nimi
precisely	this	1SG.-NEG	remember	what	3SG.GEN-SH	name

I don't precisely remember, what *it's* [*ta*] ((the ram's)) name

oli sel oinal.
be- PAST.3SG this-ADE ram- ADE
was that ram's.

When an entity is first mentioned, it is thus introduced into the framework of the discourse. After repeated mention, the entity is already familiar, and it can be referred to in a different manner than that in which it was mentioned on the second occasion. In the case of more tangible entities, especially when physical things or also living creatures are referred to, the following pattern is typical when repeatedly referring to the entity: on the first occasion the referent is mentioned with a full NP, next the demonstrative *see* and then the personal pronoun *ta*. *ta* is thus an entity activated in the discourse, whereas this is not necessarily the case with *see*. Part of the answer is, of course, that (at least) in everyday conversation, abstract referents do not so easily become activated: people generally speak of other people and things. Ideas and situations are more in the background, and add detail, although these are not discussed in greater length as a whole unit. Certain second-level entities may, in conversation, become complete, and thus in that respect resemble first-level entities. Typical examples of these are films, TV-shows, theatre performances etc. In example (7) a theatre production seen on television is discussed, and the referent pronoun changes as follows: *see- ta* (gen.)-*ta* (nom.).

(7)

Kristi: huvitav kas *see* oli mingi väga vana
 interesting Q this be-PAST.3SG some very old
 etendus= vä
 performance Q
 interesting was *that* [*see*] some very old performance=eh?

Mati: mina ei tea (.) ma pole kuulnudki vist
 1SG-LG NEG know 1SG-SH NEG-be hear-PCP-CLT probably
 I don't know (.) I think I haven't even heard of it

 millegipärast (0.5) a mis *ta* pealkiri oli
 forsome reason but what 3SG-SH title be- PAST.3SG
 for some reason (0.5) but what was *its* [*ta*] title

 [võibolla olen ka kuulnud.
 maybe be-1SG too hear-PCP
 [maybe I have heard of it.

Kristi: [meelespea, (.) meelespea oli. (1.5)
 forget-me-not forget-me-not be- PAST.3SG
 [forget-me-not, (.)forget-me-not it was. (1.5)

Kerli: see peab= olema kaheksakümnendate lõpp üheksakümnendate
 this must be-INF eighty-PL.GEN end ninghty- PL.GEN

algus.
beginning
it must=be the end of the eighties beginning of the nineties.

Kristi: ma   usun   ka   et   *ta*   vanem   vist
       1SG-SH   believe-1SG too   that 3SG-SH   old-COM   probably

       eriti   ei   saand   olla.
       especially   NEG   can-PCP   be-INF
       I think *it* [*ta*] probably couldn't have been much older either.

The same *see-ta* pattern can also be used in the case of persons, although this is not typical. I have previously described one such conversation (Pajusalu 1999: 62–63), containing a discussion of two bus drivers who are referred to with the demonstrative *see* until they are opposed to one another, and with the personal pronoun *ta* when the referent has become the main character, i.e. attention has been transferred to him alone.

When an entity is abstract, the pronoun *see* may persist even in the case of repeated mention. In (8) it is referring to an important deed, "with which one leaves one's print in history", and so *see* is repeated three times.

(8)

aga   kas   sul   näiteks   noh (0.8)   ütleme   et
but   Q   2SG-ADE   example-TRA   uh   say-1PL   that
but did you, well, (0.8) ee let's say

sul   noorena   on   mingid   õudset   ee   mingi
2SG-ADE   young-ESS   be-3SG   some-PL.NOM   terrible-PL.NOM.   uh   some
that when young you had some terrible ee some

õudne   püüdlus (.)   midagi   saavutada   midagi   erakordset
terrible   striving   RPR-PTV.+CLT   achieve-INF   RPR-PTV+CLT   exceptional-PTV
terrible striving to do something exceptional

ja   tähtsat   no   ütleme   jälg   ajalukku   vajutada   aga
and   important-PTV   uh   say- 1PL   trace   history-ILL   press-INF   but
and important, well, let's say leave your mark in history but

(.) sa   oled   vana   ja   sul   on   *see*   tegemata   ja
2.SG   be-2SG   old   and   2SG-ADE   be-3.SG   this   do-INF.ABE   and
you're old and you haven't done *it* [*see*] and

sa   saad   aru   et   sa   ei   saagi   *seda*   teha   et
2SG   get-2SG   mind   that   2SG   NEG   get-CLT   this-PTV   do-INF   that
well, you understand that you can't do *it* [*seda*]

noh   sa (.)   sul   on   juba   see   aeg   möödas   kus   sa
uh   2SG   2SG-ADE   be-3SG   already   this   time   over   where   2SG
the time is gone when you could

oleksid	saand	*seda*	teha=	ja
be-COND-2SG	get-PCP	this-PTV	do-INF	and

have done *it* [*seda*]=and

The same may be the case when an entity is indeed physical, but is a thing, a substance for instance, that lacks clear boundaries, such as soup (9). In the same example one can once again see that the entity referred to with the pronoun *see* is not particularly well defined. It may also be vague; let us refer to such incidents as indistinct reference. Thus neither we nor, apparently, the speaker himself know whether the third *see* refers to the same soup or only to the mushrooms. But that is not important.

(9)

see	võib	küll	hea	olla	aga	noh	*see*	tundub	nii
this	may-3SG	PTC	good	be-INF	but	uh	this	seem-3SG	so

it [*see*] may indeed be very good, but, well, *it* [*see*] seems so

kallis	olevat=	sest	vata		kuussada	grammi
expencive	be-PCP	because	see-IMP.2SG		six-hundred	gram-PTV

expensive, because see, six hundred grams of

mahedaid	seeni,	mis	*see*	maksab	vist
mild-PL.PTV	mushroom-PL.PTV	RPN	this	cost-3SG	probably

mild mushrooms, what does *that* [*see*] cost, probably

kolmkümmend	krooni.
thirty	kroon-PTV

thirty kroons.

To sum up, the general tendencies of anaphoric usage of pronouns *tema*, *ta* and *see* are as follows:

1) *tema* is animate, *see* is inanimate and very usually abstract, *ta* is "in between", but more concrete that *see*;
2) *tema* is emphatic and usually in opposition with some other person;
3) the less abstract the referent is, the more it tends to get *ta* as the pronoun for repeated reference;
4) in the case of competing equal (in respect to animateness and concreteness) referents in the same context, the main character (or the most salient one) tends to occupy the shortest possible pronoun *ta*.

See, tema *and* ta *in different cases*

In the previous section, the main principles of the usage of pronouns *see*, *tema* and *ta* have been discussed. Traditionally, different morphological forms of these pronouns (and of the other lexemes of natural language as well) are regarded as being semantically and pragmatically equal, that means, the meaning of a word does not change when the word is declined.

However, we have already seen in Table 1 that the percentage of occurrence of these pronouns is different in the nominative and the genitive. Below I will discuss some differences in the functions of different case forms of pronouns *see*, *tema* and *ta,* above all instances in which *see* refers to an animate and *tema* and *ta* to an inanimate referent, i.e. to the circumstances in which deviations from the typical referential relationship are possible. In the fields of Table 2, these instances are numerically presented in ordinary, not bold, type.

Singular nominative

The singular nominative is the most frequently used case in everyday conversation (a total of 648 times). In the data under examination, the pronoun *ta* occurred most frequently in the nominative (375 times, 58% of nominative forms), followed by the pronoun *see* (240 times, 37%) and least frequently the pronoun *tema* (33 times, 5%). *Tema* referred only to animate referents.

See

In accordance with the rules of written Estonian, *see* is the only of the forms examined that can be the head noun of the relative or complement clause in the main clause. In speech, of course, it is often difficult to determine whether one is dealing with a correlative of a subordinate clause or not, although one can at least say that when a speaker wishes to, using a subordinate clause, to continue his sentence by specifying the entity referred with a pronoun, he selects the demonstrative *see*. These are usually cataphoric, since the main designation of reference takes place after the uttering of the pronoun. In this kind of construction there is hardly any difference between an animate and inanimate referent. Such cases make up a large proportion of instances of *see* in my data (10–13).

(10)

ainuke	asi	on	see	et	me	ei	tea	ju
only	thing	be-3SG	this	that	1.SG	NEG	know	PTC

the only thing *is* [*see*] that we don't know, right

(11)

hästi	lahe	on	see	kui	keegi	teatris	köhib
very	cool	be-3SG	this	when	someone	theatre-INE	cough-3SG

it's [*see*] really cool when someone coughs in the theatre

(12)

see	oli	omapärane	õhkkond	mis	oli
this	be-PAST.3SG	unique	atmosphere	RPN	be-PAST.3SG

ülikooli	kliinikute
university-GEN	clinic-PL.GEN

it [*see*] was a unique atmosphere, that of the university clinic

(13)

ma	ütsin	no	*see*	õpetab	ju	kes	ei	oska
1SG	say-1SG	uh	this	teach-3SG	PTC	RPN	NEG	can

I said well, it's *the one* [*see*] who isn't able that teaches

The subordinate clause may also be said before the pronoun itself, although this is a much rarer case. In example (14) the relative clause indeed comes first, and then the various speakers offer different main clauses.

(14)

M:
kõigepealt	tehakse	nagu	nädala	jooksul	on
at first	do-PSS	as	week-GEN	during	be-3SG

at first they do like for a week there's

konkurss, (.) et	kes	toob	kõige	odavama
competition that	RPN	bring-3SG	all-GEN	cheap-COM.GEN

a competition, (.) that the one who brings the cheapest

retsepti	onju,
reciepe	PTC

recipe, right

K: mhmh
/feedback/

M:
see	saab	mingi	tasuta	lõuna
this	get-3SG	some-GEN	cost-ABE	lunch-GEN

that (one) [*see*] gets some free lunch or other,

näiteks	seal	kloaagis
example-TRA	there	cloaca-INE

for example there in the cloaca

K:
jah	*see*	saab	eesti	filoloogiasse	kõmm	viie	omale.
yes	this	get-3SG	estonian	philology	pow	five-GEN	self-ALL

yeah, *that* (one) [*see*] will get an A in Estonian philology just like that, pow.

M:
ei	*see*	saab	tasuta	lõuna	ee
NEG	this	get-3SG	cost-ABE	lunch-GEN	um

that (one) [*see*] will get a free lunch in the, uh, cafeteria,

sööklas,	seal	kloaagis	tead
cafeteria-INE	there	cloaca-INE	know-2SG

there in the cloaca, you know

Also similar to that listed above is the so-called presentational clause, which begins with the pronoun *see* and the verb *olema* 'to be' and offers a new name or definition for an entity that has already in some manner been identified. In such clauses *see* may present an animate entity, as in (15) for instance, in where the speakers discuss a person who was with the watchman, and attempt to identify that same person again. In Estonian, deictic clauses, in which the pronoun *see* is accompanied by a gesture towards the entity being referred to, are also of this variety.

(15)

siis	tuli	valvur	kellel	on	viis	last
then	come-PAST.3SG	watchman	RPN	be-3SG	five	child-PTV

then the watchman who has five children came, right,

onju	üks	mingi	kutt	kaasas	ma	ei	tea	kas	*see*	on
PTC	one	some	guy	with	1SG	NEG	know	Q	this	be-3SG

some guy was with him, I don't know if *it* [*see*] was

ta	poeg	siis	vä.
3SG.GEN-SH	son	then	Q

his son or what.

In examples (10–12 and 15), the sentence-forming verb is *olema* ['to be'], and thus one can say that the verb *olema* has a strong tendency to have the demonstrative pronoun *see* as its subject. In fact, it is even difficult to find an example of the pronoun *see* in which it does not occur in the same sentence as the verb *olema*. The contrary is not, however, the case, as some other pronoun, in our data both *ta* and *tema*, can also occur with the verb *olema*. For instance, if an entity previously referred to is further characterised but not newly identified, a personal pronoun is typically used.

(16)

aga	Ilona	ei	tahtnud.	sest	*ta*	on	nii	väsinud.
but	Ilona	NEG	want-PCP	because	3SG-SH	be-3SG	so	tired

but Ilona didn't want to. because *she* is so tired.

Since in Estonian *see* also has the function of hesitation, it can be used as person-referent when a name cannot be remembered. In example (17), one possible interpretation is that the speaker cannot immediately remember Endla's name.

(17)

aga	see=	et,	mis	*see*	siis	rääkis	Endla. (.)
but	this	that	RPN	this	then	tell-PAST.3SG	Endla

but that, uh, what did *that one* [*see*] say then Endla.

	saite	juttu	ajada?
	get-PAST.2PL	talk-PTV	push-INF

were you able to talk?

Examples (10–15) and (17) are instances of *see* where the choice of pronoun is caused syntactically, they are not changeble to *tema* or *ta* even when they are used in speaking about a person. Such instances in which *see* refers to a person, and there are no grammatical reasons or reasons due to faulty recollection, occurred in only five conversations, in two of them twice in succession, so altogether only 6 instances, which are taken in consideration in Table 2. Two of these are presented in example (6) (aunt and ram), four in examples (18–20). According to my intuition, there is no reason they could not also contain personal pronouns. The *see* used emphasises the referent and provides an opportunity to oppose it to some other. The unemphatic pronoun *ta* does not permit emphasis, although *tema* permits it just as well as *see* does. It has sometimes been thought that *see*, when used to refer to a person, is pejorative, although in my data this is not completely clear; only (20) has a pejorative content. There is nevertheless a certain emotional emphasis in such use of the demonstrative.

(18)

Maia	siis	hoidis	seda	Mairet. (1.5)	ja	siis	perastpoole =
Maia	then	keep-PAST.3SG	this	maire-PTV	and	then	later

Maia was then looking after that Maire. (1.5) and then later

oli	vanaema, (.)	aga	no	see	ei	saand	süüa
be-PAST.3SG	grandmother	but	uh	this	neg	get-PCP	eat-INF

was grandmother, (.) but well, *that one* [*see*] couldn't

minna	tooma. (2.5)	see	ei	saand	köögist	tuua.
go-INF	bring-INF	this	NEG	get-PCP	kitchen	bring-INF

go to bring food. (2.5) *that one* [*see*] couldn't bring it from the kitchen.

(19)

noh	mina	hakkasin	seda	noormeest	vaatama,	see
uh	1SG	begin-PAST.1SG	this-PTV	young-man	watch-INF	this

well I began to look at that young man, and *that one* [*see*]

hakkas	mind	ka	vaatama
begin-PAST.3SG	1SG-PTV	too	watch-INF

began to look at me too

(20) ((conversation about politics, name changed))

JN:	noh	seda	Järvelille	nüüd, (0.5)	v=	mis	ta
	uh	this-PTV	Järvelill-PTV	now	Q	what	3SG-SH

	on	no=	Järvelill
	be-3SG	uh	Järvelill

well that Järvelill, (0.5) or what was he, uh Järvelill

EP: mhmh (.) (0.5)   Riho. (0.5)
    mhm   Riho
    mhmh, Riho

JN: ega   *see*   vist   pole   suurem   asi
    NEG   this   probably   be-NEG   big-COMP   thing
    that one [see] isn't all that great, I think

Ta

ta is unemphatic and refers most often to an animate creature about whom one is speaking. In everyday conversation the same person may sometimes be referred to tens of times in succession, if there are no other "competing" characters, and in this case the referential comprehensibility is well retained. In this context it is instances in which *ta* does not refer to an animate creature that are of interest. These were 66 out of a total of 375 occurrences of *ta*, i.e. 18%. In the great majority of instances, the referents were inanimate physical entities. In (21) it is a piece of clothing, in (22) a microphone. Here it is difficult to calculate with precision whether an entity can be considered to be a physical thing or not (in the case of substance words or intellectual objects such as a performance or a text, for instance). In approximate terms one can, however, say that in the everyday conversations examined, physical things are referred to with the demonstrative *see* in about half of all cases and with the personal pronoun *ta* in the other half. Examples (21–23) contain precisely such uses of *ta* that one could, on the basis of one's intuition, also exchange for *see*.

(21) ((conversation took place about a sweater that the speaker had seen in a store and would like to buy, but cannot, because it is too expensive))

saaks   omale   ühe   riide   asja   siis=   *ta*
get-COND   self-all   one-GEN   cloth-GEN   thing-GEN   then   3.SG-SH
if I could buy myself a piece of clothing then=*it's [ta]*

on   üle   viiesaja   krooni,   no   ma   ei   saa   osta
be-3SG   more   five-hundred   kroon-PTV   uh   1SG   NEG   get   buy-INF
over five hundred kroons, you know I can't buy

siukse   palgaga   mitte   ühtegi   asja (0.5)   no   mingi
such-GEN   salary-COM   neg   one-PTV-CLT   thing- PTV   uh   some
a single thing with this kind of salary. Even something

isegi   väike   asigi,   oleks   *ta*   mingi   jope   või   sihuke   aga
even   small   thing-CLT   be-COND   3SG-SH   some   jacket   or   such   but
small, be it *[ta]* some jacket or something, but, well,

noh   kõige   väiksem   niuke   pisike   kampsun.   hästi   armas.   no
uh   all-GEN   small-COM   such   small   sweater   very   sweet   uh
the smallest, a little sweater like this. Really sweet. Well

kampsun   *ta*   ka   ei   ole   *ta*   on   nagu   jakike
sweater   3SG-SH   too   NEG   be   3SG-SH   be-3SG   as   jacket-DEM

selline.
such

it [*ta*] isn't a sweater really either, *it's* [*ta*] like a jacket sort of thing.

In example (22) the situation is distinctive in that the microphone has not previously been referred to (not in the excerpt under examination), and since the microphone tangibly exists in the situation, one can consider this to be deictic and not anaphoric use. The pronoun use is, however, that of a typical narrative.

(22) ((the microphone is being set up for the recording))

ma	pean	ta	panema	niimodi=	et	ta
1SG	must-1SG	3SG.GEN-SH	put-INF	so	that	3SG-SH

I have to put *it* [*ta*] like this=so that *it* [*ta*]

oleks (0.8)	ilmselt	frontaalselt	meie	poole (.)	ta	praegu
be-COND	apparently	facing	1PL	towards	3SG-SH	now

will be facing towards us (.) *it's* [*ta*]

ripub	meil.(.)	ma	panen	ta
hang-3SG	1PL-ADE	1SG	put-1SG	3SG.GEN-SH

hanging now. (.) I'll put *it* [*ta*]

laua	peale.
table-GEN	on.

on the table.

In certain idiomatic combinations, *ta* may occur in place of *see* even such that its referent is an abstract situation. Example (23) falls into this category.

(23)

nii	ta	ongi
so	3SG-SH	be-CLT

that's the way *it* [*ta*] is

Of other text types, I have also found uses of *ta* where it refers to abstract entities in other phrases elsewhere than in idiomatic phrases, for instance *ta* has been used to refer to a court case or work as a night watchman (Pajusalu 1995). I have personally heard sentence (24), where one *ta* refers to the radio and the other to the weather. It is possible that it is in speaking of the weather that the pronoun *ta* is often used, since the weather is one of the most common referents of discourse, and may despite its ontological abstraction nevertheless be cognitively very tangible.

(24)

ta ((raadio))	ütles	et	ta ((ilm))	läheb	varsti	jälle
3SG-SH	say-PAST.3SG	that	3SG-SH	go-3SG	soon	again

soojemaks
warm- COM.TRA
it [*ta*] ((the radio)) said that *it* [*ta*] ((the weather)) would soon warm up again

It appears that in everyday conversation reference to an abstract entity with *ta* is nevertheless a relatively rare phenomenon.

Singular genitive

Genitive pronouns occur in conversation considerably less frequently than nominative pronouns, and there were altogether only 45 of these occurences, of which only six were in the *ta* form, sixteen in the *tema* form and 23 in the *selle* form. 14 instances of *tema*, 4 of *ta* and 1 of *selle* referred to persons.

See

See is typical in referring to non-persons in the genitive form. The greatest relative number of these were made up of prepositional/postpositional phrases in which *see* referred to an abstract situation or even a proposition, such as, for instance, examples (25–26), but also syntactic objects like examples (27–28).

(25)

ega	ma	*selle*	peale	iga	päev	ei	mõtle
NEG	1SG	this-GEN	on	every	day	NEG	think

I don't think about *it* [*selle*] every day though

(26)

reageerisid	*selle*	peale	eitavalt
react-3PL	this-GEN	on	negatively

they reacted negatively to *this* [*selle*]

(27)

selle	panen	selga ((*selle* = särk))
this-GEN	put-1SG	back-ILL

I'll put this [*selle*] on ((*selle* = shirt))

(28)

selle	me	teeme	ära	järgmine	aasta
this-GEN	1PL	do-1PL	PTC	next	year

that [*selle*] we'll do next year

On one occasion *selle* also referred to a person, and it is possible that here the selection was influenced by the *see* previously used, for different reasons, to refer to the same referent.

(29)

R: see   on   see   kes   töötas   seal (.) [Veerikul=vä
   this   be-3SG this RPN   work-PAST.3SG there   Veeriku-ADE
   she's [see] the one [see] who worked there (.) [In Veeriku, eh?

A: [Veerikul   ahah
    Veeriku-ADE   yes
   [In Veeriku ahah

R: issand   *selle*   laps   on   kümne   aastane
   god   this-GEN   child   be-3SG   ten-GEN   year-old
   good heavens *her* [*selle*] child is ten years old,

   minu   meelest
   1SG-GEN mind-ELA
   I think

Ta

ta is rare in the genitive. The six forms found uniformly covered the three areas of use of the genitive, there were 2 genitive attributes (30–31) and two postpositional phrase extensions (32–33), which referred to an animate referent, and two syntactic objects (see example 22, in which the microphone is discussed), which referred to an inanimate referent.

(30)

ta   ema   käis   kaalujälgijates
3SG.GEN-SH   mother   go-PAST.3SG   weightwatchers
his [*ta*] mother attended weightwatchers

(31)

kas   see   on   *ta*   poeg   siis   vä
Q   this   be-3.SG 3SG.GEN-SH   son   then   Q
is that *her* [*ta*] son then, eh?

(32)

aga   mul   oleks   oskust   *ta*   ees
but   1SG.ADE   be-COND   ability   3SG.GEN-SH   in-front-of

vabandada
apologise- INF
but I would have the ability to apologise to *her* [*ta*]?

(33)

kui   selline   iseteadlik   inimene   tuleb   kõnnib
when   such   conceited   person   come-3SG   walk-3SG

125

ta	juurde
3SG.GEN-SH	to

when such a conceited person were to walk up to *her* [*ta*]?

Tema

Tema is typically in the genitive form when a person is being referred to, since syntactical objects with an animate referent in the genitive form occur very rarely; such cases involve genitive attributes (34) and postpositional phrases (35).

(34)

sellega	lõhutakse	*tema*	vabadust
this-COM	break-PSS	3SG.GEN-LG	freedom-PTV

with this *his* [*tema*] freedom is infringed upon

(35)

kõik	lähevad	*tema*	juurde
all	go-3PL	3SG.GEN-LG	to

everybody goes to see *him* [*tema*]

In two cases, however, an inanimate entity is involved; (36) is a quotation from a written grammatical treatise and (37) is an idiomatic expression.

(36)

tema	morfeemkoostis
3SG.GEN-LG	morpheme stucture

its [*tema*] morpheme structure

(37)

puud	tuntakse	*tema*	viljast.
tree-PTV	know-PSS	3SG.GEN-LG	fruit-ELA

a tree shall be known by *its* [*tema*] fruit.

Thus in the genitive, the long form *tema* of the personal pronoun is preferred in referring to an animate entity, and the demonstrative *selle* in referring to an inanimate entity. The fact that the genitive favours the long form also became evident from Raili Pool's research into first and second person pronouns (Pool 1999). In the case of the third person it is also important that the differentiation between inanimate and animate entities is clearer in the genitive than in the nominative. *tema*, being longer and thus a more natural genitive form, is nevertheless as if "more alive" than *ta* which in the nominative refers rather often to inanimate referents, while *tema* (nom.) refers (at least in in my data) only to animate entities. Thus the demonstrative genitive form occupies a relatively greater proportion of total use.

Locatives

Of the locatives, only the allative and adessive, which are predominantly involved with the pronoun *ta* (see Table 1), occurred more frequently. The fact that a pronoun that usually refers to persons is used predominantly can be explained by the fact that the function of the external local cases in Estonian is also to transmit a semantic role of POSSESSOR (in English grammar this often corresponds to the indirect object). A possessor is naturally a person. The fact that the short form is so greatly preferred is also a familiar phenomenon in the case of other personal pronouns (Pool 1999).

A secondary reason why person-referent pronouns are so greatly predominant in these cases is that when the entity referred to is a place, then the adverbial *seal*, which refers to an object in the distance, is used in corresponding forms instead of the demonstrative *see*. In my data there were a total of 98 instances in which the demonstrative adverbial formed an independent NP and referred anaphorically to some entity that was previously referred to in the conversation. That entity is typically a place, such as a certain section of Tallinn in example (38).

(38) ((conversation about the bad condition of buildings in Lasnamäe))

ma	pakun	välja	et	see	karp	ise	seisab	*seal*
1SG	offer-1SG	out	that	this	box	self	stand-3SG	there

püsti	kauem	kui	see	maja	siin
vertically	long-COMP	than	this	house	here

I'm willing to bet that that box itself will stand *there* [*seal*] for longer than this building here

The locative demonstrative *seal* may also often refer to an event, which may perhaps also indirectly be considered to be a place (an event is always held/occurs in a certain place, and cognitively the place is an important part of the event) (39). In the case of example (38) such demonstratives may also be considered to be deictic (they are remote from the speaker and if they were in the same location as the speaker, the demonstrative *siin* [here] would be used), usages of demonstrative *seal* are clear anaphors when referring to events. In example (39) it can also be clearly seen how *seal* belongs to the paradigm of the pronoun *see*: in other cases forms of *see* are used (twice *seda* and once *sellest*, although the latter has an indistinct reference and may also refer to the event of watching as a whole), but in locatives *seal*.

(39)

A:	kas	sina	mäletad	kui	Rakveres	mängiti	*seda*
Q		2SG	remember-2SG	when	Rakvere-INE	play-PSS.PAST	this-PTV

ee   Strindbergi   Isa. (.)
um   Strindberg-GEN   father
do you remember when that, uh, Stridberg's Father was played at the Rakvere [theatre]. (.)

B: mäletan   ja   ma   olen   *seda*   isegi   vaatamas
    remember-1SG and   1SG   be-1SG   this-PTV   even   watch-INF.INE
    I remember and I've even been to see *it* [*seda*] and

    käinud   ja =õ   ma   mäletan   ainult   seda   fakti,   et
    go-PCP   and um   1SG   remember-1SG   only   this-PTV   fact   that
    I only remember the fact that

    seda   mängiti,   ja   rohkem   ma   ei   mäleta
    this-PTV   play-PSS.PAST   and   more   1SG   NEG   remember
    it [*seda*] was played, I remember nothing more

A: aga   minul   on   *sellest*   meeles   mingi   niisugune
    but   1SG-ADE   be-3SG   this-ELA-LG   mind-INE   some   such
    but I remember about *this* [*sellest*] that

    fakt,   et   Aliis   Talvik   mängis   *seal*   kedagi
    fact   that   Aliis   Talvik   play-PAST.3SG   there   someone
    Aliis Talvik played someone *there* [*seal*]

Events and other temporal entities contain a place in a cognitive sense, but it is more complicated to interpret reference to mental objects with adverbs of place. The main such mental entities are books and other texts (40–41). This, however, is the same phenomenon as when the same entities are referred to with a noun, since then locatives are also used. Here it is not important whether one thinks that place (location) is cognitively and historically primary (as is generally believed in the metaphor theory of the Lakoff-Johnson style), or whether the place has never been just a physical entity for the person. What is important is that in locatives the adverbial of place governs a significant number of inanimate referents.

In her study of the Finnish demonstratives, Laury (1997: 139) argued that "locative forms (of the demonstratives) are used for referents conceptualised as the ground." At first sight, the use of adverbials in Estonian also appears to be connected precisely with those referents that one may cognitively consider to be the ground. Example (41), however, demonstrates that this is not necessarily the case, since a book is here still the object that is spoken of, and thus instead occupies the position of a figure.

(40)

minu   asjad   on   aint   ühe   paberi   peal   *seal*
1SG-GEN   thing-PL   be-3SG   only   one-GEN   paper   on   there

kus   on   see   jutt,   et   mul   varastati   ära
RPN   be-3SG   this   story   that   1SG-ADE   steel-PASS.PAST   PTC

pilet.
ticket
my things are on only one piece of paper [*there*] [*seal*] where it says a ticket was stolen from me.

(41)

Jaan: ega   populaarteaduslikud   raamatud   ei   ole
       NEG   popular-scientifical-PL book-PL   NEG   be

       aksiomaatilised.
       axiomatic-PL
       popular science books are not axiomatic.

Margo: ei   seda   küll   aga   saad   aru   *seal*   on
       NEG   this-PTV   PTC   but   get-2SG   mind   there   be-3SG
       no, that's true, but you know, *there/in them* is [*seal*]

           mingi   kindel   põhi   millele   nad   on   nagu   üles   ehitatud.
           some   certain   basis   RPN-ADE   3PL-SH   be-3PL   like   up   build-PCP
           a certain basis on which they are, like, constructed.

Estonian grammar would permit the use of the pronoun *see* in all of these instances, although its forms are long and they are rarely used in actual everyday conversation. It may be that one of the reasons for preferring a locative is the possibility to avoid the choice between different lexically determined local cases (for instance illative or allative) as has been suggested for Finnish by Duvallon (this volume). In the data there are a total of 1 *selles*, 4 *sellest* and 3 *sellele*, and not one of these served the function of an adverb of place, but are either heads of a subordinate clause (42–43) or complements whose case is governed by verb (44). It appears that the pronoun *see* is used in locatives by the contemporary speaker when the locative's grammatical, and not cognitive motivation is involved (although historically, cognitive metaphor connections can also usually be found).

(42)

asi   on   *selles*   et
thing   be-3SG   this-INE   that
the thing is that

(43)

tänu   *sellele*,   et
thanks   this-ALL   that
thanks to the fact that

(44)

sellest   ta   ei   kirjuta
this-ELA   3SG   NEG   write
he doesn't write about *that* [*sellest*]

In one example *sealt* is also used in a context due entirely to government that linguistic instinct does not consider usual, but also not a mistake. In example (45) it namely refers to bones from which soup is cooked, i.e. it is a source, which in other languages is also often grammaticalised into a separate locative. Evidence that this is not an error is provided by the fact that two speakers in succession use the same form.

(45) ((conversation about a rooster called Koku, who has been almost completely eaten))

M: Kokul   on   need   seljaluud (.)   need   on   järgi
   Koku-ADE be-3PL   this-PL   backbone-PL   this-PL   be-3PL   left

veel
still
Koku has got those backbones (.) those are still left over

K: aa
   /feedback/

H: [*sealt*   veel]
   from there   still

M: [sest   ega   ma]   neid   ei   pannud   *sealt*
   because   NEG   1SG   3PL.PTV   NEG   put-PCP   from there
   Because I didn't put them. From *these* [sealt]

   saab   veel   suppi   keeta
   get-3SG   still   soup-PTV   boil-INF
   one can still make some soup

Seal is part of the paradigm of the demonstrative *see* even when it is used with the function of an article: it is precisely the the adverb *seal* that is used in place-referent NPs as the pro-form that is part of the NP and expresses its definitness (Pajusalu 1997b, 2001).

Plural nominative

The nominative is the only case in wich speakers have a choice of three different forms in the plural, as can be seen in Table 1. In comparison with the singular, there are significantly fewer corresponding forms, and thus it is more difficult to make generalisations. In comparing numbers, it is noteworthy that *need* (plural for *see*) appears less frequently than the singular *see*, although there is apparently a clear explanation for this: since *see* is a typically used to refer to abstract entities, it is clear that these are simply not spoken of in the plural. In other respects the entities referred to break down between animate and inanimate like the singular: of 13 occurrences, only one referred to an inanimate entity (46).

(46)

tal	on	nisukesed	pikemad	sõrmed	kah (.)
3SG.ADE-SH	be-3PL	such-PL	long-COMP	finger-PL	too

temal	*nemad* ((=sõrmed)	on	teistsugused
3SG.ADE.-LG	3PL-LG	be-3.PL	different

she has kind of longer fingers too (.) *those* [*nemad*] of his are different

If one compares the relationship between the two personal pronouns, *nemad* (plural for *tema*) represents 18% of plural personal pronouns, while *tema* represents only 8% of singular personal pronouns. Here one can see a weak tendency towards the fact that the long form is used more often in the plural than in the singular. Generally, however, it is typical that in the case of emphasis and relatively less well-known entities are referred to with the long form. In example (47) there is a discussion of how a married couple purchased an ironing table, and initially they are referred to with the neutral form *neile* (short plural for *see, tema* and *ta*), later with the long form *nemad* (plural for *tema*), later the neutral form *neil* (short plural for *see, tema* and *ta*) and then the short form *nad* (plural for *ta*).

(47)

said	uue	korteri=	ja (.)	ja (.)	keegi
get-PAST.3PL	new-GEN	apartment	and	and	someone

got a new apartment and (.) and (.) someone

kinkis	jõuluks	*neile*	triikraua=	ja	siis
present-3SG. PAST	Christmas-TRA	3PL-ADE-SH	iron	and	then

gave *them* [*neile*] an iron for Christmas and then

nemad	mõtsid=	et	vaja	triikimislauda /.../	ja	*neil*
3PL-LG	think-3PL.PAST	that	need	ironing-board	and	3SG.ADE-SH

they [*nemad*] thought that they would need an ironing board /.../ and *they* [*neil*]

on	maja	kõrval	majatarvete	pood=	ja /.../
be-3SG	house-GEN	next-to	home-appliance-PL.GEN	shop	and

have a home appliances store nearby and/.../

ja	siis	*nad*	viisidki	selle	väiksema	tagasi.
and	then	3PL-SH	bring-PAST-CLT	this-GEN	small-COMP	back

and then *they* [*nad*] took the smaller one back.

There were, however, too few plural forms to make larger-scale generalisations about their use. One interesting tendency whose validity should be verified in future using more extensive data is the occurrence of the long personal pronoun form in the case of the first mention of collective animate entities.

In everyday conversations, collective entities are typically groups of people. They can be referred to, even upon first mention, using a pronoun, if the institution that makes up the group has already been mentioned (see Laury, this volume, for more discussion about referents that can be mentioned using a pronoun on the first mention due to an already evoked schema). In example (48) the Kaseke Restaurant, where the speaker briefly worked, is mentioned. *Nemad* (plural for *tema*) refers to the restaurant's other employees, who have not yet been mentioned (at least in the conversation under examination here) and who can be identified only through the restaurant. Here the entity that is more difficult to identify is referred to by the longer form. However, the example has another interpretation too, namely that the staff of the restaurant is opposed to the speaker ("they didn't want to peel onions but I had to") and this is the reason for using the long form.

(48) ((conversation during onion peeling))

Eha: kui   mina   olin   sääl (.)   sääl   sääl   Kasekeses   siis
     when   1SG   be-1SG. PAST   there   there   there   Kaseke-INE   then
     when I was there (.) there there in Kaseke then

   minule   antigi (1.5)   tead   ku   palju   seal
   1SG.-ADE   give-PASS-CLT   know-2SG   as   many   there
   I was given (1.5) can you imagine

   sibulaid   pidi   koorima (.)   kausitäis (.)   pesukausitäis (1.2)
   onion-PL.PTV   must-3SG.PAST   peel-INF   bowlful   washing-bowlful
   how many onions one had to peel (.) a bowlful (.) a washing bowl full (1.2)

   ja   siis   *nemad*   ise   ei   tahtnud   sibulaid   koorida
   and   then   3PL-LG   self   NEG   want-PCP   onion-PL.PTV   peel-INF
   and then you *they* [*nemad*] themselves didn't want to peel onions

Conclusion

The main anaphoric tracking devices of the Estonian language are the demonstratives *see* and *seal* and the third person pronouns *tema* and *ta*, which together form three paradigms.

Animate creatures are referred to primarily with personal pronouns. However, the demonstrative may be used in a presentational clause, or when there are two different animate referents involved, or sometimes also for pragmatic emphasis in the case of a relatively new referent. The short form *ta* is specialised above all for the nominative, although the long nominative *tema* can also occur in the case of emphasis. The genitive is expressed primarily with the long form *tema*.

Inanimate abstract entities are referred to with the various forms of the demonstrative *see*. In the case of a very familiar entity and in some idiomatic expressions, an abstract entity can also be referred to with the short personal pronoun *ta*, whereas the long personal pronoun occurs very rarely (although it is not impossible).

The most interesting is the interconnection of the paradigms of the different pro-forms in the case of inanimate physical objects. One can practically say that in the nominative these are referred to with the personal pronoun *ta*, in the genitive with the demonstrative pronoun *see* (*selle*) and in the locative with the demonstrative adverb *sinna, seal, sealt*.

	ANIMATE	INANIMATE physical	INANIMATE abstract
nominative	ta ~ tema	ta ~ see	see
genitive	tema	selle	selle
locatives	talle, tal, talt	sinna, seal, sealt	sellesse, selles, sellest
plural nom.	nemad ~ nad	nad ~ need	need

The above demonstrates that in a language with a diverse morphology such as the Estonian language, we cannot, even in such pragmatic units as deictics, forget the interaction between grammar from the one side and meaning and pragmatic factors (topicality and information flow) from the other. The Estonian language is also striving towards the differentiation of different cases, although the nominative and genitive forms of many words are the same. Thus in the genitive the longer pro-forms *tema* and *selle* are used instead of the short *ta*, which pragmatically would be suited to both animate and inanimate entities.

It would be very interesting to look at the correlation between anaphoric form and the antecedent's or pronoun's grammatical role (see also Kaiser, this volume). The genitive and partitive are the prototypical object cases in Estonian, while the nominative is prototypically the case of the subject. We can see from Table 1 that there are many more demonstratives in the "object cases". However, the Estonian cases are polyfunctional and such a generalisation would require much more research.

REFERENCES

Diessel, Holger. 1999. *Demonstratives: form, function and grammaticalization.* Amsterdam/Philadelphia: John Benjamins PC.

Gundel, Jeanette, Nancy Hedberg and Ron Zacharski. 1993. Cognitive status and the form of reffering expressions in discourse. *Language* 69: 274–307.

Etelämäki, Marja. 1998. Kuva puheenalaisena. In Lea Laitinen and Lea Rojola (ed.) *Sanan voima.* Helsinki: Suomalaisen Kirjallisuuden Seura. 34–80.

Erelt, Mati, Reet Kasik, Helle Metslang, Henno Rajandi, Kristiina Ross, Henn Saari, Kaja Tael and Silvi Vare. 1993. *Eesti keele grammatika II.* Tallinn: Eesti Teaduste Akadeemia Eesti Keele Instituut.

Himmelmann, Nikolaus P. 1996. Demonstratives in narrative discourse: A taxonomy of universal uses. – In Barbara Fox (ed.) *Studies in Anaphora.* Amsterdam: John Benjamins PC. 205–254.

Larjavaara, Matti. 1990. *Suomen deiksis.* Suomi 156. Helsinki: Suomalaisen Kirjallisuuden Seura

Laury, Ritva. 1997. *Demonstratives in interaction.* Amsterdam/Philadelphia: John Benjamins PC.

Lyons, John 1977. *Semantics.* Cambridge: Cambridge University Press.

Pajusalu, Renate. 1995. Pronominit *see, tema* ja *ta* viron puhekielessä. *Sananjalka* 37: 81–93.
Pajusalu, Renate. 1996. Pronoun systems of common Estonian and Estonian dialects in a contrastive perspective. – In Mati Erelt (ed.) *Estonian Typological Studies I*. Publications of the Department of Estonian of the University of Tartu 4. 145–164.
Pajusalu, Renate. 1997a. Eesti pronoomenid I. – *Keel ja Kirjandus*: 24–30, 106–115.
Pajusalu, Renate. 1997b. Is there an article in (spoken) Estonian? – In Mati Erelt (ed.) *Estonian Typological Studies II*. Publications of the Department of Estonian of the University of Tartu 8. 146–177.
Pajusalu, Renate. 1999. *Deiktikud eesti keeles. Dissertationes Philologiae Estonicae Universitatis Tartuensis*, Tartu: Tartu Ülikooli kirjastus.
Pajusalu, Renate. 2001. Definite and indefinite determiners in Estonian. – In Enikö Nemeth T. (ed.) *Pragmatics in 2000*. Selected Papers from the 7th International Pragmatics Conference. Antwerp. 458–469.
Pool, Raili. 1999. About the use of different forms of the first and second person singular personal pronouns in Estonian cases. – Mati Erelt (ed.) *Estonian Typological Studies III*. Publications of the Department of Estonian of the University of Tartu 11, Tartu. 158–184.
Seppänen, Eeva-Leena. 1998. *Läsnäolon pronominit*. Helsinki: Suomalaisen Kirjallisuuden Seura.

ELSI KAISER

When salience isn't enough
Pronouns, demonstratives and the quest for an antecedent

*Introduction**

According to many researchers, the form of a referring expression is connected to the accessibility or salience of its referent, and the most reduced referring expressions are used to refer to the most salient[1] referents, i.e. those which are at the center of attention, most prominent at that point in the discourse. In this paper, I present evidence from Finnish suggesting that the relation between referential expressions and salience is more complex. On the basis of psycholinguistic experiments and corpus data, I argue that two types of third person anaphors in Finnish differ in their referential properties and are sensitive to different kinds of factors. More specifically, I present evidence which indicates that the third person pronoun *hän* 's/he' is sensitive to the grammatical role of the antecedent, whereas the demonstrative anaphor *tämä* 'this' – which can also be used to refer back to human referents – is sensitive to salience. I also show that *tämä* should not be viewed simply as a disambiguation tool for contexts with more than one singular third person referent. Corpus data indicate that the salience scale that *tämä* is sensitive to is a general scale that includes the various entities present in the discourse model at that point, and not just third-person singular entities. Clearly, these patterns cannot be captured by an approach that is based on a unified notion of salience and treats pronouns as referring to more salient referents and demonstratives as referring to less salient ones. On a more speculative note, I also suggest that differences in the referential properties of the pronoun and

---

* Thanks to Cassie Creswell, Eleni Miltsakaki, Kimiko Nakanishi, Ritva Laury, Ellen Prince, Maribel Romero, John Trueswell, Jennifer Venditti and David Ahn for many useful comments and suggestions. Thanks also to audiences at various conferences at which earlier versions of some pars of this paper were presented, including the 19th Scandinavian conference in Tromsø and the 38th Chicago Linguistic Society Annual Meeting. All errors are my own.

1 The terms 'salience' and 'accessibility' are used in different ways by different groups of researchers. In this paper, I will primarily use the term 'salience.' Thus, in this paper, the most 'salient' referent is the referent that is at the center of attention at that point in the discourse.

the demonstrative suggest that perhaps these two forms access different levels of representation: It could be that *hän* taps into the syntactic level and *tämä* into the discourse level.

The starting point for this paper is the often-asked question, what makes a referent salient? In light of the well-known claim that there exists a connection between the form of a referential expression and the salience of its referent, we would like to know what makes a referent a likely candidate for subsequent mention with a reduced referential form. Two of the factors that have been claimed to have an impact on referent salience are grammatical role and word order. Here, I investigate the role they play in Finnish, a highly inflected, flexible word order language with canonical SVO order (Vilkuna 1989, 1995, Helasvuo 2001). Standard Finnish has two kinds of singular third person anaphors: the gender-neutral pronoun *hän* 's/he' and the demonstrative *tämä* 'this', which can also be used for human referents.[2] (Dialects of colloquial Finnish have somewhat different anaphoric systems, see e.g. Laitinen 1992, this volume, Seppänen 1998, this volume, Etelämäki this volume). I present here the results of two psycholinguistic experiments which investigate the referential properties of these two anaphors, and I also discuss naturally-occurring corpus data from written Finnish.

On the basis of the experimental results and patterns in the corpus data, I claim that *hän* 's/he' and *tämä* 'this' differ in their referential properties and are sensitive to different kinds of factors. The experimental results show that *hän* prefers to refer to subjects, regardless of word order, and *tämä* tends to refer to postverbal constituents, especially objects. I present a tentative hypothesis that the two forms differ with respect to which level of representation they have access to: The demonstrative *tämä* accesses the discourse level, and is associated with the low end of a salience scale, and the pronoun *hän* accesses the syntactic level, and is associated with the high end of a grammatical role scale. The corpus patterns show that the relevant salience scale (whose lower end *tämä* is hypothesized to refer to) is not restricted to third-person singular entities and includes the various entities present in the discourse model at that point. This indicates that the relevant notion of salience is very general.

On the whole, my findings indicate that instead of trying to define the referential properties of *hän* and *tämä* in terms of a single unified notion of salience, we should consider a more fine-grained notion of how different factors are relevant for different referential expressions. This has

---

[2] These are the nominative forms of the pronoun and the demonstrative. In this paper, I focus on anaphoric expressions in subject position. Research on parallelism effects (see e.g. Sheldon 1974, Chambers & Smyth 1998) indicates that pronouns in subject position prefer to refer to antecedents in the same structural position, i.e. subjects. However, as I am primarily comparing the referential properties of the pronoun *hän* in matrix subject position and the referential properties of the demonstrative *tämä* in matrix subject position, any differences in their referential properties must be due to the anaphoric forms themselves. In addition, the research presented here looks only at the singular forms. The plural forms *he* 'they (human)' and *nämä* 'these' are left for future research.

important implications for our understanding of how referential systems work. On the one hand, it might be the case that the referential properties of different elements are determined by the entire system as a whole (e.g. along an accessibility hierarchy). Alternatively, it might be the case that different forms also have their own properties, independent of the system. As we will see, the data presented here seem to favor the second option.

The structure of this paper is as follows. First, in the next section, I review existing work on referent salience. Next, I discuss the word order patterns and the anaphoric system of Finnish. After that, I present the results of two sentence-completion experiments. Finally, on the basis of corpus data, I investigate uses of *hän* and *tämä* in contexts where only one featurally-compatible referent is present. Conclusions are discussed in last section of the paper.

What makes a referent salient?

There exists a general consensus that the more reduced an anaphoric expression is, the more salient or accessible its antecedent tends to be. According to various accessibility hierarchies proposed in the literature (see e.g. Gundel, Hedberg and Zacharski 1993, Ariel 1990, see also Givón 1983), overt pronouns have more accessible referents than demonstratives, and null pronouns (in languages that have them) have more accessible referents than overt pronouns. Summarizing the hierarchies proposed in the literature, the forms can be ranked as shown below:

(1)
   null > unstressed/bound pronouns > stressed/independent pronoun > demonstrative > full NP...

Thus, in languages like English, "pronouns are used most often when the referent is represented in a prominent way in the minds of the discourse participants, but more fully specified forms are needed when the representation of the referent is less prominent" (Arnold 1998: 4). This brings up the question of what makes a referent salient. Put differently, what makes a referent a likely candidate for subsequent mention with a pronoun? This question has received a lot of attention in the literature, and a number of factors have been claimed to influence salience, including syntactic role,[3] linear role, anaphoric form, discourse connectives and verb semantics. The data presented in this paper focus specifically on the effects of grammatical role and word order, while aiming to control for the other factors (for research investigating the effects of the antecedent's anaphoric form, see Kaiser 2003). Before turning to my findings, though, let us first review the existing work on these topics.

---

3   By using the terms grammatical role or syntactic role, I do not mean that thematic role is not important. For example, in the case of psychological verbs such as 'to frighten', the mapping between syntactic roles and thematic roles differs crucially from agent-patient verbs such as 'to kick.' See e.g. Turan (1998) for discussion of how thematic roles influence referent salience. In this paper, I focus primarily on agent-patient verbs.

Syntactic role

Previous research on the effects of syntactic role indicates that subjects are more salient than non-subjects (e.g. Chafe 1976, Brennan, Friedman & Pollard 1987, Matthews & Chodorow 1988, Stevenson et al. 1994 and McDonald & MacWhinney 1995, *inter alia*). The research in this area often makes use of the finding that the most reduced anaphor refers to the most salient referent. For example, Crawley & Stevenson (1990) conducted a sentence continuation experiment where the participants' task was to write continuations for stories like "Shaun led Ben along the path and he....". The continuations were analyzed to see which of the two referents people chose as the antecedent of the pronoun. Crawley & Stevenson found that participants interpreted the pronoun as referring back to the subject significantly more often than to the object.

A subjecthood advantage has also been found in corpus work (e.g. Brennan, Friedman & Pollard 1987, Tetreault 2001 and others), as well as studies of reading time (e.g. Gordon, Grosz & Gilliom 1993, Stevenson & Urbanowicz 1995). Furthermore, sentence continuation studies without pronoun prompts (e.g. Crawley & Stevenson 1990) showed the same results, i.e. participants were more likely to continue writing about the subject than the object. Thus, there is considerable evidence suggesting that a referent's grammatical function is correlated with its salience. However, it is important to note that for languages like English with relatively rigid subject-object order, it is unclear whether the 'subjecthood advantage' is due to subjects being located linearly before the object or their semantic/thematic properties. The next section discusses research that aims to sidestep this complication by looking at languages with flexible word order.

It is worth noting that in this paper, we are looking at the effects of subjecthood on the role that the referent in subject position plays in *subsequent* discourse. This does not mean that the preceding discourse is irrelevant: It has often been noted that referents appear in subject position because they are salient in the preceding discourse (for related work, see Chafe 1976, 1994, Prince 1992, *inter alia*). The relationships between subjecthood and a referent's role in the preceding and in the subsequent discourse are two sides of the same coin: If a referent is salient in the preceding discourse and is therefore realized as the subject of utterance U, it is not surprising that, from the perspective of the utterance following U, that referent can be more salient than, say, the object of utterance U (see also work on Centering Theory, e.g. Walker, Joshi & Prince 1998). Thus, in this paper, when I refer to effects of syntactic role/subjecthood on subsequent discourse, I do not mean to exclude the effects of preceding discourse.

Word order

In order to determine whether linear position or syntactic role is the crucial factor for salience, we now turn to languages with flexible word order. Previous findings reveal considerable crosslinguistic variation.

For example, Rambow (1993) claims that in German, word order in the Mittelfeld – the positions between the finite and the nonfinite verb – correlates with salience, with entities mentioned first being more salient than those mentioned later (see also Strube & Hahn 1996, 1999). In contrast, Turan (1998) and Hoffman (1998) claim that in Turkish, referent salience correlates with grammatical (or semantic) role and is not influenced by word order. Prasad & Strube (2000) make the same claim for Hindi (see also work by Gordon, Grosz & Gilliom 1993 on subjects vs. possessives in English).

Given these seemingly conflicting data, I think we need to keep in mind that word order variation has different functions in different languages and even in different constructions in one language. A constituent can occur in a noncanonical position for various reasons, e.g. because it has already been mentioned in the discourse, or because it contrasts with something else in the discourse model (see Vilkuna 1995). In my view, the different findings about the effects of word order on pronoun reference may well be a result of the multiple functions that word order variation can have. In fact, Rambow (1993) illustrates how, in German, topicalized word orders sometimes have an impact on salience and at other times do not. According to him, whether or not salience is determined by word order depends on the discourse function of the topicalized structure. So, to better understand the connections (or lack of them) between word order and salience, we need to consider the functions of different word orders in different languages. Keeping this in mind, let's now turn to the discourse functions of the two Finnish word orders that we will be investigating here, namely SVO and OVS order.

Finnish

There are at least two main reasons why Finnish provides a promising testing ground for the question of how word order and grammatical role influence a referent's prospects of being a suitable antecedent for an anaphoric expression. First, Finnish has flexible word order (see e.g. Vilkuna 1989), which enables us to disentangle the effects of word order and grammatical role. Second, standard Finnish has two kinds of third person anaphors (the pronoun *hän* 's/he' and the demonstrative *tämä* 'this'), which – given the claims of accessibility hierarchy based approaches – can be used as 'tools' to test the salience of potential antecedents.[4] We will take a closer look at these aspects of Finnish in the next two sections.

4   Dialects of spoken Finnish differ somewhat from standard Finnish in the use and form of certain pronouns, and different dialects also differ from each other. In fact, even in a more general sense, standard Finnish differs from spoken dialects because extensive sound omission and assimilation occurs in various dialects (see Karlsson 1999:244), and there are also some additional differences (e.g. in the use of possessive suffixes, certain verb endings and other areas of grammar). In this paper, I focus on standard Finnish. The referential properties of anaphoric forms in different spoken dialects are also an important area for research (see e.g. Laitinen (this volume), Seppänen (1998), inter alia).

Discourse factors and word order

Finnish has no definite or indefinite article.[5] The canonical word order is SVO, but all six permutations of S, V and O are grammatical in the appropriate contexts (Vilkuna 1995). In this paper, we focus on the SVO/OVS variation.[6] To understand why this variation might be expected to have an impact on the referential properties of *hän* and *tämä*, let us consider the pragmatic factors guiding the alternation. In Finnish, the choice between SVO and OVS is guided by whether or not the arguments have been mentioned in the preceding discourse (e.g. Hiirikoski 1995, Chesterman 1991, see also Helasvuo 2001 on pronominal subjects). To see how this works, let's first look at subjects. Subjects in a noncanonical, postverbal position introduce discourse-new referents.[7] In (2a), the sentence-initial indefinite noun phrase in the English original is translated into Finnish as a postverbal subject. On the other hand, preverbal subjects usually refer to entities that have already been mentioned in the discourse, as shown in (2b). Usually, a preverbal subject NP is only interpreted as being discourse-new if the sentence is a discourse-initial 'all new' utterance.

(2a)

Arkkujen vieressä kökötti pieni ärhäkästi sähisevä pajukori.
Trunks-GEN next-INE squatted small-NOM briskly hissing wickerbasket-NOM
A small wickerwork basket stood beside the heap of trunks, spitting loudly.
(English: Rowling 2001: 70, Finnish translation 2000: 78)

(2b)

Tyrannosaurus oli jo hyvin lähellä.
Tyrannosaur-NOM was already very close-ADE
The tyrannosaur was very close now.
(English: Crichton 1995: 240, Finnish translation 1996: 276)

Let us now consider the pattern for objects. An object in a noncanonical preverbal position in an OVS sentence, as in (3a), is discourse-old information. Finally, objects in their canonical postverbal position can be interpreted as new *or* old information, as shown in (3b).

---

5   In dialects of spoken Finnish, the demonstrative pronoun *se* 'it' is evolving into a kind of definite article (see Laury 1997). However, this is not the case in Standard Finnish.
6   See Kaiser (2000) for discussion of the syntax and discourse function of OSV order in Finnish.
7   It seems to me that in Finnish, the distinction between old and new information depends on the discourse status of the entities (whether they have been mentioned in the preceding discourse), not on whether they are known/old to the hearer (hearer-status). This is shown by the fact that names of family members or famous people (hearer-old) can be postverbal subjects if they are discourse-new (see also ex. 3). See Prince (1992) for further discussion of discourse- and hearer-status, and Birner & Ward (1998) for a discussion of how different constructions (e.g. Italian presentational *ci*-sentences and English existential *there*-sentences) differ in whether they are sensitive to hearer-status or discourse-status.

(3a)

Tiedotteen välitti julkisuuteen kurdien uutistoimisto D.E.M
Announcement-ACC transmitted public-ILL Kurds-GEN newsoffice-NOM D.E.M
The announcement was made public by the Kurdish newsoffice D.E.M
(from the newspaper *Aamulehti* 3/16/1999. Note that the Finnish example is in the active voice.)

(3b)

Poika löysi kolikon.
Boy-NOM found coin-ACC
The boy found a/the coin.

Anaphoric forms of standard Finnish

Existing work on the pronoun *hän* 's/he' corroborates the generalization that an overt pronoun (in non-prodrop languages) refers to the most salient entity. *Hän* has been described as referring to the most central, 'foregrounded' character (Kalliokoski 1991) or to the most important character in a given situation or context (e.g. Vilppula 1989, see also Laitinen this volume). On a more syntactic level, Saarimaa (1949) claims that *hän* tends to refer to the subject of the preceding sentence, since the subject is more in the foreground than other referents.[8]

The demonstrative *tämä* 'this' can be used as a proximal demonstrative or a discourse deictic (as in English, see also Etelämäki 1996, this volume), in addition to being used to refer to human antecedents (ex. 6). Here we will only focus on *tämä* when it is used anaphorically to refer to humans, since we are comparing it to the pronoun *hän*. The referential properties of *tämä* (when used anaphorically to refer to humans) differ significantly from those of *hän*. According to Varteva (1998) and others, *tämä* refers to characters in the background, i.e. to nonsalient referents. It has also been suggested that *tämä* is used for entities that will become topics in the subsequent discourse. On the sentence level, Sulkala & Karjalainen (1992) note that *tämä* is "used to indicate the last mentioned out of two or more possible referents" (1992: 282–283). This brings up the question: Does the demonstrative refer to the last-mentioned entity regardless of grammatical role? In particular, can it refer to the postverbal subject in OVS order? According to Saarimaa (1949), grammatical role is crucial: He states that *tämä* refers to a recently mentioned non-subject, and *hän* refers to a subject. However, is this what happens in actual language use?

As we will see in the remainder of this section, the existing corpus studies on the referential properties of *hän* and *tämä* in standard Finnish (e.g. Halmari 1994, Kaiser 2000) do not provide a full answer to the question of whether word order affects the referential properties of these two forms. Halmari (1994) conducted a corpus study of a range of Finnish referential

---

[8] Third person pro-drop is also possible in Finnish, but extremely limited. Referential third person main clause subjects cannot usually be null. First and second person subjects, on the other hand, can be pro-dropped. See e.g. Vilkuna (1996) for further details.

expressions, but the pronoun-demonstrative distinction was not the main focus of her study. Her corpus of written Finnish contained 433 pronoun tokens and 15 demonstrative tokens, and Halmari herself notes that "the huge number of pronouns in the sample skews the percentages, and this is a problem that needs to be addressed in future research" (Halmari 1994: 55). However, on the whole, Halmari found that *hän* refers to subjects, and *tämä* tends to refer to objects. These findings match the claims mentioned above. However, they do not tell us how word order affects *hän* and *tämä*, as Halmari did not analyze word order in her corpus study.[9]

A related study, but looking at colloquial Finnish instead of standard Finnish, was conducted by Seppänen (1998, see also Seppänen this volume). Using ethnomethodological conversation analysis, Seppänen investigated how the pronoun *hän* and the demonstrative *tämä* – as well as the demonstrative *tuo* 'that' and the demonstrative pronoun *se* 'it' – are used to refer to co-participants in the conversation, and how a person's participant status guides the use of these forms. She found that the demonstrative *tämä* tends to be used to refer to a preceding speaker when the current speaker wants to represent that earlier speaker as an active participant in the current speech situation. The pronoun *hän*, according to her findings, is used in a variety of contexts, including when the speaker wants to indicate that s/he is taking the perspective of the person to whom *hän* refers (see also Laitinen (1992, this volume) on the use of pronouns in Finnish dialects). In fact, the differences between the anaphoric systems of colloquial dialects and standard Finnish are quite striking, and merit further study.

To gain further insight into the properties of *hän* and *tämä* in standard Finnish, I conducted a corpus study (Kaiser 2000) with a more balanced corpus than the one Halmari (1994) used; 103 occurrences of *hän* and 101 occurrences of *tämä* in the novel *Tuntematon Sotilas* by Väinö Linna (1954/1999). The data reported here are for cases where the anaphor and its antecedent are in distinct main clauses. Configurations involving subordinate clauses were also coded and analyzed, but are not included here; thus the totals in the tables are less than 101 and 103 (see Kaiser 2000 for details). The findings for *hän* are shown in Table 1. *Hän* often refers to a preceding subject (43 out of 60 cases (71.67%)). In contrast, *tämä* tends to have a non-subject antecedent (Table 2). Examples are provided in (4) and (5).

---

[9] Importantly, however, Halmari (1994) did conduct a small survey and asked seven native speakers about sentences with different word orders and anaphoric elements. She tested the OVS sentence *Kanan näki kissa ja {se/tämä} kuoli.* 'Chicken-ACC saw cat-NOM and {it/this} died.' People were presented the sentence either with *se* 'it' or with *tämä* 'this' and were asked 'Who died?' With *se* 'it', participants preferred to interpret it as referring to the object *chicken* (presumably for pragmatic reasons, as a cat seeing a chicken is likely to result in the chicken's death, rather than the cat's), and with *tämä* 'this', people did not give very clear responses and found the resulting sentence "extremely hard to process" (Halmari 1994:42).

Table 1. Antecedent of hän.

Role of antecedent	Number of occurrences
S	43 (71.67%)
Poss	10 (16.67%)
DO	1 (1.67%)
IO	3 (5%)
Oblique	3 (5%)
PP	–
Total	60

Table 2. Antecedent of tämä.

Role of antecedent	Number of occurrences
S	7 (18.92%)
Poss	5 (13.51%)
DO	13 (35.14%)
IO	1 (2.70%)
Oblique	6 (16.22%)
PP	5 (13.51%)
Total	37

(4)

1 Sitten <u>eversti</u>   piti puheen... (Linna:144)
   Then <u>colonel-NOM</u> held speech-ACC...
   Then the <u>colonel</u> gave a speech...

2 <u>Hän</u>   koetti saada ääneensä   tiettyä   toverillista   sävyä.
   <u>He-NOM</u> tried to-get voice-ILL-poss certain-PTV friendly-PTV   tone-PTV
   <u>He</u> tried to get a certain friendly tone into his voice.

(5)

Lammio huusi <u>Mielosta</u>,   ja <u>tämä</u>   tuli sisään lähetit   kannoillaan.
Lammio shouted <u>Mielonen-PTV</u>, and <u>this-NOM</u> came in   messengers heels-ADE-poss
Lammio called for <u>Mielonen</u>, and <u>he</u> (Mielonen) came in with the messengers on his heels.
(Linna:286)

In sum, the results of Halmari (1994) and Kaiser (2000) show that there exists a correlation between anaphoric form and the antecedent's grammatical role. More specifically, subjects are usually referred to with *hän* 's/he', and objects and oblique arguments with the demonstrative *tämä* 'this.' It is worth noting at this point that we should not simply equate grammatical role with discourse status. Even though discourse-new referents are usually introduced in a postverbal position (as we have seen above), not all postverbal arguments are discourse-new (see ex. (3b)), and crucially, *tämä* can refer to both discourse-old and discourse-new referents (see also below).

However, even though the corpus studies seem to imply that the antecedent's grammatical role influences the referential form used to refer to it, they leave open the question of how linear order and grammatical role interact. In order to address this question, we need to investigate the referential properties of *hän* and *tämä* in sentences where the object linearly precedes the subject. However, in an un-annotated corpus, it is difficult to find a large number of sentences that have two singular third-person human referents in object-subject order, followed by *hän* or *tämä* in the next sentence. Thus, I opted instead for a sentence completion experiment. In these kinds of experiments, which are very common in psycholinguistic research, participants are asked to provide natural-sounding continuations for sentences or sentence fragments. The participants' continuations are then analyzed to find out how they interpreted the sentences.

Predictions about the effects of word order and grammatical role

Before turning to the Finnish sentence completion experiments, it's worthwhile to spell out some predictions we can make about effects of word order and grammatical role on the referential properties of *hän* and *tämä*. I assume, for the purpose of formulating these predictions, that the pronoun *hän* is predicted to refer to highly accessible referents, and the demonstrative *tämä* to less accessible referents, in accordance with accessibility theories. We will see later that this generalization is an oversimplification, but it is useful for the purposes of sketching out the predictions.

First, we could hypothesize that syntactic function is the determining factor, and subjects are more salient than objects (illustrated schematically in option (a) in Table 3; referential relations illustrated by subscripts). In this case, we predict that, regardless of word order, *hän* will refer to the subject and *tämä* to the object. Second, if we treat word order as the determining factor (i.e. constituents to the left are more salient than those to the right, as shown in option (b)), then we predict that, regardless of grammatical role, *hän* will refer to the preverbal constituent and *tämä* to the postverbal one.

Third, we could think of word order and grammatical role as independent additive determinants of salience. According to this view, both grammatical role and word order contribute to the salience of a referent (option (c)). Under this view, subjects in SVO order are the most salient, objects in SVO are the least salient, and objects and subjects in OVS order fall somewhere in between. To see why this is the case, let us consider what happens when 'salience points' are assigned to constituents (option (c)). According to the syntactic-function criterion, subjects are more salient than objects, and as a result, the subject in SVO order receives one point, as does the subject in OVS order. According to the word-order criterion, the linearly initial constituent is more salient. Thus, in SVO order, the subject receives one point, and in OVS order, the object gets one point. Now, if we add up the points for each constituent, in SVO order the subject clearly comes out as being the more salient argument. In contrast, in OVS order, both arguments have one point. Thus, if word order and grammatical function have equal effects on referent salience, it is not clear what happens with OVS order, as the two factors are pitted against each other.[10]

---

10 This discussion raises an interesting question: Should salience be viewed as increased 'activation' ("more points"), or it is rather a matter of 'suppression' (see e.g. Gernsbacher 1990), such that less salient referents lose points or receive negative points, so to speak? The distinction is not central to the present discussion, but poses interesting questions for future research.

Table 3. Predictions.

Salience determined by: Predicted referential pattern:

(a) Syntactic function $S_iVO.$ Hän$_i$....   OVS$_i$. Hän$_i$..
(subjects > objects)   SVO$_i$. Tämä$_i$...   O$_i$VS. Tämä$_i$....

(b) Word order $S_iVO.$ Hän$_i$....   O$_i$VS. Hän$_i$..
(left > right)
                                 SVO$_i$. Tämä$_i$...   OVS$_i$. Tämä$_i$....

(c) Additive effects of both factors: S.....V.....O   O.....V.....S
(i) Syntactic function   1   0   0   1
(ii) Word order   1   0   1   0
                                              2   0   1   1
                                               \   \   \   \
                                              hän tämä   ??   ??

Sentence completion experiments

In this section I present two sentence completion experiments which investigate the effects of word order and grammatical role on the referential properties of *hän* 's/he' and *tämä* 'this'. In both experiments, participants read SVO and OVS sentences followed by the first word of the next sentence, which was either *hän* or *tämä*. The participants' task was to write a continuation using this prompt word. In Experiment 1, the SVO and OVS sentences were presented in isolation. However, given that the SVO/OVS variation in Finnish is guided by the arguments' discourse status, in Experiment 2 the sentences were preceded by short contexts which established one of the arguments as discourse-old. Thus, the two experiments differ in that one of the arguments is explicitly discourse-old (previously mentioned) in Experiment 2, whereas in Experiment 1, discourse status is signalled by word order but not supported by a context. In both experiments, both the subject and object in the SVO/OVS sentences were full NPs, and thus in this paper we only test the effects of grammatical role and linear order, leaving aside other possible factors such as the antecedent's anaphoric form (see Kaiser 2003 for research investigating the role of anaphoric form). In addition to sentence completion tasks, in other work we have also used the eyetracking paradigm to investigate the effects of grammatical role and linear order on Finnish speakers' incremental interpretation of *hän* and *tämä*. Please see Kaiser (2003), and Kaiser & Trueswell (to appear) for further details.

Experiment 1

Method
This experiment tested the effect of word order and grammatical role on the referential properties of *hän* and *tämä*. The stimuli consisted of written SVO and OVS sentences, each of which was followed by the first

word of the next sentence, either *hän* 's/he' or *tämä* 'this'. Anaphor type and word order were crossed to create four conditions, as shown below. A participant's task was to write a completion for the second sentence. Example items are in

(6)

(i) SVO.Hän...
(ii) OVS.Hän....
(iii) SVO.Tämä....
(iv) OVS.Tämä......

(6a) (SVO.Hän)
Lääkäri onnitteli opiskelijaa. Hän...
Doctor-NOM congratulated student-PTV. S/he-NOM.....
A/the doctor congratulated a/the student. S/he...

(6b) (OVS.Hän)
Lääkäriä onnitteli opiskelija. Hän...
Doctor-PTV congratulated student-NOM. S/he-NOM.....
A/the student congratulated a/the doctor. S/he...

Thirty-two native Finnish-speakers participated in this sentence completion experiment. Each participant was asked to complete 38 items whose order was randomized: 8 critical items and 30 fillers. Four presentation lists were constructed by randomly combining the 8 target stories with the 30 filler stories. Within a presentation list, four of the target trials appeared with the SVO structure and four appeared with the OVS structure. For each of these sentence structure types, two had the pronoun *hän* and two had the demonstrative *tämä*. Each target item was then rotated through these four conditions, generating four different presentation lists.

The nouns used for the subject and object in the critical items were all 'occupational labels' or labels for other kinds of 'roles' (e.g. doctor, stewardess, reporter, student). This was done in order to make the continuations easier to interpret during the coding stage. All verbs used were action/agent-patient verbs (as defined by Stevenson et al. 1994). A unified verb group was used in order to control for any possible verb focusing effects.

Participants' continuations were coded according to which of the referents in the preceding sentence (the subject or the object) the participants chose as the referent of the pronoun. There were some cases where it was not clear from the continuation which referent the participant had interpreted as being the antecedent of the pronoun or demonstrative, and these were coded as 'unclear.' In addition, with *tämä*, there were some continuations where *tämä* was not used as an anaphor for one of the two characters mentioned in the preceding sentence, and was instead used as a discourse-deictic ('*This* was a mean thing to do') or in some other way. These types of used were coded as 'demonstrative' uses, in order to set them apart from the anaphoric uses.

Results

The results are shown in Figure 1. As the graph shows, the referential properties of *hän* and *tämä* are affected in different ways by word order. The pronoun *hän* 's/he' tends to be interpreted as referring to the subject, regardless of word order. Thus, in the SVO.Hän condition, the pronoun was interpreted as referring to the preceding subject in 40 out of 64 cases (63%). In the OVS.Hän condition, we see 39/64 (61%) subject-interpretations. In contrast, in the SVO.Tämä condition, *tämä* tends to refer to the object; it was interpreted as referring to the object in 53 out of 64 cases (83%). In the OVS.Tämä condition, order, however, *tämä* is split between the subject and the object. There are 21/64 (32.8%) subject-interpretations, and 24/64 (38%) object-interpretations.

Analyses of variance (ANOVAs) show that there are significant effects of anaphor type and word order on reference to both subjects and objects. ANOVAs were conducted on participant and item means of subject and object continuations, with three factors: Word order (SVO or OVS), Anaphor type (pronoun or demonstrative), and List (4 levels) in the participant analysis and Item Group (four groups) in the item analysis. The results show that whether an anaphoric element is interpreted as referring to the preceding subject depends on anaphor type (*hän* or *tämä*, $F1(1,28)=80.36$, $p<0.01$, $F2(1,4)=104.81$, $p<0.01$) and word order (SVO or OVS, $F1(1,28)=6.81$, $p<0.05$, $F2(1,4)=6.56$, $p=0.063$). There is also a significant interaction ($F1(1,28)=8.41$, $p<.0.01$, $F2(1,4)=11.31$, $p<0.05$). Similarly, for objects, whether an anaphoric element refers to the preceding object is dependent on anaphor type ($F1(1,28)=40.16$, $p<0.01$, $F2(1,4)=66.94$, $p<0.01$) and word order ($F1(1,28)=16.30$, $p<0.01$, $F2(1,4)=8.19$, $p<0.05$). Again, there is a significant interaction ($F(1,28)=19.28$, $p<0.01$, $F2(1,4)=19.61$, $p<0.05$).[11]

Thus, whether an anaphoric expression is interpreted as referring to the preceding subject or object depends on whether the anaphor is *hän* or *tämä*, and whether the word order of the preceding sentence is SVO or OVS. In addition, the interactions between word order and anaphor type show that the value of one has an effect on the other. Looking at Figure 1, we see that the pronoun *hän* tends to refer to the subject regardless of word order, whereas this is clearly not the case for the demonstrative *tämä*. Thus, the effect of word order depends on the anaphor: with *hän*, chaging the word order does not impact the subject preference, but with *tämä*, changing the word order from SVO to OVS does have a big impact on the referential patterns.

Discussion

These results indicate that the two referential forms are sensitive to different factors. The pronoun *hän* is sensitive to the syntactic function/grammatical role of potential antecedents and prefers subjects (see also

---

11   There were reliable effects involving control variables in some of the analyses we conducted in this paper. Because we believe that they have no bearing on the proposals that we will be making, these effects will not be reported.

Figure 1. Which referent does the anaphor refer to?

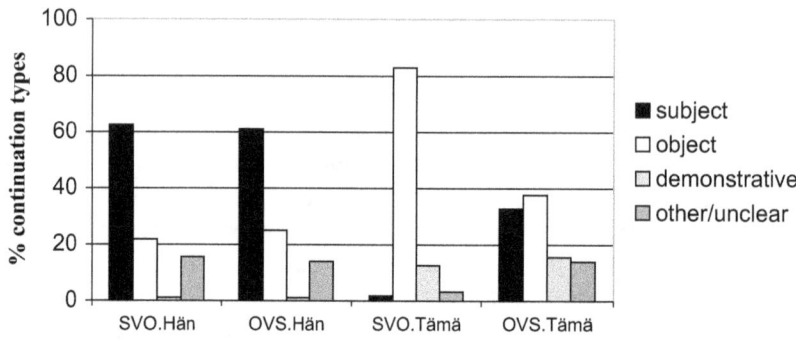

Table 4. Which referent in Sentence 1 does anaphor in Sentence 2 refer to?

	Subject	Object	Demonstrative	Unclear/other
SVO.Hän	63% (40/64)	22% (14/64)	0	16% (10/64)
OVS.Hän	61% (39/64)	25% (16/64)	0	14% (9/64)
SVO.Tämä	2% (1/64)	83% (53/64)	13 (8/64)	3% (2/64)
OVS.Tämä	33% (21/64)	38% (24/64)	16 (10/64)	14% (9/64)

Saarimaa 1949). In contrast, the demonstrative *tämä* shows a more complex pattern. In SVO order, it clearly prefers the postverbal object, but with OVS order, *tämä* is split between subject and object.

Viewed as a whole, these results do not form a pattern that matches any of the predictions discussed earlier, nor are they compatible with an accessibility hierarchy approach which assumes that all referential forms can be mapped onto a unified salience scale. Let us consider again some of the predictions sketched out above, to see why they are not compatible with the results of the sentence completion experiments. One possible prediction was that, if grammatical role determines salience, and *hän* is used for more salient referents and *tämä* for less salient referents, then *hän* is used to refer back to subjects and *tämä* to objects, regardless of word order. While this prediction fits the pattern we saw for the pronoun *hän* in the completions, it clearly does not match what we saw happen with the demonstrative *tämä*. In fact, we saw that *tämä* prefers postverbal objects with SVO order, and is split between subject and object in OVS order. This is not consistent with predictions suggesting that either grammatical role or linear order is what determines salience, but fits with the 'additive effects' prediction which claims that both word order and grammatical role matter. Thus, it seems that for *hän*, only grammatical role is relevant, and for *tämä*, both grammatical role and word order play a role.

In light of these results, we cannot maintain, at least not for Finnish, an approach that treats pronouns and demonstratives as guided by a unified notion of salience. If these forms differ only in the degree of salience that they prefer their antecedents to have, and if salience is a unified notion, then *hän* and *tämä* should not display different sensitivities to different factors – but this is exactly what we saw in the results.

Given these results, at this stage one could hypothesize that the two anaphoric forms, *hän* and *tämä*, differ in the level of linguistic representation that they 'look at' in order to locate their referents. So, on the one hand, one could say that the pronoun *hän* is sensitive to grammatical role and looks at the syntactic level to find the antecedent with the highest possible grammatical role. On the other hand, according to this hypothesis, the demonstrative *tämä* looks at the discourse level and is sensitive to a more general notion of salience – and since salience depends on factors such as word order/discourse status (e.g. Strube & Hahn 1996, 1999) and grammatical role (e.g. Crawley & Stevenson 1990), *tämä* is sensitive to these factors. More specifically, according to this approach, *tämä* prefers entities that are low in salience, entities that are not at the center of attention at that point in the discourse (see also Varteva 1998). The idea is thus that the two forms differ with respect to which level of representation they have access to: The demonstrative *tämä* accesses the discourse level, and is associated with the low-end of a salience scale, and the pronoun *hän* accesses the syntactic level, and is associated with the high-end of a grammatical role scale. To further explore the validity of this hypothesis, let us turn to the second experiment.

Experiment 2

The second experiment is an extension of the first one, and addresses the question whether the referential properties of *hän* and *tämä* are influenced by contextual oldness; that is, whether a referent has already been mentioned in the preceding discourse. As mentioned earlier, the SVO/OVS word order variation in Finnish is driven by the discourse status of the arguments. In SVO order, the subject is usually discourse-old (i.e. mentioned in the preceding discourse), and in OVS order, the object is discourse-old. However, the first experiment presented the test sentences without a preceding discourse context. The motivation behind Experiment 2, then, was to see if the same results we saw in Experiment 1 also obtain when each SVO/OVS sentence is preceded by a context which makes the preverbal argument of the SVO/OVS sentence discourse-old. In particular, given claims that discourse-old referents are more salient than discourse-new ones (Strube & Hahn 1996, 1999), we might predict that putting the sentences in context has an effect on the referential properties of the demonstrative *tämä*, which I hypothesized to be sensitive to the discourse salience level of potential antecedents.

In this experiment, as in Experiment 1, the participants' task was to complete sentence fragments. Also, just as in Experiment 1, the critical sentence had SVO or OVS word order. However, now this sentence was preceded by a two-sentence context which mentions one of the two referents. In fact, it is always the preverbal argument of the critical sentence (i.e. S in SVO, O in OVS) that is discourse-old by virtue of having been mentioned in the context. In contrast, the postverbal argument (SVO, OVS) is introduced for the first time, i.e. it is discourse-new. Thus, in contrast to Experiment 1, in Experiment 2 both SVO and OVS sentences are now felicitous, given the pragmatic word order constraints of Finnish (see above). As before, the nouns used for the subject and object were all occupational labels, and all verbs were agent-patient verbs. The four conditions were the same as in Experiment 1: SVO.Hän, OVS.Hän, SVO.Tämä, OVS.Tämä. Sixteen native Finnish speakers participated in the experiment. There were 16 critical items and 32 fillers.

The results of this experiment provide an interesting comparison to those of Experiment 1. For three out of four conditions, the results of this experiment basically replicate the findings of the first experiment. Let's first consider the results for the pronoun *hän*. In the second experiment, in both the SVO.Hän condition and the OVS.Hän condition, there are five times more subject-interpretations than object-interpretations. This replicates the subject-preference we saw for the pronoun *hän* in the first experiment.

Now, let us turn to the demonstrative *tämä*. As in Experiment 1, in the SVO.Tämä condition of Experiment 2, *tämä* has a very strong preference to refer to the postverbal argument of the preceding sentence (over 80% object-interpretations). In the OVS.Tämä condition of Experiment 2, *tämä* shows a clear preference for the postverbal subject over the preverbal object: there are almost five times more subject-continuations than object-continuations. This is unlike Experiment 1, where in OVS order *tämä* was split between the subject (33%) and the object (38%). We can sum up the behavior of *tämä* in Experiment 2 by saying that it displays a preference to refer to the postverbal referent regardless of word order. However, this postverbal tendency is much more pronounced with SVO order than with OVS order. In the OVS condition, almost a third of the continuations are 'demonstrative continuations', i.e. continuations in which *tämä* is not treated as a third-person anaphor, but used in some other way, e.g. as a discourse-deictic (as in '*This* was a mean thing to do'). A possible explanation for this pattern is discussed below. (For more details concerning the results of Experiment 2, see Kaiser (2003)).

Summary of the experiments

The results of the second experiment complement those of the first. In both experiments, the pronoun *hän* tends to refer to subjects, regardless of whether the subjects are pre- or postverbal. Thus, it seems that what matters is grammatical role, not word order. This 'grammatical role effect' for *hän* shows up in both experiments, which suggests that it is a robust finding, at least for the types of configurations investigated here. In addition, Experiment 2 shows that it does not matter whether the subject is discourse-old (which was the case with SVO target sentences) or discourse-new (which was the case with OVS target sentences). This lends support to my hypothesis that the pronoun *hän* only 'sees' the syntactic level of representation and is used to refer to antecedents that are syntactically high-ranked.

As for the demonstrative *tämä*, we hypothesized above that it has access to the discourse level and is sensitive to the general salience of antecedents. More specifically, we saw in Experiment 1 that in SVO order *tämä* refers to the postverbal object, but is split between subject and object in OVS order. In Experiment 2, we see that once the OVS sentence is situated in a supportive discourse context, *tämä* prefers the postverbal (discourse-new) referent in both SVO and OVS conditions. So, basically, the results of Experiments 1 and 2 are the same for the SVO.Tämä condition but differ for the OVS.Tämä condition, in which Experiment 1 reveals a split between subjects and objects, but Experiment 2 shows a clear postverbal preference.

This difference between the two experiments can be attributed to the presence of a preceding discourse context in Experiment 2. In Experiment 1, only word order provided information about the discourse status of the two arguments (remember that in Finnish, OVS order is used when the object is old and the subject new), but Experiment 2 included a context which supported the discourse-statuses signalled by the word order. Now, in light of the claim that discourse status affects salience (e.g. Strube & Hahn 1996, 1999),[12] it is not surprising that making the postverbal subject in the OVS condition more clearly discourse-new by means of the context leads to a stronger effect of discourse status on salience. Thus, given the claim that *tämä* prefers entities that are low in salience, it is not surprising that it shows a stronger preference for the postverbal subject in OVS order in Experiment 2 than in Experiment 1. However, we shouldn't forget that grammatical role also has an effect on the referential properties of *tämä* – this is illustrated by the differences in the continuation results in Experiment 2 for the SVO.Tämä condition (with a postverbal, discourse-new object) and the OVS.Tämä condition (with a postverbal, discourse-new subject). We see that even when both word order and discourse-status are pitted against grammatical role, grammatical role nevertheless has somewhat of an impact.

The effect of grammatical role (i.e., the demonstrative's preference for objects over subjects) is also hinted at by the large number of 'demonstrative' continuations in condition OVS.Tämä of Experiment 2. What would prompt such a larger number of non-anaphoric uses? If *tämä* prefers nonsalient referents, then maybe the problem with the OVS.Tämä condition is that neither the preverbal object nor the postverbal subject is an 'ideal' antecedent for *tämä*. The postverbal subject presumably loses salience because of its discourse-newness, but at the same time, it is still a

---

12 As mentioned earlier, *tämä* can also refer to discourse-old referents, as is shown by corpus data. If it is preceded by a transitive sentence that contains two discourse-old arguments, which in Finnish will normally occur in S-O order, it prefers the object.

subject and hence to some degree inherently salient. The preverbal object is nonsalient because it is an object – but at the same time, it is preverbal and discourse old. This is a very different situation from SVO.Tämä, where the salience contributions of discourse-status and grammatical role do not conflict in this way.

When discussing non-anaphoric uses of *tämä*, it is worth emphasizing that participants could treat *tämä* either as a personal anaphor or as something else (e.g. discourse deictic) in *both* SVO and OVS conditions. However, the occurrence of non-anaphoric uses was much higher in the OVS.Tämä configuration than in the SVO.Tämä configuration. In my view, this is because the latter configuration has an 'ideal' (i.e. low-salience) antecedent for *tämä*, namely the postverbal object, whereas in the former configuration, neither the subject nor object has quite the right properties to be a good antecedent for the demonstrative anaphor *tämä*.[13]

On the whole, the results of Experiment 2 support the hypothesis formulated on the basis of Experiment 1, namely that *hän* is associated with the high end of a scale and *tämä* with the low end of a scale, but the scales are different. For the pronoun, the relevant scale is hypothesized to be the hierarchy of grammatical relations, whereas the scale relevant for the demonstrative is a salience scale. For related psycholinguistic work in the eye-tracking paradigm, i.e. using people's eye-movements to track their incremental interpretation of *hän* and *tämä* in Finnish, see Kaiser (2003), Kaiser & Trueswell (to appear).

(7)

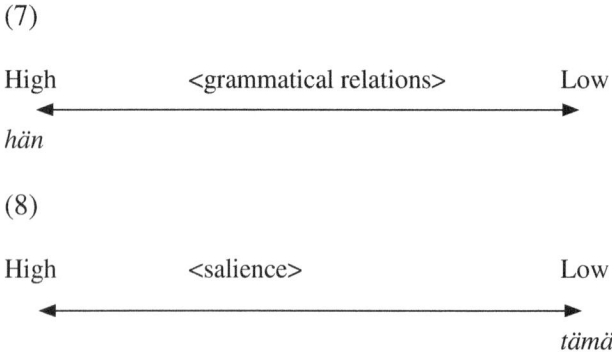

(8)

This idea is, however, only a hypothesis at this point, and needs to be tested further – in particular the hypothesis about the pronoun *hän* having a subject preference. In future work I hope to look at experiencer/psych verbs as well as the Finnish impersonal passive construction, in order to better understand the relation between the syntactic notion of subjecthood and the preferred antecedent of the pronoun *hän*. In the sentence completion experiments reported here, the subject of the preceding sentence

---

13 Interestingly, it seems that a demonstrative interpretation may not have been as easy to use as an 'escape hatch' in Experiment 1 as in Experiment 2 – perhaps because of the lack of a preceding discourse context in the first experiment.

was also the agent. It might thus turn out that the pronoun *hän* is actually sensitive not to subjecthood *per se*, but to agentivity associated with it in these experiments. In future work, by looking at different constructions and verb types, I plan to investigate these kinds of questions in detail.

Absence vs. presence of competing referents

The hypothesis presented in the preceding sections, namely that *hän* is associated with the high-end of a grammatical role scale and *tämä* with the low end of a salience scale, raises a number of questions concerning the consequences of the presence of other referents in the discourse. More specifically, will the presence of other, featurally different (i.e. not singular third person) referents impact the referential properties of *hän* and *tämä*? Or, to put it a different way, is use of the demonstrative *tämä* inextricably linked to the need for disambiguation, in contexts where there are multiple third-person singular referents?

These questions have important consequences for my hypothesis that *tämä* is used to refer to entities at the lower end of a salience scale. Consider two possible scenarios: (a) *tämä* is used for low-salience referents in contexts where there are two third-person referents and thus disambiguation is necessary, or (b) *tämä* is also used in contexts with only one featurally-compatible referent (i.e. disambiguation is not necessary), if that referent is low in salience. These two scenarios are represented schematically below:

(a) *Disambiguation use*
Referent A (high salience, 3rd person singular)
Referent B (low salience, 3rd person singular) ¬ *tämä*

(b) *General low salience use*
Referent A (high salience, not necessarily 3rd person singular)
Referent B (low salience, 3rd person singular) ¬ *tämä*

In the experiments discussed in the preceding sections, there were always two third person singular human referents present. Thus, there were always two referents that were featurally compatible (in this case, 3rd sg human) with the anaphor. This is the situation represented in scenario (a). We did not yet investigate scenario (b). In this final section, in order to find out whether *tämä* can be used to refer to low-salience referents even if the higher-salience referents present in the discourse are not featurally-compatible (as sketched out in scenario (b)), I look at naturally-occurring corpus data. As we will see, *tämä* can indeed be used in such contexts. This indicates that *tämä* is not simply used to disambiguate in contexts where there is more than one possible referent. More specifically, the corpus patterns show that the salience scale that *tämä* is sensitive to is a general scale that includes the various entities present in the discourse model at that point, and not just third-person singular entities. We will say more about this below.

In the corpus data, I focus primarily on examples where the anaphoric expression is in subject position and in a clause other than the clause containing the antecedent. This was done in order to control for effects of parallelism (Sheldon 1974, Chambers & Smyth 1998). Since I am comparing the referring properties of the pronoun *hän* in subject position and the demonstrative *tämä* in subject position, any differences in the referential properties of the anaphoric expressions must be due to the anaphoric forms themselves.

Corpus data

The discussion here will be limited primarily to two main construction types, namely (i) sentences with third-person postverbal subjects, and (ii) sentences that have non-third person matrix subjects but that contain a singular third-person referent in some other position. (There are of course various other contexts that we could also have considered, but for reasons of brevity, we will focus on these two here.) As we will see, both the pronoun *hän* and the demonstrative *tämä* can be used to refer to third-person singular referents in these constructions.

Let us first consider postverbal third-person subjects in contexts which contain no other singular third person referents. Given the experimental result that *hän* prefers to refer to a preceding subject regardless of word order, we predict that in sentences such as (11a), a pronoun can be used to refer back to the postverbal subject. Naturally-occurring data shows that this prediction is borne out (11b, see also Kaiser 2000).

(11a)

    Tapahtumaa   oli seuraamassa   kanavainsinööri   John Scott Russell
    Event-PTV   was following-INE   canal-engineer-NOM   John Scott Russell
    Canal engineer John Scott Russell was following the event

(11b)

    ja   hän   lähti   ratsain   seuraamaan tätä   aaltoa.
    And   <u>he-NOM</u> left on-horseback following   this-PTV   wave-PTV
    and <u>he</u> started to follow this wave on horseback.

(11c) [subsequent sentences]

    Aalto oli vajaat puoli metriä korkea ja muutaman metrin pituinen, siisti ja sileä vesimassa, joka siis kulki eteenpäin lähes muuttumattomana. Russell pystyi seuraamaan tämän aallon etenemistä muutaman kilometrin...

    The wave was less than half a meter in height and a few meters in length, a neat and smooth mass of water, which moved forward almost without changing. Russell was able to follow the progress of this wave for a few kilometers...
    (www.physics.utu.fi/theory/kaaos_koherenssi.html)

What about the demonstrative *tämä*? Is it also used to refer back to postverbal subjects in contexts with only one third-person singular referent? We saw earlier, in the sentence completion tasks, that in contexts with two third-person singular referents, in the SVO condition *tämä* has a strong preference to refer back to the postverbal object. In OVS condition, the postverbal preference is somewhat weaker, but in Experiment 2, with an appropriate context, *tämä* nevertheless has a preference for the postverbal subject over the preverbal object. If we turn to naturally-occurring data and look at contexts with only one third-person singular referent, we do occasionally see *tämä* being used to refer to postverbal subjects in the absence of any featurally appropriate competing referents (ex. (12)). However, use of *tämä* for postverbal subjects in these kinds of contexts is clearly less frequent than use of the pronoun *hän*. This pattern is not surprising, given that in the OVS conditions of the sentence completion studies, the subject preference of *hän* was found to be stronger than the subject preference of *tämä*.

(12)

1 Yhdyshaudan kulman takaa häämötti mies,
  Trench-GEN corner-GEN behind loomed man-NOM
  Behind the corner of the trench loomed a man

2 ja vain silmänräpäyksen tämä ehti epäröidä.... (Linna:331)
  and only eyeblink-GEN this-NOM had-time to-hesitate...
  and he only had a moment to hesitate....

(12c) [subsequent sentences]

...tuliko sieltä hänen pakeneva toverinsa vaiko vihollinen. Hän myöhästyi samanlaisesta syystä kuin Rokka äsken. (Linna: 331–332).

...whether it was his fleeing friend or an enemy. He was too late for the same reason that Rokka [another character in the story] had been late earlier.

Now, having looked at postverbal subjects, let us turn to a context where 'unnecessarily' use of *tämä* is very common – namely when referring to non-subjects in contexts which lack competing third-person referents. In example (13a), *tämä* is used to refer to a genitive modifier of a NP inside a relative clause, and in (13b), it is used for the head of a relative clause-type structure (see Kaiser 2000 for more details on use of *tämä* for referents in embedded clauses).

(13a)

[Context: Formula 1 chief Ecclestone has demanded that FIA (International Automobile Federation) return to Ferrari world championship points that had been taken away.]

FIA julkaisi keskiviikkona tiedotteen, jossa se kummasteli Ecclestonen lausuntoa. Tämä väitti taistelleensa jo vuosia F1-sääntöjen tiukkuutta vastaan. "FIA on hämmästynyt, sillä herra Ecclestone on ainakin kaksi kertaa äänestänyt nykyisten sääntöjen puolesta."

FIA published yesterday an announcement in which it expressed surprise at Ecclestone's statement. He claimed to have been fighting for years against the strict F-1 regulations. "The FIA is surprised, because Mr. Ecclestone has voted for the current regulations at least twice [quote from FIA spokesman]."
(from the newspaper *Helsingin Sanomat*, 21.20.1999)

(13b)

[Context: Finland's attempts to be chosen as the host of the 2006 Winter Olympics]
Helsingin hankkeen markkinamieheksi on värvätty myös tasavallan presidentti Martti Ahtisaari. Helsingin hakukomitea yritti kovasti saada kansainväliseen maineeseen nousseen Ahtisaaren paikalle, mutta tämä ei kiireiltään ehtinyt. Suomalaiset olivat myös valmiita järjestämään suoran videoyhteyden Helsingistä, mutta se taas ei sopinut KOK:lle.
Nyt Ahtisaari kertoo nauhalta itsensä ja suomalaisten suuresta kiinnostuksesta urheiluun....

The president of the republic, Martti Ahtisaari has been enlisted as the marketing man for the Helsinki project. The Helsinki search committee tried hard to get risen-to-international-fame[14] Ahtisaari [i.e. Ahtisaari, who had risen to international fame] there, but he couldn't make it. The Finns were also ready to organize a live video connection from Helsinki, but that didn't work for the International Olympic Committee.
Now Ahtisaari speaks on tape about his and the Finnish people's deep interest in sports...
(from the newspaper *Helsingin Sanomat*, 16.6.1999)

Of course, not every non-subject in these kinds of contexts is referred to with *tämä*. In some cases, the pronoun *hän* is used instead, as in the examples below. In (14a), the direct object is referred to with *hän* in the next sentence, and in (14b), the oblique argument is referred to with *hän*.

(14a)

[Context: Formula 1 driver Senna's fatal accident]
Väsyneet vapunviettäjät havahtuvat kotisohvillaan, kun Ayrton Sennan auto paiskautuu rajusti betoniseinään. Lääkintämiehet nostavat Sennan pois romuttuneesta autostaan, mutta hän kuolee radalle miljoonien tv-katsojien silmien edessä. Sennan viimeiset päivät nostattivat joukon kysymyksiä...

Tired First-of-May celebrators wake up on their couches when Ayrton Senna's car crashes violently into a concrete wall. Medics lift Senna out of his destroyed car, but he dies on the track in front of millions of TV viewers. Senna's final days raised many questions...
(from the newspaper *Helsingin Sanomat*, 13.11.1999)

14 The construction used here is sometimes called the 'Agent construction', which, according to Karlsson (1999), "is a way of contracting relative clauses...in most cases these clauses then become premodifiers, with the verb functioning as an adjective" (Karlsson 1999:207).

(14b)

[Context: A recap of Swedish skier Jernberg's success in Cortina, Italy]
Cortinassa viidenkympin lähtöasemat olivat Sixten Jernbergille herkulliset. Hän pääsi taipaleelle kovimman kilpakumppaninsa Veikko Hakulisen jälkeen. Takaa-ajoasemansa turvin Jernberg hallitsi kilpailua mestarillisesti alusta alkaen. Tasaisen varmasti hän pystyi pitämään jatkuvan turvavälin Hakuliseen, joka lopulta jäi toiseksi.

In Cortina, the starting positions for the fifty-kilometer race were ideal for Sixten Jernberg. He got to start the race after his toughest competitor Veikko Hakulinen. From his chasing position, Jernberg ruled the race masterfully from the very beginning. Reliably, he was able to keep a continuous safety distance to Hakulinen, who came in second in the end.
(from the newspaper *Helsingin Sanomat*, coverage of Nagano olympics 4.2.1998)

In sum, the examples presented in this section show that in contexts that only contain one singular human third person referent, both *hän* and *tämä* can be used to refer back to that one referent. In other words, even though the 'regular' pronoun *hän* is unambiguous in these contexts, sometimes the more marked option, *tämä*, is nevertheless used. This shows that *tämä* should not be viewed as merely a means of disambiguating between two or more possible third person referents. If it were only a 'disambiguation tool', we would not expect it to surface in contexts where there is no need to disambiguate. In fact, the 'unnecessary' uses of *tämä* tell us that the relevant salience scale (whose lower end *tämä* is hypothesized to refer to) is one that includes the various entities present in the discourse model at that point, and not just third-person singular entities. In other words, the relevant notion of salience appears to be a very general one.

A question that we have not yet addressed concerns the division of labor between *hän* and *tämä*. Given that both anaphoric forms can be used to refer to human third person referents in the absence of featural competitors, the question arises: what guides the choice between them? The corpus data suggests that factors such as agentiveness, information status, and degree of embeddedness may influence uses of *hän* and *tämä*. As an example, let us take a look at information status. As mentioned above, postverbal subjects in Finnish are discourse-new – i.e., they have not yet been mentioned in the current discourse. However, this does not mean that they cannot be hearer-old, i.e. already known to the hearer (see Prince 1992 for discussion of hearer-status and discourse-status). For instance, in ex. (11), which is from a speech given at a physics department, the postverbal discourse-new subject is John Scott Russell who was the discoverer of the solitary wave and in all likelihood someone whom the hearers all knew about, i.e. hearer-old but discourse-new. He is referred to with the pronoun *hän*. In contrast, in ex. (12), the postverbal subject is 'a man visible behind the corner of the trench' – a character mentioned in the story for the first time, i.e. hearer-new and discourse-new. He is referred to with the demonstrative *tämä*. In light of previous research, the influence of information status on anaphoric form is not surprising – for example, Strube & Hahn (1996, 1999) claim that hearer-old entities are more salient than hearer-new entities.[15]

In future work, I hope to look in more detail at the division of labor between *hän* and *tämä* in contexts to see if this hypothesis about the role information status is tenable, and also to explore the possible effects of other factors in more detail, including degree of embeddedness (compare, for example, (13a, b) with (14a, b)) and agentivity.

Role of subsequent discourse

Another factor that one might expect to guide the choice between *hän* and *tämä* in the absence of competitors – namely the role played by the relevant referent in subsequent discourse (see e.g. Givón 1983, Arnold 1998, as well as work within Centering Theory). For example, following the claim of accessibility-hierarchy approaches that pronouns are used for more salient referents than demonstratives, we could hypothesize that the demonstrative *tämä* is used for referents that are not mentioned again in the subsequent discourse and/or referents that are only briefly relevant in the discourse, and that the pronoun *hän* is used for more central, more 'important' referents.

However, at least at this stage, this hypothesis does not receive clear support from my corpus data. In the examples given above, there does not appear to be a clear correlation between anaphor type and importance of the referent in the subsequent discourse (however, see Seppänen 1998). Further evidence that the choice of *hän* vs. *tämä* does not seem to be determined by the role the referent plays in subsequent discourse is the occurrence of 'switching.' More specifically, an entity that is first referred to with *tämä* is often referred to with *hän* later on, often in the very next clause, e.g example (12c). If *tämä* and *hän* differ in terms of the role that their referents play in the subsequent discourse, we do not expect to see this kind of 'switching.' I thus tentatively conclude that the role a referent plays in the subsequent discourse does not appear to satisfactorily account for the patterns of *hän*/*tämä* use that we have been discussing here, but I also emphasize that this area would benefit from future work.

Conclusions

In this paper, on the basis of the results of two sentence completion studies and a preliminary corpus investigation, I argued that *hän* 's/he'

---

15 It is not clear whether hearer-status plays a role in the *hän*/*tämä* variation for non-subjects. Both hearer-old (e.g. 13b) and hearer-new (example below) non-subject constituents can be referred to with *hän*. Further corpus work to determine the frequency with which anaphoric form occurs in this context would be very useful.
(a) Lähetin eräälle kaverilleni pitkiä ja perusteellisia sähköpostiviestejä. Hän vastasi niihin aina parilla rivillä ja hyvin ylimalkaisesti. (http://www.helsinginsanomat.fi/klik/akvaario/20010724akvaario.html) 'I sent long and thorough emails to one of my friends. He answered them with only a few lines, very cursorily.'

and *tämä* 'this' differ in their referential properties and are sensitive to different kinds of factors. More specifically, I hypothesized that (i) the pronoun *hän* is associated with the high end of a grammatical role scale, and that (ii) the demonstrative *tämä* is not simply a 'disambiguation tool' for contexts with multiple third-person singular referents, and is actually associated with the low end of a very general salience scale that includes various entities present in the discourse model at that point, not just third-person singular entities. The claim that the referential properties of *hän* and *tämä* are not subject to a single common factor is also supported by related psycholinguistic research using the eye-tracking paradigm (Kaiser 2003, Kaiser & Trueswell to appear), i.e. using people's eye-movements to track their incremental interpretation of *hän* and *tämä* in Finnish.

Taken as a whole, the results show that we cannot maintain, at least not for Finnish, an approach in which pronouns and demonstratives are guided by a unified notion of salience. If *hän* and *tämä* differ only in the degree of salience than they prefer their antecedents to have, they should not display different sensitivities to different factors – yet this is what we see in the results. This claim that we shouldn't try to define the referential properties of *hän* and *tämä* in terms of a single unified notion of salience has important implications for our understanding of how referential systems – and perhaps also other linguistic systems – work. On the one hand, we could imagine a system that assigns jobs to the elements, such that the functions of one element are dependent on the functions of other elements in the system. This type of approach seems to be implicit in accessibility hierarchies which suggest that null pronouns are used for more accessible referents than pronouns, which in turn are used for more accessible referents than demonstratives, and so on. On the other hand, an alternative option is that the different elements that are part of the system have properties of their own that are independent of the system. In this case, though, since the elements are part of the same system, there may well be some situations in which these properties come into conflict. The findings presented in this paper seem to support the second option.

Of course, many questions still remain open. For example, the differences between the anaphoric systems of standard Finnish and colloquial Finnish bring up the question of how the findings presented here relate to dialects of colloquial Finnish. Conducting experiments similar to the ones reported here, but using colloquial Finnish, would be very interesting. Another important question concerns the grammatical role scale and salience scale that I hypothesize *hän* and *tämä* relate to respectively. If we hypothesize that *hän* is associated with the high end of a grammatical role scale and *tämä* with the low end of a salience scale, then we are faced with the question of how these scales relate to each other. For a particular referent that falls somewhere on each of the scales, how is the 'division of labor' between *hän* and *tämä* worked out? At what point is a referent sufficiently non-salient to be referred to with *tämä*, or sufficient high up on the grammatical role hierarchy for *hän* to be used? Answers to these questions are beyond the scope of this paper, but they merit further research.

SOURCES

Aamulehti, Finnish newspaper
Crichton, Michael. 1995. *The Lost World.* New York: Knoepf.
Crichton, Michael. 1996. *Kadonnut Maailma.* Helsinki: Otava. (Finnish translation)
Linna, Väinö. 1954/1999. *Tuntematon Sotilas.* Helsinki: WSOY
Rowling, J. K. 2001. *Harry Potter and the Prisoner of Azkaban.* New York: Scholastic.
Rowling, J. K. 2000. *Harry Potter ja Azkabanin vanki.* Helsinki: Tammi. (Finnish translation)
Helsingin Sanomat (Finnish newspaper web archives), and other texts on the web.

REFERENCES

Ariel, Mira. 1990. *Accessing NP antecedents.* London: Routledge, Croom Helm.
Arnold, Jennifer. 1998. *Reference form and discourse patterns.* Unpublished Ph. D. dissertation, Stanford University, Stanford, CA.
Birner, Betty and Gregory Ward. 1998. *Information status and noncanonical word order in English.* Amsterdam/Philadelphia: John Benjamins.
Brennan, Susan E., Marilyn A. Friedman and Charles J. Pollard. 1987. A Centering approach to pronouns. *Proceedings of the 25th Annual Meeting of the Association for Computational Linguistics*, Stanford, Calif., 155–162.
Chafe, Wallace L. 1976. Givenness, contrastiveness, definiteness, subjects, topics, and point of view. In C. N. Li (ed.) *Subject and topic*, 25–55. New York: Academic Press.
Chafe, Wallace L. 1994. *Discourse, Consciousness and Time.* Chicago: University of Chicago Press.
Chambers, Craig and Ron Smyth. 1998. Structural parallelism and discourse coherence: A test of Centering Theory. *Journal of Memory and Language* 39: 593–608.
Chesterman, Andrew. 1991. *On definiteness.* Cambridge, England: Cambridge University Press.
Crawley, Rosalind J. and Rosemary J. Stevenson. 1990. Reference in single sentences and in texts. Journal of Psycholinguistic Research, 19(3), 191–210.
Etelämäki, Marja. 1996. *Keskustelu tarkoitteesta kamerataiteen oppitunnilla – ja pronominit tuo, se, tämä.* Thesis, Department of Finnish, University of Helsinki.
Gernsbacher, Morton Ann. 1990. *Language Comprehension as Structure Building.* Hillsdale, N. J: Lawrence Erlbaum.
Givón, Talmy. 1983. *Topic continuity in discourse: A quantitative cross-language study.* Amsterdam: John Benjamins.
Gordon, Peter C., Barbara J. Grosz and Laura A. Gilliom. 1993. Pronouns, names, and the Centering of attention in discourse. *Cognitive Science* 17, 311–347
Gundel, Jeanette K., Nancy Hedberg and Ron Zacharski. 1993. Cognitive status and the form of referring Expressions in Discourse. *Language* 69, 274–307.
Halmari, Helena. 1994. On accessibility and coreference. *Nordic Journal of Linguistics*, 17, 35–59.
Helasvuo, Marja-Liisa. 2001. *Syntax in the Making – the emergence of syntactic units in Finnish conversation.* Amsterdam/Philadelphia: John Benjamins.
Hiirikoski, Juhani. 1995. Correlations between some morphosyntactic features and word order in Finnish and English: Some preliminary results of testing the transitivity hypothesis. In B. Wårwik, S. K. Tanskanen and R. Hiltunen (eds.) *Organization in Discourse, Proceedings from the Turku Conference (Anglicana Turkuensia 14)*, 289–299.

Hoffman, Beryl. 1998. Word order, information structure and Centering in Turkish. In Marilyn A. Walker, Aravind K. Joshi and Ellen F. Prince (eds.) *Centering Theory in Discourse*, 251–272. Oxford: Oxford University Press.

Kaiser, Elsi. 2000. Pronouns and demonstratives in Finnish: Indicators of referent salience. In Paul Baker, Andrew Hardie, Tony McEnery and Anna Siewierska (eds.) *Proceedings of the Discourse Anaphora and Reference Resolution Conference (DAARC 2000)*, 20–27.

Kaiser, Elsi. 2003. *The quest for a referent: A crosslinguistic look at reference resolution.* Ph. D. dissertation, University of Pennsylvania.

Kaiser, Elsi and John Trueswell. to appear. Investigating the interpretation of pronouns and demonstratives in Finnish: Going beyond salience. In Edward Gibson and Neil Pearlmutter (eds.) *The processing and acquisition of reference.* Cambridge: MIT Press.

Kalliokoski, Jyrki. 1991. Emphathy as motivation for style shifting in narrative. In Jef Verschueren (ed.) *Levels of linguistic adaptation. Selected papers of the International Pragmatics Conference* v. II, 147–161. John Benjamins, Amsterdam.

Karlsson, Fred. 1999. Finnish – An essential grammar. London/New York: Routledge.

Laury, Ritva. 1997. *Demonstratives in Interaction.* John Benjamins, Philadelphia/Amsterdam.

Matthews, Alison and Martin S. Chodorow 1988. Pronoun resolution in two-clause sentences: Effects of ambiguity, antecedent location, and depth of embedding. *Journal of Memory and Language*, 27, 245–260.

McDonald, Janet L. and Brian MacWhinney. 1995. The time course of anaphor resolution: Effects of implicit verb causality and gender. *Journal of Memory and Language*, 34, 543–566.

Prasad, Rashmi and Michael Strube. 2000. Discourse salience and pronoun resolution in Hindi. In Alexander Williams & Elsi Kaiser (eds.) *U. Penn Working Papers in Linguistics*, vol. 6.3, 189–208.

Prince, Ellen F. 1992. 'The ZPG letter: subjects, definiteness and information status.' In Sandra A. Thompson & William C. Mann (eds.) *Discourse description: diverse analyses of a fund raising text*, 295–325. Philadelphia/Amsterdam: John Benjamins.

Rambow, Owen. 1993. 'Pragmatic aspects of scrambling and topicalization in German.' Paper presented at the Workshop on Naturally-Occurring Discourse, Institute for Research in Cognitive Science, University of Pennsylvania.

Saarimaa, E. A. 1949. Kielemme käytäntö. Pronominivirheistä. *Virittäjä* 49. 250–257.

Seppänen, Eeva-Leena. 1998. *Läsnäolon pronominit. Tämä, tuo, se ja hän viittaamassa keskustelun osallistujaan.* Helsinki: Suomalaisen Kirjallisuuden Seura.

Sheldon, Amy. 1974. The role of parallel function in the acquisition of relative clauses in English. *Journal of Verbal Learning and Verbal Behavior,* 13.272–281.

Stevenson, Rosemary and Agnieszka Urbanowicz. 1995. Structural focusing, thematic role focusing and the comprehension of pronouns. *Proceedings of the 17th Annual Conference of the Cognitive Science Society*, 328–332. Pittsburgh, PA.

Stevenson, Rosemary J., Rosalind J. Crawley and David Kleinman. 1994. Thematic roles, focus and the represenation of events. *Language and Cognitive Processes*, 9, 519–548.

Strube, Michael and Udo Hahn. 1996. Functional Centering. *Proceedings of ACL '96*, 270–277.

Strube, Michael and Udo Hahn. 1999. Functional Centering: Grounding Referential Coherence in Information Structure. *Computational Linguistics*, 25(3).

Sulkala, Helena and Merja Karjalainen. 1992. *Finnish.* London: Routledge.

Tetreault, Joel. 2001. *A Corpus-Based Evaluation of Centering and Pronoun Resolution.*

Turan, Ümit Deniz. 1998. Ranking forward-looking centers in Turkish. In Marilyn A. Walker, Aravind K. Joshi and Ellen F. Prince (eds.) *Centering Theory in Discourse*, 136–160. Oxford: Oxford University Press.
Varteva, Annukka. 1998. Pronominit hän ja tämä tekstissä. *Virittäjä*, 2/1998, 202–223.
Vilkuna, Maria. 1989. *Free word order in Finnish*. Helsinki: Suomalaisen Kirjallisuuden Seura.
Vilkuna, Maria. 1995. Discourse configurationality in Finnish. In Katalin Kiss (ed.) *Discourse Configurational Languages*, 244–268. New York: Oxford University Press.
Vilkuna, Maria. 1996. *Suomen lauseopin perusteet*. Helsinki: Edita.
Vilppula, Matti. 1989. Havaintoja hän- ja he-pronominien käytöstä suomen murteissa. *Virittäjä* 93, 389–399.
Walker, Marilyn A., Aravind K. Joshi and Ellen F. Prince. 1998. Centering Theory in Discourse. Oxford: Oxford University Press.

OUTI DUVALLON

The pronoun *se* in the context of syntactic and discursive ruptures of spoken texts

Introduction

This paper proposes a syntactic approach to the use and interpretation of the Finnish pronoun *se* 'it, s/he' in spoken texts. The analysis is concentrated on a particular context of use in which the host construction of the pronoun is an utterance that suspends another ongoing verbal construction, as in example (1).[1] The pronoun *se* 'it' points to a referent whose lexical description is unachieved in the context previous to its occurrences:

(1)

 – – – nin näil on kuulemma valtavan s- hieno niinku *ei se mikään mökki o vaan se on semmonen hirsitupa + oikeen* ja sit siel on kaikki mikroaaltouunista ja astianpesukoneest lähtien

 – – – so I heard they have a very b- splendid uh *it's not at all any cottage but it is a timbered house + really* and then there is everything from a microwave oven and a dishwasher (Summer plans 079)

This example is different from a prototypical case of anaphora in which the pronoun is preceded by a full lexical antecedent. However, I will argue that the interpretation of the pronoun *se* 'it' takes place here essentially inside the linguistic context, i.e. by establishing a connexion between its host constructions and the sequence suspended.

In order to analyse this kind of use of the pronoun *se*, I take a viewpoint of production of verbal constructions in spoken discourse. My aim is to

---

1   All examples are drawn from a corpus of conversational data. I have use in this study audiotaped data provided by the department of Finnish at the University of Helsinki (number of tape is indicated) and my personal collection (without number). The transcriptions are adapted for a syntactic approach and contain only some prosodic indications, e.g. the places of pauses, marked by the symbol "+". When necessary, prosodic patterns are commented in the text. See the appendix for a description of data, transcription symbols and other notations used in this paper.

pay attention, on the one hand, to some characteristics of lexical naming processes and to show, on the other hand, that the pronoun *se* is an original referring expression: it can be used for picking out a referent with a minimum of descriptive content not only when lexical descriptions of the referent are already made, but also when they are still in progress or still being negotiated, and even when they are momentary unavailable.

This paper is organized as follows. I will first briefly present the pronoun *se* in light of the Finnish third person pronoun system. Secondly, I will define the basic notions of the syntactic framework adopted here. Then I will discuss some models by which lexical descriptions are built up in oral productions. Finally, I will analyze extracts of the type presented above from the perspective of the emergence of the linguistic context in which pronouns are used. The first part of the paper examines sequences which have a clearly metalinguistic function and the second part presents an example of a non-metalinguistic parenthetical insert.

The pronoun se *in the Finnish pronominal system*

Finnish grammars have traditionally classified the pronoun *se* as a demonstrative pronoun, but many authors have also, more or less explicitly, integrated this pronoun into the category of personal pronouns (see for instance Penttilä 1963: 508–511; Saukkonen 1967; A. Hakulinen 1985, 1988; Hakulinen et al. 1994: 215). In the system of three demonstratives *tämä, tuo* and *se*, the first two have been described in terms of proximity, i.e. proximal or distal with regard to the speaker, whereas the pronoun *se* has been considered more neutral in relation to the distance and is said to have its referential landmark in the addressee. Compared with the other two forms, the pronoun *se* has thus been deemed less clearly demonstrative and particularly suited for "anaphoric" uses (cf. Setälä 1891: 76–77; Penttilä 1963: 510–514; Hakulinen 1985; Larjavaara 1985, 1990: 93–157, 2001).

More recently, Etelämäki (1996, in this volume), Laury (1997) and Seppänen (1998) have revisited the Finnish demonstrative system within interactional and conversational frameworks. Rejecting the static, distance-based view, these studies claim that demonstratives allow the speaker to assign different statuses to referents, to organize structures of interaction and to manage participant roles in conversation. According to Laury (1997: 59), by using the pronoun *se*, the speaker places the referent in the addressee's social and cognitive sphere (cf. Itkonen 1966: 421). Seppänen (1998), who treats the use of third person pronouns as devices for referring to co-participants in conversation, suggests that the pronoun *se* invites the recipients to seek its interpretation source in the world of discourse even if the referent is present in the current speech situation (see also Etelämäki 1996: 62–66). In the most typical cases, the pronoun *se* seems to refer to referents that have already been introduced into discourse by other forms or that are otherwise already in the participants' centre of attention (Laury 1997: 77–87). Thus the recent studies, as well as traditional descriptions, see the pronoun *se* primarily as an "anaphoric" pronoun.

Note that according to the classic theory of anaphora, the anaphoric status of third person pronouns results from the fact that these forms lack a lexical content (see e.g. Milner 1982: 20). In order to be interpreted, the third person pronouns should be related to lexical content available in their linguistic context (Milner, op. cit.: 31).[2] Functionally oriented approaches have abandoned this purely textual conception in favour of a re-definition of anaphora as a procedure by which the speaker invites the hearer to sustain his attention on a referent previously introduced in focus of discourse (Ehlich 1982; see also Givón 1983; Chafe 1987; Ariel 1988; Gundel et al. 1993).

However, although the pronoun *se* typically serves as a tracking form, its use is not constrained by a previous lexical mention of the referent or by the presence of the referent in the situation of utterance. For instance Laury (1994, 1997: 125–128, in this volume) has examined the use of the pronoun *se* as a first mention pronoun (see also Fox 1987: 67–69; Ziv 1996). This kind of use, and more generally all cases in which the referential target of the pronoun is not explicitly and unequivocally given in its immediate context of use, draw attention to the role the host construction plays in the interpretation process. In fact, instructions carried by the host construction of the pronoun and the position of this construction in the larger linguistic context offer crucial criteria for the pronominal reference resolution.

By its inherent semantic properties, the pronoun *se* sets few restrictions on its potential referents. Like the other Finnish third person pronouns, it distinguishes between singular and plural number. However, Finnish lacks grammatical gender. Furthermore, in non-standard Finnish, the referent of the pronoun *se* can be human or non-human, animate or inanimate, a discrete entity or a propositional content. Note that the pronoun *hän* which is reserved in standard Finnish to refer to human referents is used in most varieties of spoken Finnish as a logophoric pronoun by which the speaker displays his identification with another individual referent's viewpoint (Laitinen 2002, this volyme).

In what follows, I will describe patterns by which the referential anchoring of the pronoun *se* can be defined in textual domains of the linguistic context.

Some preliminary considerations

The governing verb and rection places opened by it

The framework of my syntactic analysis is the Pronominal Approach developed by Blanche-Benveniste et al. 1987 (see also Blanche-Benveniste 1997; for an application to Finnish, see Tiainen-Duvallon 2002). In this theory, the syntactic description is grounded on the notion of the verb.

---

2   The linguistic segment that is supposed to confer a descriptive content on a pronoun is called *antecedent*.

Verbs are governing elements which are endowed with a constructional power, i.e. an ability to organise other elements around them. The syntactic slots a verb creates in its environment will be referred to as *rection places* (places de rection) in this paper.

The constructional power of a verb is taken to be an inseparable property from its lexical content (Blanche-Benveniste 1997: 99). In contrast, rection places opened by a verb can be identified without any lexical content, by using pronouns, and more generally, different kinds of pro-forms. In Finnish, among the latter, there are the "true" pronouns with the complete declension in cases, but also pro-adverbs (Airila 1940) such as locative demonstratives (e.g. *siellä* 'there') and temporal adverbs (e.g. *silloin* 'then').[3]

Pro-forms are indeed surer syntactic indicators than lexical forms of nouns (cf. also Helasvuo 2001: 34). First, pro-forms can present rectional features imposed by a verb regardless of the probability of lexical combinations. Secondly, pro-forms bring out differences in rectional features that nouns do not always show (cf. Tarvainen 1977: 43–44; Hakulinen & Karlsson 1979: 175):

(2)

Hän meni *sinne ~ Pariisiin$_{ILL}$ ~ Venäjälle$_{ALL}$*.
'He went *there(to) ~ to Paris ~ to Russia.*'

(3)

Hän ihastui *siihen$_{ILL}$ ~ Pariisiin$_{ILL}$ ~ Venäjään$_{ILL}$ ~ ranskalaiseen$_{ILL}$ keittiöön$_{ILL}$*.
'He fell in love *with it ~ with Paris ~ with Russia ~ with French food.*'

For instance the verb *mennä* 'to go' in (2) has in its construction a locative element which indicates the directional feature of "movement towards". This feature is one of the three distinctions ("position", "movement from" and "movement towards") made on the dimension of "direction" in the Finnish case system (Siro 1960: 29–30; see the appendix). However, the verb *mennä* 'to go' does not impose on its locative complement the choice between the illative and the allative cases which belong to two different series of cases on the dimension of "quality" in the local case system. This choice depends on the nominal lexeme which realizes the locative rection place. Syntactically, the two lexical realizations *Pariisiin$_{ILL}$* 'to Paris' and *Venäjälle$_{ALL}$* 'to Russia' are equivalent to the proadverb *sinne* 'there(to)' which distinguishes only three forms indicating the features on the dimension of "direction": *siellä* 'there' (position), *sieltä* 'from there' (movement from) and *sinne* 'there(to)' (movement towards).

---

3   Note that the term *rection* is used here to speak about two kinds of elements: verb-specific valency elements and non-verb-specific elements, as temporal and spatial complements, which are however concerned by the modalities of the verb and which can be identified by pro-forms. The term *rectional element* contrasts with the term *associated element* that is reserved to speak about elements that are not constructed by a verb (cf. *clausal complement* in the more traditional terminology).

The verb *ihastua* 'to fall in love' in (3) has in its construction an element in the illative case, and all realizations of this rection place are syntactically equivalent to the pronoun *se* in the illative case, *siihen*$_{ILL}$ 'with it'.

The syntactic equivalence between pro-forms and lexical realizations of rection places serves to distinguish elements that are constructed by a verb from elements that are not (see note 3), and it serves also to recognise idiomatic expressions in which the lexical element having an appearance of a complement is more or less set, like *huomioon*$_{ILL}$ in *ottaa huomioon*$_{ILL}$ 'to take into consideration' (?*ottaa siihen*$_{ILL}$ '?to take into it').

In brief, pro-forms function as grammatical tools in the syntactic description of units constructed by a verb. We can consider them basic forms compared with lexical forms of nouns. A pro-form is syntactically equivalent to a paradigm of different lexical realizations in a rection place opened by a verb. In addition, note that this equivalence between pro-forms and lexical forms is not limited to verbal constructions, but it concerns also constructions of other grammatical categories, like postpositions in Finnish.

The rection paradigms

In both oral and written productions, rection places are likely to receive multiple realizations. Put differently, we can expect to find in the spoken chain elements that do not combine to form syntagmatic units, but which instantiate the same rection place and form paradigmatic lists (cf. Blanche-Benveniste 1987: 137–142, 1990: 13–19). It is thus advisable to distinguish in the spoken chain two kinds of relations and respectively two axes of progression, the syntagmatic axis and the paradigmatic axis.

The idea of these two basic axes of language was formulated by F. de Saussure in his *Course in general linguistics* (1983[1916]), and we find it later also in the works of R. Jakobson (see for instance 1956). According to the former, linguistic production processes bring into play a double system of syntagmatic units and associative groupings:

> Our memory holds in store all the various complex types of syntagma, of every kind and length. When a syntagma is brought into use, we call upon associative groups in order to make our choice. - - - In uttering the words *que vous dit-il?* ('what does he say to you?'), we vary one element in a latent syntagmatic type of which other examples would be *que te dit-il?*, *que nous dit-il?* etc. ('what does he say to you/us/them…?' etc.). This is the process involved in our selection of the pronoun *vous* in *que vous dit-il?* In this process, which involves eliminating mentally everything which does not lead to the desired differentiation at the point required, associative groupings and syntagmatic types are both involved. (Saussure 1983[1916]: 128–129.)

Utterances seem then to be constructed and perceived as combinations of different elements, selected from paradigmatic sets of possible alternatives.

The constituents of a context are in a status of *contiguity*, while in a substitution set signs are linked by various degrees of *similarity* which fluctuate between the equivalence of synonyms and the common core of antonyms. (Jakobson 1956: 61.)

To Saussure and Jakobson, syntagmatic relations of combination (or contexture) are realized in discourse, while associative or paradigmatic relations of selection (or substitution) belong only to the code, i.e. to an abstract system that constitutes a language, and are not realised in discourse.

However, empirical data show that lexical selection processes are not exclusively a matter of the speaker's memory (Blanche-Benveniste 1990: 14). Selection processes leave traces in the actual linguistic production and sometimes they occupy an important place in it. The syntagmatic advancement of an utterance can be stopped on a rection place that is instantiated several times. In fact, the introduction of lexical elements into rection places follows regular patterns in oral productions. By way of illustration, consider the following four examples.

The first realization of a rection place can be done with an element without any lexical content. In example (4), the locative complement of the verb *lentää* 'to fall' is announced by the element *sinne* 'thereto', a locative demonstrative indicating the directional feature of "movement towards". This demonstrative is followed by a pause and then it is repeated in front of a noun in the allative case, *tielle* 'road', which expresses the same directional feature ("movement towards") as the demonstrative:

(4)

> minä lensin pyllylleni *sinne + sinne tielle*$_{ALL}$
> I fell on my behind *on the + on the road* (Hairdressing salon 105)

In Finnish, the autonomous pro-forms and the demonstrative determiners are morphologically identical. It could then be possible to analyze example (4) as a figure of right dislocation, with the first realization of the locative rection place made by a pro-form closely attached to the verb and a lexical realization of the same place being located in the periphery of the construction. But we can also see here a repetition typical of oral productions at the beginning of a syntagmatic unit before the introduction of lexical elements (cf. Blanche-Benveniste 1987: 133).[4] If these two analytical possibilities exist in theory, the interpretation of a particular occurrence is likely to be guided by prosodic features and the larger context of use, in particular by the presence or absence of a referential anchoring to the pro-form.

---

4   For the discussion about the status of locative demonstratives, see Laury 1997: 128–145. In *Iso suomen kielioppi* (Hakulinen et al. 2004) the syntagmatic units formed by a locative demonstrative and a noun in a local case as *sinne tielle* 'on the road' are called *fixed apposition construction* (*kiinteä appositiorakenne*).

The second analysis is a hypothesis on the suspension of the syntagmatic axis of the utterance. This hypothesis is visualised below in a figure that exploits the horizontal and vertical axes of the page (see Blanche-Benveniste 1990). When paradigmatic elements are placed one below the other in a vertical column, the syntacmatic axis emerges on the horizontal dimension:

Table 1.

minä	lensin	pyllylleni	sinne	
I	fell	on my behind	on the	
			sinne	tielle$_{ALL}$
			on the	road

In any case, whatever the syntactic analysis may be, we have here an example in which a rection place is announced by a non-lexical element before the lexical realization.

Secondly, a rection place can be reinstantiated in order to increase the degree of lexical specification. In example (5), paradigmatic reiterations target the place of the valency complement of the verb *kiittää* 'to thank'. This rection place is first realized by the noun phrase *kaikkia*$_{PART}$ *naisia*$_{PART}$ 'all women' in which the lexical head (*naisia* 'women') is a basic level categorization (cf. Rosch 1977; Cornish 1996: 33). After having completed the syntagmatic axis of the utterance (by the sequence *kuten tapana on* 'as is customary' encircled by the addressee's responses *joo joo, niin*), the speaker re-edits the valency complement of the verb *kiittää* 'to thank'. The elements *Hannaa*$_{PART}$ 'Hanna', *äitiänsä*$_{PART}$ 'his mother' and *ketä*$_{PART}$ *kaikkiansa*$_{PART}$ 'everybody' form a list in which the noun phrases are, as in the first realization, in the partitive case which the verb *kiittää* 'to thank' imposes on its valency complement:

(5)

S1   ku se esipuheessaan kato kiittää *kaikkia*$_{PART}$ *naisia*$_{PART}$
because he in his preface you see thanks *all women*
S2   joo joo
oh
S1   kuten tapana on
as is customary
S2   niin
yes
S1   *Hannaa*$_{PART}$ ja *äitiänsä*$_{PART}$ ja *ketä*$_{PART}$ *kaikkiansa*PAR
Hanna and *his mother* and *everybody* (Summer plans 079)

Table 2.

se esipuheessaan	kato	kiittää	kaikkia$_{PART}$	naisia$_{PART}$	kuten	tapana	on
he in his preface	you see	thanks	all	women	as	customary	is
				Hannaa$_{PART}$			
				Hanna			
			ja	äitiänsä$_{PART+POS}$			
			and	his mother			
			ja	ketä$_{PART}$ kaikkiansa$_{PART+POS}$			
			and	everybody			

The reiterations constitute an additive enumeration, explicitly marked by the element *ja* 'and', which specifies the designation made by the first realization. We can also note that the last realization *ketä kaikkiansa* 'whom else ~ everybody' closes the list by inviting at the same time to consider the listing as non-complete (cf. Jefferson 1990: 65–68).

Thirdly, the assignment of lexical elements can be made by opposing different designations. In (6), the noun phrases *niitä kortteja* 'those post cards' and *pieniä kirjeitä* 'small letters' realize the valency complement of the verb *olla* 'to be'. The first realization is within the scope of the negative modality of the verb. Then the elements *vaan siis* 'but PRT' introduce into the same rection place a second realization that is endowed with its own modality, i.e. it escapes the negative modality affecting the first realization:

(6)

> ((a season worker in a post office explains what her job entails))
> se ei oo nyt *niitä kortteja* vaan siis + *pieniä kirjeitä*
> this time it's not *those post cards* but + *small letters* (Childhood friends 101)

Table 3.

se	ei	oo	nyt		niitä$_{PART}$		kortteja$_{PART}$
it	is not		this time		those		post cards
				vaan siis		pieniä$_{PART}$	kirjeitä$_{PART}$
				but PRT		small	letters

The first noun is preceded by the demonstrative determiner *niitä* 'those' (plural form of the demonstrative *se*) that seems to function here as an invitation to the addressee to link information carried by the utterance with an already shared knowledge (cf. Vilkuna 1992: 134). The first realization *kortteja* 'post cards' is indeed introduced as a presupposed element with which the second realization *pieniä kirjeitä* 'small letters' is contrasted. Neither the second, nor the first is supposed to assume the designation alone, but these two realizations, by defining each other, constitute together the lexical description.

Finally, the overt negotiation about different naming possibilities is particularly obvious in examples of repairs. In (7), the speaker stops the syntagmatic axis of the utterance after having pronounced the verb *väitti* 'said', followed by the beginning of the element *et(tä)* 'that', and returns to a rectional element in the allative case (*sille*$_{ALL}$ *poliisille*$_{ALL}$ 'to the policeman') which has been realized already before the governing verb.[5]

(7)

vaikka hän sille *poliisille* väitti e- tai *kuulustelijalle* väitti että + hän oli juonu viinaa
even though *to the policeman* he said tha- or *to the investigator* he said that + he had drunk alcohol (Hairdressing salon 105)

Table 4.

vaikka	hän	sille$_{ALL}$	poliisille$_{ALL}$		väitti	e-				
even though	he	to the	policeman		said	tha-				
			tai	kuulustelijalle$_{ALL}$	väitti	että	hän	oli	juonu	viinaa
			or	to [the] investigator	said	that	he	had	drunk	alcohol

The second realization *kuulustelijalle*$_{ALL}$ 'to [the] investigator' that is introduced by the element *tai* 'or' proposes an alternative designation,[6] after which the verb is reproduced and its construction is completed.

The instability of lexical descriptions

Repairs that take place with a delay show that lexical descriptions remain an object of negotiation even when a lexical designation has momentarily been made. On the other hand, paradigmatic lists with the contrastive effect evidence the fact that lexical realizations of a rection place do not reduce to the selection of a unique term among the paradigm of possible realizations (cf. Blanche-Benveniste 1987: 142). In paradigmatic developments anchored to a rection place, lexical designations are built up progressively. They may advance for example by specification, the first realization only announcing a rectional element by indicating its syntactic type or making a basic level categorization of the referent.

The introduction of lexical elements into rection places may then consist of an entire task during which a referent is constructed by using

---

5   This word order is sometimes used in sequences which contain information supposed to be already known (see for instance Sorjonen 2002; Duvallon 2003).
6   Only the lexical head of the noun phrase is reproduced, but not the determiner. A careful reader may have noticed a difference in the figures of this example and example (6) in which the second realization equally contains no demonstrative determiner. In the analysis of (6), I have placed the editing terms *vaan siis* in front of the empty column of the determiner, while in the analysis of (7), the editing element *tai* is placed after the column of the determiner. This difference reflects an intuition based interpretation that in (6) the re-edition concerns the whole noun phrase, but in (7) only the lexical head noun. I would like to emphasize that figures representing syntactic organization of utterances are rather robust. The grammatical status of Finnish demonstrative determiners is a question that could not be treated here (see Laury 1997; Juvonen 2000; Larjavaara 2001).

different descriptions depending on viewpoints from which the speaker picks out the referent or perspectives in which s/he places the referent (cf. for instance Blanche-Benveniste 1985; Apothéloz & Reichler-Béguelin 1995; Mondada & Dubois 1995). Even a simple lexical designation gets its value in relation to a paradigm of other potential designations (see also Schegloff 1996: 458, note 25).[7] The instability of lexical elements can also be explicitly stated by the speaker in metalinguistic sequences produced during the lexical selection process.

Metalinguistic sequences

The realization of rection places is sometimes accompanied by which do not constitute the main sequences line of discourse, but rather make linguistic production processes explicit by providing comments on how to put propositional content into words. In this section, I will first examine three models by which a metalinguistic sequence can be inserted in the body of a frame construction. Then, I will formulate a hypothesis on the referential anchoring of the pronoun *se* used in metalinguistic sequences.

Three insertion models

It happens that instead of providing a rection place with a lexical element, the speaker produces a verbal sequence which explicates the request or inaccessibility of a lexical description. In example (8), the verb *hyppiä* 'to jump' has in its construction a valency complement which is first instantiated by the element *niit* 'those'. Although the form *niit* could function as an independent pronoun, the preceding linguistic context does not contain here any explicit interpretation source (cf. ex. (4)). Prosodic cues equally contribute to expect a syntagmatic continuation.[8] So, we can see here a pro-element that is used as a determiner anticipating a lexical head of a noun phrase. After a pause and a hesitation sound *ö*- 'uh', the speaker pronounces however not a nominal element but a sequence which requests a lexical designation: *mitä ne nyt on* 'what they PRT are ~ what are they called':

(8)

S1 – – – nythän se on hyppiny niit + ö- *mitä ne nyt on* +
    – – – it's true that now he has been jumping those + uh *what are they called* +
S2 laskuvarjo-
    parachute-
S1 niin niit   laskuvarjohyppyi
    yes those parachute jumps (Summer plans 079)

---

7   My remarks on lexical naming processes are limited to a syntactic approach.
8   For more information about prosodic cues used in the turn-holding, such as a level intonation and a pause initiated by glottal closure, see for instance Local 1992; Local & Kelly 1986; Ogden 2001. I thank Sara Routarinne for these references.

Table 5.

nythän	se	on	hyppiny	niit	ö-			
now-PRT	he	has	been jumping	those	uh			
						mitä	ne nyt	on
						what	they PRT	are

In example (9), a metalinguistic sequence is integrated into the construction of the postposition *kanssa* 'with'. The rection place opened by this postposition is realized at the first time by the noun in the genitive case *vaimonsa*$_{GEN-POS}$ 'his wife'. The first realization is followed by the element *ja* 'and', that gives cause for expecting to a second realization in the same syntactic place (note that the governing element, i.e. the postposition which follows its rectional element in the spoken chain, is still in suspense). But after a pause, the speaker produces the metalinguistic sequence *en mä tiiä kuka se oli* 'I don't know who s/he was' with which she declines to provide a lexical designation. After that, the syntagmatic axis is completed by the governing postposition:

(9)

Aaro oli siel vaimonsa ja + *en mä tiiä kuka se oli* + kanssa
Aaro was there with his wife and *I don't know who s/he was* (Three high school scholars 099)

Table 6.

Aaro	oli	siel	vaimonsa$_{GEN-POS}$					
Aaro	was	there	his wife					
			ja					
			and					
			en	mä	tiiä	kuka	se	oli
			NEG	I	[don't] know	who	s/he	was
								kanssa
								with

In these two cases, it looks as if the metalinguistic sequence takes provisionally the place of a noun or a noun phrase.[9] Note that in (8) a lexical designation is suggested later on by the addressee (S2) who pronounces the beginning of a lexical element (*laskuvarjo-*, the first part of a compound word). The initial speaker approves it (*niin* 'yes') and then, by reiterating

---

9   In figures I have separated the metalinguistic sequences from the frame constructions in order to indicate the passage from the main discourse to the metalanguage, but on the other hand, the metalinguistic sequences are aligned with the syntactic slot of the frame construction they seem to occupy.

the determiner, she introduces it explicitly into the syntactic matrix of the frame construction:[10]

Table 7.

S1 nythän	se on	hyppiny	niit$_{PART}$	ö-		
now+PRT	he has	been jumping	those	uh		
S2				*mitä*	*ne nyt on*	
				what	*they PRT are*	
				laskuvarjo-		
				parachute-		
S1			niin	niit$_{PART}$	laskuvarjohyppyi$_{PART}$	
			yes	those	parachute jumps	

In (9), in contrast, the metalinguistic sequence is integrated into a rection paradigm without adding any lexical designation subsequently.

In the second type of cases, the metalinguistic sequence takes over from the categorization of a referent. The extract in example (10) (quoted already at the beginning of this paper) starts with a sequence that gives the impression of a syntactic and semantic incompletion (*näil on kuulemma valtavan s- hieno* 'I heard they have a very b- splendid'):

(10)

– – – nin näil on kuulemma valtavan s- hieno niinku *ei se mikään mökki o vaan se on semmonen hirsitupa + oikeen* ja sit siel on kaikki mikroaaltouunista ja astianpesukoneest lähtien
– – – so I heard they have a very b- splendid uh *it's not at all any cottage but it is a timbered house + really* and then there is everything from a microwave oven and a dishwasher (Summer plans 079)

Table 8.

näil$_{ADE}$	on	kuulemma	valtavan	s-		
they	have	I heard	[a] very	b-		
				hieno$_{NOM}$	niinku	
				splendid	PRT	

10 According to Schegloff *et al.* 1977, repairs in conversation are organised in the way that the initial speaker has the privilege of resolving a problem that arises in the production of an utterance. The particle *nyt* used in word search sequences is indeed a mark of the rhetorical nature of these sequences (cf. Hakulinen & Saari 1995: 490–491). In example (8), the immediate participation of the addressee in the lexical selection process may be related to the fact that the whole utterance calls for a shared knowledge: on the one hand, in the head of the frame construction, there is the enclitic particle *-hAn* which marks that the utterance contains information supposed to be already known by the addressee (A. Hakulinen 2001[1976]), and on the other hand, the determiner *niit*, whose use seems to go hand in hand with the particle, invites the addressee to link the propositional content of the utterance with an already shared knowledge (Vilkuna 1992: 133–135; Duvallon 2004). (Cf. Goodwin 1987, who pays attention to the role that apparent hesitations play in the management of participant roles in speech situations in which the access to information conveyed in discourse is shared by several participants.)

The pronoun in the adessive case *näil*$_{ADE}$ 'they' and the verb *on* seem to begin a possessive construction (*näil on*... 'they have...'). We could then expect the valency complement to be realized by a noun phrase. After the verb, the element *kuulemma* 'I heard' (frozen form of the verb *kuulla* 'to hear') indicates that the speaker is reporting second hand information (cf. Kuiri 1984: 201, 207–209). Then the realization of the valency complement is started by the adjective phrase *valtavan s- hieno* 'very b- splendid' (the sound *s-* preceding the adjective *hieno* could be perceived in this context as a beginning of the adjective *suuri* 'big').[11] The particle *niinku* functions as a signal that the utterance will be continued.

Suojala (1989: 121–122) has observed that this particle is used in contexts in which the continuation involves a syntactic rupture, as in this example. Instead of providing directly a lexical head noun, the speaker produces two sequences in which the verb *olla* 'to be' is used first in the scope of the negative modality (*ei se mikään mökki o* 'it's not at all any cottage') and then in the scope of the affirmative modality (*se on semmonen hirsitupa oikeen* 'it is a timbered house really'). The contrasting relation between these sequences is explicitly marked by the element *vaan* 'but':

Table 9.

näil$_{ADE}$ on kuulemma they have I heard	valtavan s-[a] very b-				
	hieno$_{NOM}$ splendid	niinku PRT			
		ei NEG	se it	mikään any	mökki o cottage is [not]
	vaan but		se it		on semmonen hirsitupa oikeen is a timbered house really

In the first metalinguistic sequence, the negative auxiliary verb begins the construction and the realization of the valency complement *mikään mökki* 'any cottage' is placed between the subject pronoun *se* 'it' and the governing verb *o* 'is'. This constituent order creates the effect of rejecting a presupposition. That effect is still intensified by the indefinite negative determiner *mikään* 'any'. Indeed, the first realization of the valency complement reiterates a lexeme (*mökki* 'cottage') which has already been used in the preceding context of this extract. The first realization is contrasted with the noun phrase *semmonen hirsitupa* 'a timbered house'[12] which is placed in the second sequence in the neutral position after the verb.

Example (11) presents a similar case. At the end of line 2, there is the sequence *kyllä tosiasiassa tehdään poliittisia* 'in reality they make

---

11 It is well known that adjectives may sometimes be used as nouns. In example (10), this interpretation is not very satisfactory.

12 The demonstrative adjective *semmonen* that means literally 'that kind of' can serve as a mark of a lexical approximation. It is used as a kind of indefinite article in order to introduce a lexical description or a categorization of a referent (note that Finnish lacks the category of indefinite article; see Juvonen in this volume).

political' in which the adjective *poliittisia* 'political' starts the realization of the valency complement of the verb *tehdä* 'to make'. After a pause, the speaker continues not with a lexical head which we could be waiting for, but by producing the metalinguistic sequence *ehkei ne ole paketteja mutta jonkun sortin sopimuksia kuitenkin* 'perhaps they are not packages but some kinds of contracts anyway':

(11)

1 nykyäänhän puhutaan hyvin paljon siitä ettei solmita poliittisia virkapaketteja + mutta sitten m- minusta näyttää siltä
  it's true that nowadays it is very often said that they don't make any packages of political posts + but it seems to
2 että kuitenkin + kansa + hyvin näkee ja ja kyllä minusta olen itsekin voinut nähdä että kyllä tosiasiassa tehdään poliittisia +
  me that however + people + see very well and and me too I could have seen that in reality they make political +
3 *ehkei ne ole paketteja mutta jonkun sortin sopimuksia kuitenkin*
  perhaps they are not packages but some kinds of contracts anyway (Professional life)

Table 10.

kyllä	tosiasiassa	tehdään$_{PASS}$	poliittisia					
PRT	in reality	they make	political					
				ehkei	ne	ole	paketteja	
				perhaps-NEG	they	are [not]	packages	
						mutta	jonkun sortin	sopimuksia	kuitenkin
						but	some kinds of contracts	anyway

Within the metalinguistic sequence, the first realization of the valency complement of the verb *olla* 'to be' reiterates a lexeme used in the preceding context (line 1: ...*ettei solmita poliittisia virka*paketteja '... that they don't make any *packages* of political posts'). The first realization is within the scope of a modal adverb and the negative modality of the verb (*ehk-ei* 'perhaps-NEG'). Then the element *mutta* 'but' introduces a second realization which is endowed with its own modality, i.e. the affirmative modality without any explicit mark, and accompanied by the adverb *kuitenkin* 'anyway'.[13]

In these two examples, the metalinguistic sequences interrupt an ongoing syntactic construction before the speaker provides a nominal head of a noun phrase whose realization has been started by a modifier. Unlike example (6) above, in which the opposition of different lexical descriptions is done directly in the main line of discourse, the naming process is carried out here

13 In Finnish, two elements can serve as contrastive markers: *vaan* and *mutta* 'but'. The element *vaan* seems to be used in contexts in which the contrasting relation involves only the negative and the affirmative modalities and in which the negative modality is expressed before the affirmative one. In example (11), in addition to the negative modality, the first sequence contains an expression of the epistemic modality (the adverb *ehk(ei)*) and the contrastive marker is *mutta*.

by means of metalinguistic sequences. The nominal head nouns are not provided at all at the level of the frame constructions. However, note that in (10) the following construction which is introduced by the elements *ja sit* 'and then' begins with the pro-form *siel* 'there' which points to the referent whose lexical description is achieved in the metalinguistic sequences.

The last two examples contain a metalinguistic sequence whose form seems to be more or less lexicalised. This third type of metalinguistic sequences produces the effect of modalising a lexical choice in a rection place. In (12), the valency complement of the verb *saada* 'to get, to obtain' is realized by the noun phrase *joku puoltoist viikkoo sairaslomaa* 'about one and a half weeks of sick leave' in front of which is grafted an interrogative sequence (*o- o- oisko se nyt ollu* 'w- w- would it PRT have been'):

(12)

sit se sai niinku + *o- o- oisko se nyt ollu* joku puoltoist viikkoo sairaslomaa
then he got uh + *w- w- would it* PRT *have been* about one and a half weeks of sick leave (Childhood friends 101)

Table 11.

sit	se	sai	niinku	o-				
then	he	got	PRT	w-				
				o-				
				w-				
				oisko	se nyt ollu	joku	puoltoist$_{NOM \sim ACC}$ viikkoo$_{PART}$	sairaslomaa$_{PART}$
				would-Q	it PRT have been	about	one and a half weeks of	sick leave

In (13), the locative complement of the verb *muuttaa* 'to move' is first instantiated by the element *jonneki* 'to someplace' (a pro-adverb corresponding to the indefinite pronoun *jokin* 'some, a' and expressing the directional feature of "movement towards"), and the interrogative sequence *oliks se nyt* 'was it PRT' is inserted within the nominal syntagm, just before the proper noun *Tampereelle*$_{ALL}$ 'to Tampere':

(13)

ne muuttaa jonneki + *oliks se nyt* Tampereelle$_{ALL}$ tai jotain[14]
they will move to some(place) + *was it* PRT to Tampere or something
(Women's conversations 081)

[14] Like the locative demonstratives (cf. the discussion in the section concerning the rection paradigms), the element *jonneki(n)* can be used as an autonomous form (with the meaning 'somewhere'). On the other hand, it is also used as a kind of determiner before nouns. When it is followed by a proper noun as in (13), the element *jonneki(n)* produces a special type of approximation effect: the proposed lexical element that refers to a specific referent is to be taken as an example. In fact, three different elements contribute here to that kind of interpretation: firstly, the element *jonneki*, then the metalinguistic sequence that puts the lexical realization into the scope of the interrogative modality and finally the sequence *tai jotain* 'or something', added at the end (cf. Salo 2000: 54–57, 76–83).

Table 12.

ne	muuttaa	jonneki	*oliks*	*se*	*nyt*	Tampereelle_ALL
they	[will] move	to some(place)	*was-Q*	*it*	*PRT*	to Tampere

The metalinguistic sequences are formed by the verb *olla* 'to be' that is used in the past tense (past conditional in (12) and preterit in (13)) and endowed with the interrogative modality. The verb is accompanied by the subject pronoun *se* 'it' and the particle *nyt* which makes the interrogation explicitly rhetoric (cf. (8) above; Hakulinen & Saari 1995: 490; Kurhila forthcoming).

In (12), we could hesitate over the analysis of the noun phrase *joku puoltoist viikkoo sairaslomaa* 'about one and a half weeks of sick leave': does it belong to the construction of the verb *olla* 'to be' or the verb *saada* 'to get, to obtain'? The quantifier *puoltoist* 'one and a half' is in the nominative case and governs the form of the other elements in this noun phrase.[15] It is preceded by the indefinite element *joku* 'some' that marks here the approximation of the numeral expression (*joku puoltoist viikkoo* 'about one and a half weeks'). On the one hand, this noun phrase in the nominative case seems to realize the valency complement of the verb *olla* 'to be', but on the other hand, we could take it too as a realization of the valency complement of the verb *saada* 'to get, to obtain', since the accusative case of numeral expressions such as *puol(i)toist(a)* 'one and a half' is identical to the nominative case.[16]

Example (13) provides us with a clearer case favouring the second type of analysis. The noun phrase *Tampereelle*_ALL 'to Tampere' is in the allative case that expresses the same directional feature of "movement towards" than the indefinite element *jonneki* 'to some(place)'. The noun phrase *Tampereelle*_ALL 'to Tampere' is then governed by the verb *muuttaa* 'to move', and not by the verb *olla* 'to be'. Instead of having the status of a governing verb that selects its complements, the verb *olla* is used here as a support of modalities that target the lexical choice in a rection place opened by the governing verb in the frame construction (cf. sequences such as *sanotaan (nyt)* 'let's say').

To sum up, the metalinguistic sequences may have different degrees of integration into the frame construction. They could be grafted in front of (see (12)) or within (see (13)) a nominal syntagm, and sometimes they seem to stand provisionally in the place of a noun in the frame construction (see (8) and (9)). In other cases, the syntactic rupture is more

---

15 As other numerals in the nominative case, it is followed by an element in the partitive case. The element *puoltoist* 'one and a half' quantifies first the noun *viikkoo*_PART 'week', then the elements *puoltoist viikkoo* 'one and a half weeks' function as a quantifier of the noun *sairaslomaa*_PART 'sick leave':
[[*puoltoist*_NOM   [*viikkoo*_PART]]   *sairaslomaa*_PART]
'one and a half   weeks of   sick leave'

16 The indefinite element *joku* could serve as a counterargument: formally, it is in the nominative case (cf. the accusative case *jonkun*). But it seems to me that this element can remain invariable in particular in front of numerals.

perceptible (see (10) and (11)). However, in all cases, the interpretations of the frame construction and the metalinguistic sequences are closely interdependent.

The referential anchoring of the pronoun *se*

In all the examples above, the metalinguistic sequences are formed round the verb *olla* 'to be' with the subject slot realized by the singular or plural pronoun *se* 'it, s/he' ~ *ne* 'they'. In this section, I will formulate a hypothesis on the referential anchoring of these subject pronouns.

We can suppose that the recipients make the first hypothesis on the referential interpretation of the pronoun *se* in relation to its preceding context, if there is any potential interpretation source (cf. Reichler-Béguelin 1988: 36–39; Zay 1995: 208). In the case of syntactic ruptures, it seems that the suspension of a construction and the insertion process give to the interrupted construction a particular saliency in the interpretation of referring expressions used in inserted sequences (cf. Zay 1995: 212).

In example (8), the suspension of the frame construction is preceded by the element *niit* 'those' which instantiates the valency complement of the verb *hyppiä* 'to jump':

(8)

S1   – – – nythän se on hyppiny niit + ö- mitä *ne* nyt on +
     – – – it's true that now he has been jumping those + uh what are *they* called
S2   laskuvarjo-
     parachute-
S1   niin niit laskuvarjohyppyi
     yes those parachute jumps (Summer plans 079)

This form announces a realization of the valency complement in the plural. In addition, the governing verb itself attributes to its valency complement the semantic property of "something that can be jumped" (cf. Cornish 1996: 30–31). It is this rection place, announced in the frame construction, but still being without any lexical element, that offers the most immediately available referential anchoring to the subject pronoun *ne* 'they' of the metalinguistic sequence *mitä* ne *nyt on* 'what *they* PRT are ~ what are *they* called'. Note that the pronoun *ne* is here interpretable in its linguistic context without any previous lexical designation of the referent (during the telephone conversation from which this example is extracted) and before the subsequent lexical designation. Indeed, as we have already seen above, the addressee (S2) comes to aid – in spite of the rhetorical nature of the question – by suggesting a designation (*laskuvarjo-* 'parachute'). In so doing, she shows indirectly that she has localised the referential anchoring of the pronoun *ne* 'they'.

In (9), the reference resolution is equally done without relying on any lexical designation of the referent. The pronoun *se* is used in the sequence *en mä tiiä kuka se oli* 'I don't know who *s/he* was' which is inserted within the construction of the postposition *kanssa* 'with'. The pronoun finds its referential anchoring in the rection place governed by this postposition. It points to a referent whose designation is to be expected after the first realization of the rectional element of the postposition (*vaimonsa* 'his wife') followed by the element *ja* 'and', but which the speaker is unable to name (according to the very host sequence of the pronoun):

(9)

> Aaro oli siel vaimonsa ja + en mä tiiä kuka *se* oli + kanssa
> Aaro was there with his wife and + I don't know who *s/he* was (Three high school scholars 099)

The first realization *vaimonsa* 'his wife' actualizes a semantic field and in this way, it also orients the expectations for the second realization. In the metalinguistic sequence, the interrogative pronoun *kuka* 'who' which realizes the valence complement of the verb *olla* 'to be' indicates that the referent of the subject pronoun is human. In view of the semantic field opened by the first lexical realization, the referent's sex is probably also female, but neither this property nor the property [+human] is displayed by the Finnish pronoun *se*.

In examples (10) and (11), the interruption of the frame construction takes place after an adjectival modifier, before the apparition of the lexical head of the noun phrase. The subject pronouns of the metalinguistic sequences, *se* 'it' and *ne* 'they', find their referential anchoring in the rection slot whose realization has been started in the frame construction, but not achieved: in the place of the valency complement in the possessive construction *näil on...* 'they have...' of (10) and in the place of the valency complement of the verb *tehdä* 'to make' in (11):

(10)

> – – – nin näil on kuulemma valtavan s- hieno niinku ei *se* mikään mökki o vaan *se* on semmonen hirsitupa + oikeen
> – – – so I heard they have a very b- splendid uh *it*'s not at all any cottage but *it* is a timbered house really (Summer plans 079)

(11)

> – – – kyllä tosiasiassa tehdään poliittisia + ehkei *ne* ole paketteja mutta jonkun sortin sopimuksia kuitenkin
> – – – in reality they make political + perhaps *they* are not packages but some kinds of contracts anyway (Professional life)

These referential anchorings are confirmed by the compatibility between the propositional content of the frame construction and the categorization of the referent accomplished in the metalinguistic sequences (cf. Zay 1995: 212):

Table 13.

näil$_{ADE}$ on	kuulemma	valtavan	s-				
they have	I heard	[a] very	b-				
			hieno$_{NOM}$	niinku			
			splendid	PRT			
	ei	se	mikään	mökki	o		
	NEG	it	any	cottage	is [not]		
	vaan	se			on	semmonen *hirsitupa*	oikeen
	but	it			is	a *timbered house*	really
näil on valtavan hieno hirsitupa 'they have a very splendid timbered house'							

Table 14.

kyllä	*tosiasiassa*	*tehdään*$_{PASS}$	*poliittisia*				
PTR	in reality	they make	political				
		ehkei	ne	ole			paketteja
		perhaps-NEG	they	are [not]			packages
					mutta	jonkun sortin	*sopimuksia* kuitenkin
					but	some kinds of	*contracts* anyway
tosiasiassa tehdään poliittisia sopimuksia 'in reality they make political contracts'							

We can propose the same kind of analysis on the referential anchoring of the pronouns *se* in examples (12) and (13) in which the metalinguistic sequences are grafted on a realization of a rection place with the effect of modalizing the lexical choice. In (13), the referential target of the pronoun *se* 'it' is the locative rection place of the verb *muuttaa* 'to move' that has been instantiated by the element *jonneki* 'to some(place)' before the use of the pronoun:

(13)

ne muuttaa jonneki + oliks *se* nyt Tampereelle$_{ALL}$ tai jotain
they will move to some(place) + was *it* PRT to Tampere or something (Women's conversations 081)

In (12), the referential anchoring of the pronoun *se* 'it' is provided by the place of the valency complement of the verb *saada* 'to get, to obtain'. Note that the insertion of the metalinguistic sequence happens before any element instantiates the valency complement in the frame construction:

(12)

sit se sai niinku + o- o- oisko *se* nyt ollu joku puoltoist viikkoo sairaslomaa
then he got uh + w- w- would *it* PRT have been about one and a half weeks of sick leave (Childhood friends 101)

The verb *saada* 'to get, to obtain' itself creates an expectation for a valency complement, and in addition, the following particle *niinku* serves as a signal that the utterance will be continued (cf. example (10) in the previous section). The identification of the rection place offering the referential anchoring to the pronoun *se* is based here on the knowledge we have on the complementation of the governing verb.

To sum up, in all of the examples, the host construction of the pronoun *se* is a metalinguistic sequence that is integrated into another verbal construction or that suspends an ongoing verbal construction. The referential anchoring of the pronoun is provided by the frame construction, and to be precise, by a rection slot which is expected and whose realization has eventually begun, but which is still devoid of full lexical content. The analyses have tried to show that a governing element and a beginning of a syntagm that instantiates a rection slot (and sometimes even the governing element alone) are enough to provide referential anchoring for the pronoun *se* which is used in sequences creating a syntactic and discursive rupture in the text.

In the examples above, the pronoun *se ~ ne* 'it, s/he ~ they' could hardly be described as a "substitute of a noun". On the contrary, it serves to point to a referent that has not yet been named, in order to question its possible designations, to accomplish its categorization or a lexical description in an attributive construction, or to modalize a lexical choice. We have seen, too, that in certain cases the pronoun *se* can be interpreted in its linguistic context without any previous or subsequent lexical mention of the referent. It could be possible, of course, to replace in these examples the pronoun *se ~ ne* by a semantically non-specific noun phrase, as in (8) by *ne jutut* 'these things': *mitä ne jutut on* 'what are these things (called)'. Nevertheless, it seems to me that the interpretation of the analysed occurrences of the pronoun *se* does not involve this kind of non-specific designations. The recourse to non-specific noun phrases is another strategy, and a real one exploited by speakers, but also a more marked one compared to the use of the pronominal pointers.[17]

An example of parenthetical inserts

In the final example, the host construction of the pronoun *se* 'it, s/he' is slightly different from the preceding ones. The metalinguistic sequences analysed above which break in during a lexical selection process are a particular case of the syntactic and discursive heterogeneity of spoken texts: being inserted into the body of a frame construction, they are likely

---

17   Note that the other Finnish demonstratives *tämä* 'that' and *tuo* 'this' can be used, too, in metalinguistic sequences. The hypothesis formulated above on the interpretation of the pronoun *se* could be applied also to these forms, but in addition we should take in consideration the specific demonstrative features of these forms, for instance the fact that their referential origo is in the speaker (see for example Laury 1997: 59; cf. also the description of the Finnish demonstratives by Etelämäki in this volume).

to provide or serve to introduce a lexical description the frame construction is devoid of.

This section presents an insert which can be called *parenthesis* (cf. Ravila 1945; Duvallon & Routarinne 2001). Even if they are semantically related, the frame construction and the parenthetical insert remain syntactically non-integrated and seem to have distinct cognitive goals and more or less independent planning processes as well (see Berrendonner 1993; Zay 1995; Mondada & Zay 1999).

The example below illustrates one more way the referential target of the pronoun *se* can be defined in textual domains of the linguistic context. As we have seen, the pronoun *se* is not always interpretable at the very moment it appears in the text. Among the contexts propitious to deferred interpretation, there is the one in which the parenthetical insert containing the pronoun is interpolated within a noun phrase, between the lexical head and a relative clause that completes it. Consider example (14):

(14)

> mä: ajattelin tehdä tietokoneella tämmösen + aa nelosen *se oli kai Naavan Sakarin idea* mikä toimis lippuna ja + ohjelmana + saman tien mikä taitetaan näin ja + täällä sitten lukee blaa blaa – – –
> I thought of doing by computer an + A4 size page like this *it was perhaps Sakari Naava's idea* which could serve as a ticket and + a program + at the same time which is fold up like this and + then here is the text blah blah – – – (Neighbourhood association 089, 090)

As already noted, it is probable that an initial hypothesis on the referential anchoring of the pronoun *se* is formulated in relation to the preceding context, provided that it contains an interpretation source (cf. Reichler-Béguelin 1988: 36–39; Zay 1995: 208). In example (14), the pronoun *se* is used in the sequence *se oli kai Naavan Sakarin idea* 'it was perhaps Sakari Naava's idea'. The preceding context contains the noun phrase *tämmösen aa nelosen* 'an A4 size page like this' which offers to the pronoun *se* the most immediately available interpretation source. However, the host construction and in particular the realization of the valency complement (*Naavan Sakarin idea* 'Sakari Naava's idea') are likely to orient the interpretation of the subject pronoun *se* towards a propositional content, and not a discrete entity.

From the viewpoint of the linear advancement of the text, the interpretation of the pronoun *se* remains more or less uncertain when its host construction is achieved, since the propositional content of the preceding sequence *mä: ajattelin tehdä...* 'I thought of doing…' is not very compatible with the predication 'to be someone else's idea' (?'it ["*that I thought of doing something*"] was perhaps S. N.'s idea').[18] Next the

---

[18] When we look at the insert from the point of view of the achieved production, we can see however that the parenthesis serves to repair an interpretation to which the beginning of the sequence eventually gives rise, i.e. the interpretation that the speaker is responsible for the idea she is presenting.

speaker produces two relative clauses (*mikä toimis lippuna ja + ohjelmana + saman tien* 'which could serve as a ticket and + a program + at the same time' and *mikä taitetaan näin* 'which is fold up like this') which complete syntactically the noun phrase *tämmösen aa nelosen* 'an A4 size page like this'. The pronoun *se* and its host construction are thus encased within a noun phrase:

Table 15.

mä: ajattelin tehdä	tietokoneella			*tämmösen aa nelosen*		
I thought of doing	by computer			*an A4 size page like this*		
		se	oli	kai	Naavan Sakarin idea	
		it	was	perhaps	Sakari Naava's idea	
				mikä	toimis	lippuna
				which	could serve as	a ticket
					ja	ohjelmana saman tien
					and	a program at the same time
				mikä	taitetaan	näin
				which	is folded up	like this

Finally, the pronoun *se* 'it' finds its interpretation source in this complex noun phrase (in italics above) which is constructed around the parenthetical insert. Put differently, the pronoun picks out a referent whose lexical content is still being formulated in the frame construction. It is in fact this "resumptive" pronoun (Maillard 1974) that creates the referent and introduces it in the text, even though it is not possible to exactly determine the limits of the reference (cf. Zay 1995: 208, 213–214).

Unlike the examples in the preceding section, the host construction of the pronoun does not participate here directly to the process of lexical designation of the referent, but it proposes rather supplementary information about the propositional content that is being formulated in the frame construction. It seems to me that the resolution of that kind of passages consists in putting in relation two different perspectives on a scene described, rather than seeing in the text a progressive accumulation of information. The frame construction and the insert form separate textual domains, the first one enclosing the second one. The interpretation of the pronoun *se* necessitates figuring out this textual organisation and could not be achieved before the whole constructional figure has been finished.

Conclusion

The pronoun *se* is not solely a tracking form used to refer to referents already introduced in the interlocutors' centre of attention. It serves also to capture referents whose existence is only expectable on the bases of the linguistic context. In the context of syntactic and discursive ruptures examined above, the pronoun *se* points to referents which are still being introduced in the utterance within which the host construction of the pronoun shelters. The pronoun *se* allows constructing the reference in cases in which lexical designations are momentarily unavailable or must be negotiated. On the other hand, it also enables a referential act to target a lexical content still in progress within another textual domain.

I have tried to show, on the one hand, that semantic information conveyed by the host construction and the position of this host construction in the larger linguistic context play an undeniable role in the determination of the referential anchoring of a pronoun. In the context of syntactic ruptures, the insertion process itself seems to make out of the frame construction, and not only of elements already realized, but also of rection slots left in suspense, a particularly salient interpretation domain for pronouns used in inserted sequences. On the other hand, I have wanted to underline the fact that reference resolution is not always possible at the very moment a pronoun appears in the text. The categorization or the lexical content of a referent can be confirmed only later on. Moreover, pronouns can find their referential anchoring even without any lexical designation of the referent in the preceding or subsequent context.

Uses that speakers make of different types of referring expressions in oral productions lead me to see the pronoun *se* as an original referring form which is not necessarily identical with a lexical content identified in the linguistic context. In comparison with lexical descriptions whose value is determined in relation to the whole paradigm of other potential lexical representations and which could, in principle, at any moment, be changed over other designations depending on different points of view and perspectives, the pronoun *se*, with its minimal descriptive content, is a more stable referring expression. I propose that pro-forms such as the pronoun *se* be considered not only as surer syntactic indicators than lexical forms of nouns (Blanche-Benveniste et al. 1987: 237), but also as unmarked referring expressions, as neutral designations and, so to say, controllers of lexical descriptions of referents.

REFERENCES

Airila, Martti. 1940. Pronominit. *Virittäjä* 44: 301–314.
Apothéloz, Denis and Marie-José Reichler-Béguelin. 1995. Construction de la référence et stratégies de désignation. *TRANEL* 23: 227–271.
Ariel, Mira. 1988. Referring and accessibility. *Journal of Linguistics* 24: 65–87.
Berrendonner, Alain. 1993. Périodes. In H. Parret (ed.) *Temps et discours*. Louvain: Presses universitaires de Louvain.
Blanche-Benveniste, Claire. 1985. La dénomination dans le français parlé: une interprétation pour les « répétitions » et les « hésitations ». *Recherches sur le français parlé* 6: 109–130.
Blanche-Benveniste, Claire. 1987. Syntaxe, choix de lexique, et lieux de bafouillage. *DRLAV* 36–37: 123–157.
Blanche-Benveniste, Claire. 1990. Un modèle d'analyse syntaxique «en grilles» pour les productions orales. *Anuario de Psicologia* 47: 11–28.
Blanche-Benveniste, Claire. 1997. L'approche pronominale et référenciation. In F. Cordier and J.-E. Tyvaert (eds) *La place de l'image dans la cognition. Le pronom et son rôle dans la référenciation*. Reims: Presses Universitaires de Reims.

Blanche-Benveniste, Claire, José Deulofeu, Jean Stefanini and Karel van den Eynde. 1987. *Pronom et Syntaxe. L'approche pronominale et son application au français.* Paris: SELAF.
Chafe, Wallace. 1987. Cognitive constraints on information flow. In R. S. Tomlin (ed.) *Coherence and Grounding in Discourse.* Amsterdam: Benjamins.
Cornish, Francis. 1996. 'Antecedentless' anaphors: deixis, anaphora, or what? Some evidence from English and French. *Journal of Linguistics* 32: 19–41.
Duvallon, Outi. 2003. L'ordre sujet-complément-verbe dans les textes oraux en finnois. *Études finno-ougriennes* 35: 131–160.
Duvallon, Outi. 2004. Observations sur les déterminants dans les productions orales. *Actes du 6ᵉ colloque franco-finlandais de linguistique contrastive.* Publications du Département des Langues Romanes de l'Université de Helsinki, Helsinki.
Duvallon, Outi and Sara Routarinne. 2001. Parenteesi keskustelun kieliopin voimavarana. In Mia Halonen and Sara Routarinne (eds.) *Keskustelunanalyysin näkymiä.* Kieli 13. Helsinki: Helsingin yliopiston suomen kielen laitos.
Ehlich, Konrad. 1982. Anaphora and Deixis: Same, Similar, or Different? In R. J. Jarvella and W. Klein (eds.) *Speech, Place, and Action.* Chichester: John Wiley & Son Ltd.
Etelämäki, Marja. 1996. *Keskustelu tarkoitteesta kuvataiteen oppitunnilla – ja pronominit tuo, se, tämä.* Pro gradu -tutkielma. Helsingin yliopiston suomen kielen laitos.
Fox, Barbara. 1987. *Discourse structure and anaphora.* Cambridge: Cambridge University Press.
Givón, Talmy (ed.). 1983. *Topic continuity in discourse: A quantitative cross-language study.* Amsterdam: Benjamins.
Goodwin, Charles. 1987. Forgetfulness as an Interactive Resource. *Social Psychology Quarterly* Vol. 50, No. 2: 115–131.
Gundel, Jeanette, Nancy Hedberg and Ron Zacharski. 1993. Cognitive status and the form of referring expressions in discourse. *Language* 69/2: 274–307.
Hakulinen, Auli. 1985. On cohesive devices in Finnish. In E. Sözer (ed.) *Text connexity, text coherence: aspects, methods, results.* Hamburg: Buske.
Hakulinen, Auli. 1988. Miten nainen liikkuu Veijo Meren romaaneissa. In L. Laitinen (ed.) *Isosuinen nainen. Tutkielmia naisesta ja kielestä.* Helsinki: Yliopistopaino.
Hakulinen, Auli. 2001[1976]. Liitepartikkelin *-han/-hän* syntaksia ja pragmatiikkaa. In L. Laitinen et al. (eds.) *Auli Hakulinen: Lukemisto. Kirjoituksia kolmelta vuosikymmeneltä.* Helsinki: Suomalaisen Kirjallisuuden Seura.
Hakulinen, Auli and Fred Karlsson. 1979. *Nykysuomen lauseoppia.* Helsinki: Suomalaisen Kirjallisuuden Seura.
Hakulinen, Auli et al. 1994. *Kieli ja sen kieliopit. Opetuksen suuntaviivoja.* Helsinki: Edita.
Hakulinen, Auli and Mirja Saari. 1995. Temporaalisesta adverbista diskurssipartikkeliksi. *Virittäjä* 99: 481–500.
Hakulinen, Auli et al. 2004. *Iso suomen kielioppi.* Helsinki: Suomalaisen Kirjallisuuden Seura.
Helasvuo, Marja-Liisa. 2001. *Syntax in the making: the emergence of syntactic units in Finnish conversation.* Amsterdam: John Benjamins.
Itkonen, Terho. 1966. Tutkimus suomen asyndetonista. *Virittäjä* 70: 402–423.
Jakobson, Roman. 1956. Two Aspects of Language and Two Types of Aphasic Disturbances. In Roman Jakobson and Morris Halle, *Fundamentals of Language.* The Hague: Mouton.
Jefferson, Gail. 1990. List-Construction as a Task and Resource. In G. Psathas (ed.) *Interaction Competence.* Washington, D. C.: Interactional Institute for Ethnomethodology and Conversation Analysis and University of America Press.
Juvonen, Päivi. 2000. *Grammaticalizing the definite article. A study of definite adnominal determiners in a genre of spoken Finnish.* Doctoral dissertation. Stockholm University, Department of Linguistics.
Kuiri, Kaija. 1984. *Referointi Kainuun ja Pohjois-Karjalan murteissa.* Helsinki: Suomalaisen Kirjallisuuden Seura.

Kurhila, Salla. forthcoming. The particle *nyt* 'now' in word search sequences. Unpublished manuscript.
Laitinen, Lea. 2002. From logophoric pronoun to discourse particle: A case study of Finnish and Saami. In I. Wischer and G. Diewald (eds.) *New Reflections on Grammaticalization*. Amsterdam: John Benjamins.
Larjavaara, Matti. 1985. Suomen demonstratiivisysteemin rakenne. *Sananjalka* 27: 15–31.
Larjavaara, Matti. 1990. *Suomen deiksis*. Helsinki: Suomalaisen Kirjallisuuden Seura.
Larjavaara, Matti. 2001. Tämä, tuo vai se? *Kielikello* 4/2001: 17–22.
Laury, Ritva. 1994. *Se* ensimaininnan pronominina puhutussa suomessa. *Virittäjä* 98: 449–453.
Laury, Ritva. 1997. *Demonstratives in Interaction. The emergence of a definite article in Finnish*. Amsterdam: Benjamins.
Local, John. 1992. Continuing and restarting. In P. Auer and A. Di Luzio (eds.) *The contextualization of Language*. Amsterdam: John Benjamins.
Local, John and John Kelly. 1986. Projection and 'silences': Notes on phonetic and conversational structure. *Human Studies* 9: 185–204.
Maillard, Michel. 1974. Essai de typologie des substituts diaphoriques. *Langue française* 21: 55–71.
Milner, J.-C. 1982. *Ordres et raisons de la langue*. Paris: Seuil.
Mondada, Lorenza and Danièle Dubois. 1995. Construction des objets de discours et catégorisation: une approche des processus de référenciation. *TRANEL* 23: 273–302.
Mondada, Lorenza and Françoise Zay. 1999. Parenthèses et processus de configuration thématique: vers une redéfinition de la notion de topic. In J. Verschueren (ed.) *Pragmatics in 1998. Selected Papers from the 6th International Pragmatics Conference*. Vol 2. Antwerp : IprA.
Ogden, Richard. 2001. Turn-holding, turn-yielding and laryngeal activity in Finnish talk-in-interaction. In K. Kohler and A. Simpson (eds.) *Journal of the International Phonetic Association* 31: 139–152. –
Onikki-Rantajääskö, Tiina. 2001. *Sarjoja – nykysuomen paikallissijaiset olotilanilmaukset kielen analogisuuden ilmentäjinä*. Helsinki: Suomalaisen Kirjallisuuden Seura.
Penttilä, Aarni. 1963. *Suomen kielioppi*. Porvoo: WSOY.
Ravila, Paavo. 1945. Lauseeseen liittyneet irralliset ainekset. *Virittäjä* 49: 1–16.
Reichler-Béguelin, Marie-José. 1988. Anaphore, cataphore et mémoire discursive. *Pratiques* 57: 15–43.
Rosch, Eleanor. 1977. Classification of real-world objects: Origins and representations in cognition. In P. N. Johnson-Laird and P. C. Wason (eds.) *Thinking. Readings in Cognitive Science*. Cambridge: Cambridge University Press.
Salo, Juha. 2000. *Joku gradu – sanojen* joku ja jokin *merkitys puheessa*. Pro gradu -tutkielma. Helsingin yliopiston suomen kielen laitos.
Saukkonen, Pauli. 1967. Persoonapronominien *hän : se, he : ne* distinktiivinen oppositio. *Virittäjä* 71: 286–292.
Saussure, Ferdinand de. 1983 [1916]. *Course in general linguistics*. London: Duckworth.
Schegloff, Emanuel. 1996. Some Practices for Referring to Persons in Talk-in-Interaction: A Partial Sketch of a Systematics. In B. A. Fox (ed.) *Studies in anaphora*. Amsterdam: Benjamins.
Schegloff, Emanuel, Gail Jefferson and Harvey Sacks. 1977. The preference for self-correction in the organisation of repair in conversation. *Language* 53/2: 361–382.
Seppänen, Eeva-Leena. 1998. *Läsnäolon pronominit. Tämä, tuo, se ja hän viittaamassa keskustelun osallistujaan*. Helsinki: Suomalaisen Kirjallisuuden Seura.
Setälä, Emil Nestor. 1891. *Suomen kielen lauseoppi*[3]. Helsinki: K. E. Holm'in kustannuksella.
Siro, Paavo. 1964. *Suomen kielen lauseoppi*. Helsinki: Tietosanakirja OY.
Sorjonen, Marja-Leena. 2002. Word order and interaction. Paper presented at the Euro-Conference on Linguistic Structures and their Deployment in the Organisation of Conversation, Interactional Linguistics, Helsinki 6–11 September, 2002.

Suojala, Marja. 1989. Varaukset. In A. Hakulinen (ed.) *Suomalaisen keskustelun keinoja I.* Kieli 4. Helsinki: Helsingin yliopiston suomen kielen laitos.

Tarvainen, Kalevi. 1977. *Dependenssikielioppi*. Helsinki: Gaudeamus.

Tiainen-Duvallon, Outi. 2002. *Le pronom anaphorique et l'architecture de l'oral en finnois et en français*. Thèse de doctorat non publiée. École pratique des hautes études, Paris.

Vilkuna, Maria. 1992. *Referenssi ja määräisyys suomenkielisten tekstien tulkinnassa*. Suomi 163. Helsinki: Suomalaisen Kirjallisuuden Seura.

Zay, Françoise. 1995. Notes sur l'interprétation des expressions référentielles dans les parenthèses. *TRANEL* 23: 203–223.

Ziv, Yael. 1996. Pronominal reference to inferred antecedents. In L. Tasmowski and W. De Mulder (eds.) *Coherence and Anaphora. Belgian Journal of Linguistics* 10. Amsterdam: Benjamins.

APPENDIX

Transcription symbols and other notations
+   pause (length non specified)
sa-   truncated word
a: lengthening
NEG   negation
PRT   particle
Q   interrogative particle
sen$_{CASE}$ grammatical indications: NOM nominative, GEN genitive, PAR partitive, ADE adessive, ILL illative, ALL allative; PASS (impersonal) passive, POS possessive suffix
[the]   in the translation line, a grammatical element absent from the original production or placed elsewhere in it

Corpus
Summer plans 079: telephone conversation
Childhood friends 101: telephone conversation
Neighbourhood association 089, 090: face-to-face conversation
Hairdressing salon 105: face-to-face conversation
Women's conversations 081: telephone conversation
Three high school scholars 099: face-to-face conversation
Professional life: radio conversation

Local case system in Finnish (cf. Onikki-Rantajääskö 2001: 14).

Table 16.

The dimension of DIRECTION→	Static cases	Dynamic cases	
	"position"	"movement from"	"movement towards"
The dimension of QUALITÉ↓			
Intern cases	INESSIVE talossa 'in a/the house'	ELATIVE talosta 'from a/the house'	ILLATIVE taloon 'into a/the house'
Extern cases	ADESSIVE pöydällä 'on a/the table'	ABLATIVE pöydältä 'from a/the table'	ALLATIVE pöydälle 'onto a/the table'

PÄIVI JUVONEN

On the pragmatics of indefinite determiners in spoken Finnish[1]

Introduction

In their independent use, pronouns fill a number of different functions as richly illustrated by the articles in this volume. In the present paper, the focus is on both indefinite pronouns and other parts-of-speech elements as determiners, as manifested in a corpus of spoken Finnish. Hence, the often mentioned other means of expressing definiteness or partitive indefiniteness in Finnish, such as word order or case alternation, are not discussed here (see e.g. Chesterman 1991; Lyons 1999 for discussions of these. For an example, see Kaiser, this volume).

Traditionally, Finnish is said to have neither a definite nor an indefinite article. The sometimes rather article-like use of both definite and indefinite adnominal determiners has, however, been noticed by several Finnish grammarians and, led to proposals of the existence of both an indefinite and a definite article in colloquial spoken Finnish (see e.g. Vilkuna 1992 for a discussion of the former and Laury 1997 for the latter). For a dissenting view in the case of a definite article, see Juvonen (Juvonen 2000a).

This paper first addresses the question of a possible functional differentiation between three types of adnominal indefinite determiners: the indefinite determiner/numeral *yks* 'a, one', the indefinite pronoun *joku/jokin* 'some' and the adnominal demonstrative adjectives *semmonen*, *tämmönen* 'that/this kind of' etc. Second, it briefly discusses the findings of the use of the determiners in a cross-linguistic grammaticalization perspective.

A note on the data studied

The data used to exemplify the use of adnominal determiners in this study consist of two corpora of spoken Finnish from the early 1990s. The first corpus consists of 138 retellings of a story on a silent cartoon

---

[1] I would like to thank Östen Dahl, Maria Koptjevskaja Tamm, Ritva Laury and Mikael Parkvall for helpful comments on this paper.

by 40 ten- to fifteen-year old Finnish-Swedish bilingual adolescents who report Finnish to be the language of their homes, their 20 monolingual Finnish age mates and a group of 19 monolingual Finnish university students. These are the data used also in (Juvonen 1996; Juvonen 2000a; Juvonen 2000b), where all the 2650 referring lexical NPs in the data were analysed. Indefinite adnominal determiners appear in these data either as isolated, single mentions of referents or as first mentions of referents mentioned several times. Of totally 628 first mentions of referents, 79 had *semmonen* etc (12.6%), 32 had *joku* (5.1%) and 71 had *yks* (11.3%) as a determiner. Of totally 1043 isolated mentions only 10 contain an explicit indefinite marker.

The second corpus consists of 45–60 minute long interviews on various subjects with the same adolescents as in the retelling data. This latter corpus has not been systematically analysed in terms of statistical calculations so no total number of NPs is available. It has, for the present purpose, been manually searched for examples. All the bilingual subjects are resident in the Stockholm area (Sweden). The Finnish adolescents reside in the municipality of Vantaa and the university students are from the nearby Helsinki (Finland).

The puzzle

Definiteness and the form-function relationships among different linguistic expressions traditionally called definite or indefinite have been in focus in a lot of work. A commonly held view (Ariel 1988; Ariel 1990; Givón 1983; Givón 1995; Haspelmath 2000; Hawkins 1978; 1991; Lyons 1999 among others) is that indefiniteness has to do with the identifiability, familiarity or accessibility of a referent: using an indefinite expression implies that the speaker does not presuppose that his/her interlocutors can identify the referent of the expression used.

Apart from definiteness in terms of identifiability, indefinite noun phrases are commonly analysed in terms of their specificity. Somewhat simplified (for the intricacies of the markers of this relational, context-dependent concept in Finnish, see Vilkuna 1992; especially pages 77–105), specificity has to do with whether or not a specific individual or a specific group of individuals can be pointed out as the referent of an NP by any participant within the current verbal exchange. Hence, in example a) below, the speaker indeed has a specific car in mind, whereas in example b) the NP *a car* does not refer to a specific specimen. Instead, it points out any one member of the class of cars as the possible object of the speaker's future purchase.

   a) I am going to buy a car, an old Sierra a friend of mine is selling.
   b) I am going to buy a car, but I haven't decided what kind yet.

Thus, indefinite expressions can be either specific as in a) or, non-specific, as in b). A specific interpretation seems to entail existence. Also, specificity need not automatically mean speaker-specific, even though the rather standard example[2] above may suggest so. The referent of an NP may for example be non-specific for the speaker, but either specific or non-specific for the person talked about, as in

c) He realised that there was a letter missing in the head-lines.[3]

As the above English examples illustrate, languages with a category of indefinite articles can use them to indicate the degree of identifiability, i.e. the definiteness, of the referent talked about by means of an NP. Speakers of Finnish can choose to use one of a number of indefinite determiners to indicate the status of an NP in terms of definiteness. The puzzle that initiated the examination of their uses conducted here is the fact that they can be used in seemingly identical syntactic, semantic and pragmatic contexts, for example as first mentions of main participants in a story retold, as shortly illustrated. So, the question is: what is the difference, if any?

Recently, the referential identifiability approach to (in)definiteness has been challenged in favour of a more interactive approach, allowing for the active creation or construction of discourse referents. Notably, Epstein (Epstein 2002 see especially pp. 333–334; see also e.g. Fraurud 1990; Maes and Noordman 1995; Kaiser, this volume, for discussions of the usefulness of the identifiability approach) has argued for a more flexible analysis of the English definite article *the*. Inspired by the theory of mental spaces as proposed by Fauconnier (Fauconnier 1994) and the accessibility theory of Ariel (Ariel 1990), he proposes an account of the use of *the* in terms of "the availability of an "access path" through a configuration of mental spaces" (p. 334). In this way, he argues, he can not only account for the uses where indeed identification of a referent seems to be the main reason for using the definite article, but also for the cases where speakers for various pragmatic reasons such as the prominence of a discourse entity have used the article where not expected in terms of identifiability.

The account of the use of the English definite article in terms of mental spaces proposed by Epstein is intuitively appealing. However, as I am at least not yet convinced about the advantages of combining this approach specifically with accessibility theory, I will not base my analysis on it. I will though occasionally make reference to possible mental space explanations in a less technical manner and generally take the interactive and discourse constructive path when examining the use of adnominal *yks* 'a, one', adnominal *joku/jokin* 'some' and adnominal *semmonen* 'this kind of, such' in similar contexts.[4] First, however, briefly about the determiners studied.

2 This particular example is mine, but it is clearly inspired by the numerous examples involving cars that have flourished in the literature of linguistic definiteness since at least (Prince 1981)
3 This example is a free translation of example 3, page 79 in (Vilkuna 1992).
4 For a similar approach in analysing the Estonian indefinites *üks*, *mingi* and *kôik*, see (Pajusalu 2004).

Yks, joku and *semmonen*

The indefinite determiner *yks(i)* 'a, one' is formally identical with the numeral 'one'. Thus, as indefinite articles often develop historically from the numeral 'one' (Givón 1981; Heine 1997), it would be a good candidate for an indefinite article in Finnish as well.

Joku 'some, somebody'[5] and *jokin* 'something' are indefinite pronouns used both independently and as indefinite adnominal determiners. There are three series of indefinite pronouns in Finnish occurring partly in overlap, partly in different indefinite contexts (Haspelmath 2000: 293). For example, there are forms corresponding to *joku/jokin* (a member of the non-emphatic *-kin*-series) used in direct and indirect negation, *kukaan/ mikään* 'nobody/nothing' (member of the basically negative *-kaan*-series), and a free-choice series form *kuka hyvänsä* 'whoever'. The use of these latter forms will not, however, be studied here due to the limited number of occurrences in the data studied. Also, the form *jokin* seems to be confined to literary use, leaving *joku* as the spoken Finnish form for reference to both animate and inanimate beings.

Demonstrative pronouns and adverbs are usually described as definite in nature. This also seems to be the case with the Finnish pronouns *tämä* 'this', *tuo* 'that' and *se* 'this/that' and the corresponding adverbs. However, the derived adjectival forms of Finnish demonstrative pronouns – *semmo(i)nen, sella(i)nen, tämmö(i)nen, tälla(i)nen, tuommo(i)nen* and *tuolla(i)nen* (all meaning approximately 'this/that kind of, such') – have been argued to be basically indefinite (cf. Juvonen 2000a; Larjavaara 1986; 1990).[6] For details of their etymology, see (Juvonen 2000a: 29–40). As adjectival forms, they usually occupy the adjective slot[7] in an NP and can thus co-occur with determiners; both definite and indefinite (see below).[8] However, they also occur as sole modifiers of nouns in indefinite NPs. These are the uses that are in focus here. By far the most frequent of the demonstrative adjectives is *semmonen*. In what follows, I will use only

---

5   As an independent pronoun *joku/jokin* also refers to persons and things, i.e. as equivalent to 'somebody' and 'something'. For the indefinite pronominal uses in a typological perspective, cf. (Haspelmath 2000). For a recent study of the use of the Swedish indefinite pronoun *någon* in adnominal position, cf. (Nivre 2002).

6   C. Lyons has argued, in order to sustain a basic assumption of all demonstrative elements as definite, that this kind of elements in the languages of the world are not in fact demonstratives at all, even though they "contain a demonstrative element as part of [their] meaning" (Lyons 1999: 151). As the demonstrative element is indeed strongly present also in the Finnish three-term demonstrative adjective paradigm, I find it hard to argue that they would be anything but demonstratives.

7   This seems always to be the case in combination with definite determiners, whereas in combination with indefinite determiners the order may vary: in the retelling corpus studied here we find both *semmonen yks N*, *yks semmonen N* and *se semmonen N*, but never **semmonen se N*. The consequences of this empirical observation for e.g. the degree of grammaticalization of definite and indefinite articles in spoken Finnish go beyond the purposes of the present paper, but would be interesting to explore systematically elsewhere.

8   The Swedish *sådan* and the English *such* also co-occur with indefinite articles. Not, however, to my knowledge, with definite articles.

semmonen to illustrate their uses, as it is the form found in all contexts studied. It is thus possible, that the other members of the paradigm may not behave exactly the same in all contexts, even though I here assume it.

Basically all Finnish adjectives, pronouns and determiners are inflected in number and case and can be accompanied by bound particles. This is also the case with the adnominal determiners[9] studied here. Also, they all occur with nouns referring to animate as well as inanimate referents, in subject, object as well as oblique syntactic position,[10] even though only one example per usage type is illustrated below, due to space limits. In the following subsections I will illustrate the use of these determiners in a number of contexts frequently connected with the use of indefinite expressions that could be identified in the data.

To summarize then, the items to be discussed in what follows are *yks* 'a, one', *joku/jokin* 'some' and the demonstrative adjectives of the form *semmonen* 'this kind of, such' as adnominal determiners in different semantic and pragmatic contexts.

First mention specific indefinites

One of the contexts where all three determiners are used in the data studied is when a new referent that is also mentioned later on in the discourse, is introduced. Examples (1–3) illustrate this kind of use. They are all introducing the main participant(s) in the story retold. As participants in the story, the man, the woman and the boy are all specific; the interlocutor as well as the storytellers can (concretely) point out the individuals talked about.

---

9   Despite what I myself just said about the demonstratives behaving like adjectives, I will in the remainder of this paper sometimes call all the adnominal indefinites determiners. I hope the more formally oriented reader will excuse this sloppy use.
10 In the retelling data, a clear majority of all NPs determined by the determiners studied were animate subjects. The percentage varied from 67% for *joku N* to 82% for *semmonen N* and 87,5% for *yks N* as subjects.

(1) (Indefinite phrases with *yks*. Bilingual girl, age 10. Retelling data[11].)

1 <u>yks</u>   eeh, / äiti   ja,   / poika   o-   / poika   leikki,
   YKS   er   / mother   and   / boy   we- / boy   played
   a er mother and son we-/ (a) boy was playing

2 / pikkupoika   leikki   hiekkalaatikolla=
   / little.boy   played   sandbox-ADE
   (a) little boy was playing in (a) sandbox

3 =ja   äiti   istu   penkillä   ja   katteli.
   and   mother   sat   bench-ADE   and   watched
   and (his) mother was sitting on (a) bench watching

4 sitte   siihen   tuli   <u>yks</u>   mies=
   then   to-there   came   YKS   man
   then there arrived a man

5 =mikä,   / istu   sen,   /
   who   / sat   SE-GEN   /
   who sat down beside

6 viittos=   =että   vo-/,   / saaks   se   istua
   pointed   that   co-/   / could   SE   sit
   indicated with his finger asking whether he could sit down

11 *Transcript notation*
   /   a short pause
   .   a period indicates falling intonation
   ,   a comma indicates a continuing intonation
   ?   a question mark indicates a rising intonation pattern
   :   a semicolon indicates a continuing intonation with a weak rise
   -/ a single dash followed by a slash indicates an abrupt cut-off

Translation conventions
The examples have been translated both with a word-by-word translation and with a free translation. The word-by-word translation indicates only nominal inflection. Nominative case and singular number are used as default. An unmarked noun, e.g. 'man' in the word-by-word translation indicates that the original Finnish word is nominative singular. The glossing 'man-PL' stands for 'men' (nominative plural) and 'man-ALL' for 'to (the) man' (allative singular).

The free translation is intended as a help in understanding the original example. It follows the information structure of the original as much as possible, and is, thus, not an idiomatic translation. In translating the Finnish determiners or the absence thereof, the following principles have been applied.

JOKU translated with 'a/some'
SE   translated with 'the'
SEL   translated with 'a sort of, a kind of'
SEM   translated with 'a sort of, a kind of'
TOM   translated with 'that sort of'
TOI   translated with 'that'
TÄL   translated with 'this sort of'
TÄM   translated with 'this sort of'
TÄÄ   translated with 'this'
YKS   translated with ' a'

Bare NPs mentioned for the first time are translated with an indefinite article and later mention bare NPs with a definite article.

7	siihen	sen,	.hhh	äitin	viereen	ni,	(MM)	/
	to.there	SE-GEN	inhale	mother-GEN	beside	so	(mm)	/

there beside the mother

8	ja,	sit	se	istu. o-/	oikeen	lähelle	ni, /
	and	then	SE	sat re/	really	close	so /

and then he sat down really close

9	.hhh	se,	pik-/	pikkupoika	ni, /	se	heitti, /
	inhale	SE	li-/	little.boy	so /	SE	threw /

the little boy, he threw

10	lapiom	menemään	ja. /	(HUOKAISEE)	eeh, /
	spade-GEN	away	and /	(sighs)	er /

his spade away and er

11	katto	tota,	katto	tuimas-/ vähän	tuimasti	niitä.
	looked.at	PRT	looked.at	angr-/ little	angrily	SE-PTV.PL

looked kind of looked angr-/ (a) bit angrily at them

The scope of the determiner *yks* in line 1 is not entirely clear, even though the continuing intonation pattern on the conjunction *ja* within an NP together with the abruption of the syntactic construction strongly suggests that the mother and the boy are jointly determined.

Interestingly, there are no *yks*-marked first mention specific indefinites in the young adult retelling data; a fact I will shortly come back to.

According to Vilkuna (Vilkuna 1992), adnominal *yks* is used in spoken Finnish to mark speaker-specific indefiniteness in two cases. First, it is used when the speaker intends to say something more about the referent later on, i.e. in introducing new referents expected to reappear during the same discourse. This is exactly the kind of use illustrated in example (1). Second, it is also used in an almost opposite case: when the referent mentioned is not at all important (p. 129). She especially mentions the common use of adnominal *yks* together with proper names, a use illustrated and discussed below. First, however, an illustration of the use of *joku* in exactly the same context:

(2) (Indefinite phrases with *joku*. Monolingual boy, age 15. Retelling data.)

1	no	siin	oli	tota	nii,	<u>joku</u>	hoitaja tai,
	well	there	COP	PRT	PRT	JOKU	nurse or

well there was some nurse or

2	lastenhoitaja	tai	joku	sellanen	ja, /	sit	lapsi
	babysitter	or	JOKU	SEL	and /	then	child

(a) babysitter or some such and, then (a) child

3	leikki	siinä	ja, /	sit	siihen	tuli	<u>joku</u>
	played	there	and	then	to-there	came	JOKU

played there and, then some charmeur

4	eeh,	hurmuri	paikalle	joka,	yritti	hurmata	sen	hoitajan
	er	charmer	place-ADE	REL	tried	charm	SE-GEN	nurse-GEN

who tried to charm the nurse arrived

Example (2) is a typical example of the young adults' as well as the adolescents' retellings. As example (1) above, this is also from the very beginning of the story retold, and all the characters introduced here are mentioned several times later – they are the main participants the actions of whom the story is all about. As can be seen in line 2, the use of a marker when introducing even main participants (in this case the child) is, however, not necessary in Finnish. A bare NP functions just as well.[12]

According to Vilkuna, adnominal *joku* fulfills much the same kind of functions as adnominal *yks*. The difference between them is said to lie in their identifiability. *Yks*-marked NPs have speaker-specific indefinite reference and are as such identifiable for the speaker. *Joku*-marked NPs are not, according to her, identifiable neither for the speaker nor the interlocutor (Vilkuna 1992: 132).

The proposed non-identifiability of *joku*-marked NPs is not in accordance with these data. Obviously in the retelling data the participants talked about are specific, identifiable individuals appearing in the cartoon retold.[13] However, Vilkuna (Vilkuna 1992) does also mention something else that seems to me to be a plausible explanation as to why there is variation between the use of *yks*-marked and *joku*-marked NPs in the same syntactic and semantic/pragmatic contexts in these data. On page 33 she mentions that "The *joku*-marked cases are, thus, about the kind of reference the speaker has inferred or accepted from some third source" (my translation). And, on page 132, with reference to Lepäsmaa (Lepäsmaa 1978) she adds that *joku*-marked NPs are easily interpreted as if the speaker was indifferent about the identity of the referent. In my view, this kind of hearsay or indifference interpretation, perhaps combined with a pinch of uncertainty about the identity of the referent, could be an explanation as to the absence of *yks*-marked NPs in the university student retelling data as there is enough evidence that adults use the construction in conversational data. It could also explain why some of the adolescents choose *joku*-marked instead of *yks*-marked constructions. They are, thus, besides introducing a new referent into the discourse, actively distancing

---

12 At first glance, the construction in example 2 resembles that of example 1, where I argued that *yks* jointly determined both the mother and the boy introduced. Here, however, the NPs introducing the participants clearly belong to different syntactic constructions and thus, the second NP is a bare NP.

13 The interviewer and the interviewee watched in fact the cartoon together, so in a way there is no need whatsoever to use any indefinite introductions. Indeed, many of the adolescents use definite descriptions directly, as reported in (Juvonen 2000a). The fact that we do find explicitly indefinite first mentions of obviously familiar or known referents may perhaps be attributed to the task of retelling a story.

themselves from the story, or rather, marking that they are not the original source of the story; they are retelling someone else's story.[14]

(3) (Indefinite phrases with *semmonen*. Bilingual boy, age 15. Retelling data.)

1   ja   sitten tota tulee   <u>semmonen</u> mies. se   istuu   s-/
    and   then   PRT   comes   SEM   man   SE   sits.down   abrupted
    and then this man arrives. He sits down beside(abrupted)

2   tai   eka   se   seisoo   siinä   ja   kattelee
    or   first SE   stands   there   and   watches
    or first he stands there and watches

As illustrated in example (3), *semmonen*-marked nouns can in these data also be used as first mention specific indefinites. As already mentioned, adnominal *semmonen* usually behaves syntactically as an adjective, and as a demonstrative it contrasts with other Finnish demonstratives in where in the (concrete or abstract) space the referent is situated (see Larjavaara 1986; Laury 1997 for a discussion of Finnish demonstratives). It has, however, also been suggested that they can be used in article-like fashion (Helasvuo 1988; Vilkuna 1992) to indicate, among other things, a listener-non-specific reference. Also, as Vilkuna (Vilkuna 1992: 132–133) puts it: it is used to indicate a class or type rather than to identify an individual.

To me, this sounds very much like the recognitional use of demonstratives (see Himmelmann 1996 for the term). A recognitional use of a demonstrative implies that the interlocutor should be able to identify not the specific individual, but the type or class that individual belongs to by way of appealing to shared knowledge[15] (Diessel 1999; Himmelmann 1996; Himmelmann 1997). According to Lindström (Lindström 2000) the use of demonstratives (adnominal or independent) in this function in spoken Swedish carries an implication of either "you know what I am talking about" or "you know *what kind* of thing I am talking about; you can imagine" (p. 8).

In the case of the man introduced into the discourse by *semmonen mies* 'this man' (or rather, 'this-kind-of man, such a man') in example (3), I would like to propose a recognitional use interpretation: the speaker indicates that the interlocutor should be able to recognize the type/class which the individual belongs to. This suggestion may seem contradictory: the essence of indefiniteness was above described as the absence of a presupposition that one's interlocutor should be able to identify a referent and now I am claiming that *semmonen* is indefinite, but used here to mark that the interlocutor should be able to identify the *type of referent* talked about. There is, however, no real contradiction involved: by using

---

14   Combined with a quantifying expression, the use of *joku* implies that the exact amount talked about is uncertain for the speaker. See Duvallon, this volume, for an example and a discussion of this kind of approximating effect of *joku*.

adnominal *semmonen*, the speaker partly complies with the (optional) norms of discourse in marking the NP as indefinite and, partly (vaguely) classifies the type of referent we are talking about.

In this subsection, I have illustrated that all three adnominal indefinites studied here can be used to introduce participants referred to even later on, i.e. important referents. In all cases discussed the reference has been speaker-specific in the sense that the speaker has a specific individual in mind. The use of *any* indefinite in this context implies that the speaker does not presuppose that the interlocutor should be able to identify the individual in question *within the discourse*. By using *yks* as the determiner, the speaker indicates this and the fact that this is an important referent that will reappear later. By using *joku* as the determiner, the speaker additionally informs the interlocutor, that he/she is not the original source of the story, that it *is* a retelling. By using *semmonen* as the determiner, the speaker adds a "you know what kind of"-classification to the referent. The classificatory power of *semmonen* need not, however, be strong: it may merely state that we are talking about one of many possible individuals in a group; give an example of the individuals in the class. Hence, there does indeed seem to be a division of labour between the determiners *yks*, *joku* and *semmonen*, based on the speakers' interpretation of the situation at hand. In terms of mental spaces, one could perhaps characterize the use of *yks* in terms of creating a simple base space for the purpose of introducing a new, formerly not mentioned but important discourse referent; the use of *joku* as building up an alternative base space with the additional 'hearsay'-component that represents the reality of somebody else than the story teller; and, finally, the use of *semmonen* as a blend of two mental spaces, the one active in the use of *yks* (i.e. a neutral introduce a new referent-space) and a new one where types of referents are classified and thus characterized by the common features of a typical member of the class. The blend would then involve identifying both the type of referent and accepting it as a new referent for the discourse at hand.[16] In the remainder of this paper, I will not pursue an analysis in mental space terms, but invite the reader to do so.

In what follows, I will examine the use of these determiners in still other semantic/pragmatic contexts in order to see, whether this preliminary description of their use gains more generality.

Non-specific indefinites

Heine delimits the use of a non-specific marker to contexts where participants "whose referential identity neither the hearer nor the speaker knows or cares to know" (Heine 1997: 73) are introduced. As mentioned

---

15   Cf. with the use of the demonstrative determiners in indefinite phrases, as in 'this man I met yesterday', in (Wright & Givón 1987).
16   I am not claiming that this is the best way to describe these uses within a mental spaces account – see e.g. (Harder 2003) for a discussion of the use of blending as a mechanism. I do, however, find the mental spaces approach promising enough for future analyses to start playing with the idea.

above, Vilkuna (Vilkuna 1992) has indirectly claimed that adnominal *yks* cannot be used with non-specific referents. Indeed, there were no examples of this kind of use in the data with *yks* as the determiner. Both *joku* and *semmonen*, however, occur in non-specific contexts defined in Heine's sense.

In example (4), the girl interviewed has been telling me, the interviewer, about a holiday trip to Stockholm and how her family almost missed the ferry back to Helsinki as the subway line they were supposed to take was out of order. As the interested interviewer I then ask her how the situation was resolved and she tells me that she and her family were standing in a long line for a taxi when they found out that the subway was eventually working again. Example (4) is the answer to my follow-up question as to how they found out that it was no longer out of order.

(4) (Non-specific use of *joku*. Monolingual girl, age 15. Interview data.)

<u>joku</u>   mies   tuli   varmaan   sit   sanoon   et   ne
JOKU   man   came   surely   then   to.say   that   SE-PL
some man must have come to tell that they [i.e. trains]

toimii   taas.
function   again
were functioning again

The identity of the messenger is clearly of minor importance in this case. The non-specific reading is also enforced by the use of *varmaan*, glossed here as 'surely, certainly', but more idiomatically translated as 'some man must have come'. Hence, rather than marking that the speaker is not the original source of the story, we here have a case of *joku* marking the speakers indifference towards or uncertainty about the exact identity of the individual referent.

In example (5), *semmonen* is used in a context where it is quite clear that there exists no specific camera.

(5) (Non-specific use of *semmonen*. Bilingual girl, age 10. Interview data.)

1   ois   ollu   hyvä   ku   ois   ollu   kamera.
     COP   COP   good   if   COP   COP   camera
     (It) would have been good if (we) had had (a) camera.

2   .hhh   <u>semmonen</u>   videokamera.
     inhale   SEM   video.camera
     One of these video cameras.

In this example the *kamera* in line 1 is non-specific. The following *semmonen videokamera* in line 2 is obviously a specification of the kind of camera intended. However, it does not refer to a particular specimen of its sort – in fact it does not refer at all. Hence, even as a specification it is non-specific as regards an individual item – the specification yields rather class or type membership (see Givón 1981; Vilkuna 1992; also Lindström 2000).

Indefinite determiners with proper names

One use of indefinite markers characteristic of spoken Finnish is that they can be used with proper names. Most commonly, the determiner in these cases is *yks*, but as the following examples illustrate, the other two determiners under my loop also occur in this function. The most common use in these data is as introductions of new referents that are talked about for a while (cf. above about first mention specific indefinites). However, there are also examples where the individual owner of the proper name seems to be of minor importance. I have chosen to illustrate these latter uses in examples (6–8).

(6) (Indefinite *yks* with proper names. Bilingual boy, age 13. Interview data.)

1 mutta me on totuttu sanoon että, / yhtä Mattia
   but 1PL COP used.to to.say that / YKS-PTV proper name-PTV
   but we are used to saying that,(short pause) it's only this guy Marko

2 me sanotaan Hämäläiseks sukunimen perusteella
   1PL say proper name-TRA last.name-GEN ground-ADE
   whom we call Häkkinen, (using) his last name

In example (6) we see a proper name determined by *yks* used as an example of a person, who is usually referred to by means of his last name. The current topic of the interview is the different ways students with the same first name are addressed both in the classroom and among the students.

As mentioned, the other indefinite determiners are not as common with proper names as *yks*. I have found only one example of the use of adnominal *joku* with proper names in the data, given here as example (7). Here, the girl is telling me about a TV game show that she likes to watch, and as I am not familiar with it, she tries to explain to me what the program is all about.

(7) (*Joku* with proper names. Monolingual girl, age 13. Interview data.)

1 siin oli joku henkilö sanottu, vaikka joku
   there COP JOKU person mentioned for.example JOKU
   well in it a person was mentioned for example (some)

2 Eva-Riitta Siitonen ja sit, piti laittaa niinku, mikä sen
   (proper name) and then must put sort.of what SE-GEN
   Eva-Riitta Siitonen and then one was meant to put sort of what his/her

3	asema	on	ja,	mikä	puolue	ja,	semmosii	kaikkee.
	position	COP	and	what	party	and	SEM-PTV.PL	all

position was and which political party (he/she belonged to) and all such (things)

The *joku*-marked *Eva-Riitta Siitonen*[17] in line 2 is mentioned as an example of the kind of people we are talking about, in this case politicians and celebrities – not really as an individual. The NP does not refer. Once again, thus, we see *joku* as the indifference-marker, it really does not matter that much what the individual name used is. What matters is that it is a name of a celebrity.

There are a lot of NPs in the interview data with one of the demonstrative adjectives as a modifier. Some of them contain proper names. In example (8), the girl is telling me about a circus she once visited and mentions a group of artists by proper name determined by *semmonen*.

(8) *Semmonen* with a proper name. Bilingual girl, age 10. Interview data.

siel	oli	semmonen,	eeh,	<u>semmonen</u>	Kenny ja boy
there	COP	SEM	hesitation	SEM	proper name

There was this er this Kenny ja boy

niitten	nimi	oli.	ne	oli	hirveen	notkeita	ja	sillee.
SE-GEN.PL	name	COP	SE-PL	COP	very	flexible	and	so

their name was. They were very flexible and so.

This is all that is said about the artist group within the almost 60-minute long interview. This specific group is mentioned as an example of what kind of performing artist groups there were in the circus visited, not as an important discourse referent.

The use of an indefinite determiner with a proper name can initially seem problematic. Proper names are *definite* descriptions, how come they can be combined with an indefinite determiner? One fact to consider in the case of *yks* is its origins as a numeral. In some contexts it is hard to tell the two uses apart. In languages with grammaticalized indefinite articles, we do not usually find indefinite articles with most definite descriptions, but they obviously sometimes occur with proper names. It is perfectly alright to use an indefinite article also in English in cases like <u>a</u> *James Smith came to see you*. In Swedish, as in English, it is also perfectly alright to talk about <u>a</u> *future Stockholm*, <u>ett</u> *framtida Stockholm* and <u>a</u> *disappointed Parkvall*, <u>en</u> *besviken Parkvall*. Also, other indefinite determiners such as *one* in English and *en viss* 'a certain' in Swedish can be used together with proper names. In for example witness-statements, we can thus find something like *the witness met <u>one</u> Jonathan Smith* or *vittnet såg <u>en viss</u> Pettersson* ('the witness saw a certain Pettersson') when

---

17 At the time of the interview, Eva-Riitta Siitonen was the mayor of the municipality of Vantaa and as such known at least by name to this girl.

a person is mentioned for the first time or in isolation. Among definite descriptions, constructions with proper names thus seem to be treated specially in many languages.

A possible solution to the question how something as definite as proper names can receive an indefinite marker lies however, I believe, in the nature of indefiniteness. I agree with Lyons (Lyons 1999) in that indefiniteness does not seem to be as clear-cut a matter as definiteness – there simply is something more to it than just not being definite, not being identifiable (cf. also Epstein 2002 and above about the identifiability view of definiteness). In my view, this something more has to do with the presupposition part of identifiability. We should understand the presupposition connected to the use of indefinites that the interlocutor need not be able to identify a referent partly discourse internally, partly as a speaker's choice. Hence, the speaker *can choose to present* a referent with an indefinite marker even if the speaker him/herself (and sometimes also the interlocutor) knows what or whom they are talking about. The speaker's choice in its turn may give rise to different pragmatic effects, such as: if somebody uses an indefinite marker with a proper name, either ignore the referent (because it's unimportant) or, keep track of this new referent, it is an important one (cf. above about Vilkuna's two main uses for adnominal *yks* in Finnish) or; we may engage in name dropping in order to give an example of the class in question, as in all the above examples. Hence, the speaker can actively construct and place the discourse entities in different mental spaces, regardless whether or not they are referred to or just mentioned.

Plural indefinites

In most languages, indefinite pronouns can be inflected for number and/or appear with plural nouns. We thus find English sentences such as <u>Some guys</u> never learn or Swedish sentences such as *Jag träffade <u>några vänner</u> igår* ('I met <u>some</u> friends yesterday'). Indefinite articles do not, however, regularly co-occur with plurals as their sole modifiers, even though we can find forms such as the Swedish *ena* as in *De var ena latmaskar*, 'They were a bunch of lazybones' (note the English translation with a pseudo-partitive construction; see Koptjevskaja-Tamm 2001, for partitive and pseudo-partitive constructions). Also, in some German dialects, specifically Bavarian dialects, indefinite articles do have regular plural forms (Glaser 1996; Kolmer 1999). All the indefinite determiners studied here, as well the indefinite pronoun *joku* as the other parts-of-speech categories, can appear as determiners of plural nouns in Finnish.

(9) (Plural indefinite *yks,* bilingual boy, age 12. Interview data.)

1 <u>yhet</u>   pojat   vaihto   sen   pikkuharjan   isoon   harjaan
  YKS-PL   boy-PL   changed   SE-GEN   small.brush-GEN   big-ILL   brush-ILL
  Some boys swapped the small brush for (a) big brush

The NP *yhet pojat* in example (9) is the only mention of the boys in question. Hence, it is an example of how *yks* can be used to indicate a speaker-specific and speaker-identifiable mention of referents whose exact identity is of less importance. As with the singular *yks*-marked NPs, plural yks can also, however, be used to introduce important participants into the discourse. In the case of example (9), the boys were never mentioned again – but they could have easily become important had the boy continued talking about them after this introduction. In a way, the use of yks as a determiner leaves the speaker with an option to pick up a referent later on and make it important.

Example (10) illustrates the use of joku in plural.

(10) (*Joku* with a plural noun. Monolingual girl, age 15. Interview data.)

1 sit   jos   Se   on   vaan   niinku   lintsaus   niin,
   then   if   SE   COP   only   sort.of   truancy   PRT
   Then if it is just a kind of truancy

2 sit   <u>jotkut</u>   maikat   antaa   ihan   jälkkärin.
   then   JOKU-PL   teacher-PL   give   just   detention
   then some teachers even give (you) detention

In example (10) we see *joku* as a determiner of a plural noun, also here an only mention of the teachers at the very end of an episode where the student has been talking about skipping classes in general and in her case in particular. As Ritva Laury pointed out to me upon seeing this example, one wouldn't expect this kind of examples with *yks*. There is no way to know whether the speaker has specific teachers in mind, but she clearly chooses not to present them as clearly specific by using *yks*. It may be that *joku* is more non-specific here, even though the entailment of existence typical of specific NPs holds. It may also be that *jotkut* is here used simply to imply that the group of teachers behaving in this way is not empty.

(11) (*Semmonen* with plural reference. Monolingual boy, age 15. Interview data.)

1 niitä   rantoja   missä   ei   ketään   muita oo,
   SE-PTV.PL   beach-PTV.PL   where   NEG   nobody   other COP
   The beaches where there is nobody else,

2 <u>semmosii</u>   laguuneja.
   SEM-PTV.PL   lagoon-PTV.PL
   these kind of lagoons

The use of *semmonen* in example (11) also conforms to the suggested interpretation of type membership/recognitional use of adnominal demonstrative adjectives in Finnish.

Indefinites with mass nouns

The last context of use for the Finnish indefinites studied here is that of NPs denoting "homogenous undifferentiated stuff without any certain shape or precise limits" (Koptjevskaja-Tamm in press); i.e. what is often called mass nouns (for an excellent discussion of the intricacies of the syntax and semantics of mass nouns, collectives and the like, see Koptjevskaja-Tamm in press). The majority of languages that have an indefinite article (which are a minority of the languages of the world) do not allow it to appear together with mass nouns (Bavarian dialects being an exception again, see Kolmer 1999: 23–25). And yet other languages, such as French, have a separate, so called partitive article used with mass nouns (and also plural nouns) to indicate unspecified quantity. In light of the present data, Finnish allows for at least two of the determiners studied to co-occur with mass nouns. I have not encountered any examples of *yks* as a determiner in these constructions in these data, but as in many languages, both the indefinite pronoun *joku* and the demonstrative adjective *semmonen* do occur.

(12) (*Joku* with mass nouns. Monolingual boy, age 12. Retelling data.)

1   sitte siinä joku toinem mies tilas <u>jotain</u> lihaa
    then there JOKU other man ordered JOKU-PVT meat-PVT
    then there (was) some other man (who) ordered some meat

2   ja <u>jotain</u> muuta. <u>jotain</u> juomist <u>jotain</u>
    and JOKU-PVT else JOKU-PVT drink-PVT JOKU-PVT
    and something else. something to drink some

3   viinii varmaan ja,
    wine-PVT surely and
    wine I think and,

In example (12), the student is retelling a short episode from a Charlie Chaplin film. In example (13), another student is telling me about visiting the school nurse after a minor accident.

(13) (*Semmonen* with a mass noun. Bilingual boy, age 10. Interview data.)

1   ne olis laittanu <u>semmosta</u> kirvelevää ainetta siihe
    SE-PL COP put SEM-PVT stingy-PVT substance-PVT to.there
    They would have put this stingy stuff there

To me, the most straightforward interpretation of the use of the determiners here is once again in accordance with the preliminary description of their division of labour above: with joku, the speaker marks indifference towards the referent, inferred/reported source of knowledge or uncertainty about the exact identity of the referent; with semmonen type or class membership.

Functional specialization of adnominal indefinites in spoken Finnish

In light of the data presented, there does seem to be a functional differentiation between the indefinite determiners studied according to how the speaker wishes to present a referent to his/her interlocutor(s) within the current discourse, i.e. how he/she actively constructs the discourse entity.

First, all the three determiners occurred in most contexts exemplified. There were, however, two contexts where no examples of *yks* as a determiner were found. One of them was with nouns typically used to denote masses. However, typical mass nouns can often be used as countable nouns (for different ways of describing this, see e.g. Löbner 1985; Jackendoff 1991; Koptjevskaja-Tamm in press) – one way to do this in Finnish seems to be by using *yks* as a determiner. Even though I did not find examples of this in the data studied, I can easily imagine a situation where at least I as a native speaker could use *yks* with a typical mass noun. If I wanted to discuss let us say a specific brand of wine with somebody, I could introduce it into the discourse by means of e.g. *Mä join kerran yhtä viiniä joka...* 'I once drank this wine that...' (Notice the English translation with the indefinite *this*, which I think is the most proper one here.) Note, however, how the use of *yks* changes the meaning of 'wine' from undividable or mass to countable – so we have to conclude that *yks* cannot occur with mass nouns.

Whether this is due to the fact that the form is identical to the numeral 'one' is not entirely clear. It is, however, worth noting, that any numeral used as a determiner of a typical mass noun would have the same effect – i.e. the noun would be interpreted as a count noun (a sort of X as above or a typical amount of X, as in *A beer, please!*). It is also worth noting that it is often claimed that indefinite articles do not usually combine in this way with mass nouns without losing the mass interpretation (Koptjevskaja-Tamm in press).

The other context where no *yks* could be found was the speaker non-specific context. All the examples above with *yks* as a determiner can be argued to be speaker-specific. Thus, the first conclusion to be drawn here is that there is a division of labour between *yks* on the one hand, and *joku* and *semmonen* on the other, so that whereas the latter can be used in both specific and non-specific contexts, *yks* can in these data only be used in speaker-specific contexts. Also, there were no examples of non-referring uses of *yks*-NP, whereas the other two determiners were found also in non-referring contexts.

Second, there is a functional differentiation between the three determiners in speaker-specific contexts. This specialization of the elements originates in how the speaker perceives the discourse for the moment, more specifically the referents talked about, and how he/she anticipates/plans for the continuation of the discourse. The first choice yields whether or not to use a marker of indefiniteness at all. In the retelling condition, 45% of all first or isolated mentions of referents have no determiner at all, i.e. a bare NP is used as in example (2) above when introducing the boy appearing in the cartoon. The second choice then basically yields one of the determiners studied here. I would like to summarize this choice in terms of the main functions of the determiners as revealed in the data studied as a preference in terms of frequency, as follows:

The main function of *yks* as an adnominal determiner in these data is to introduce a specific referent into the discourse in a rather neutral fashion, i.e. with no other implication than that the interlocutor(s) need not make an effort to try to identify the referent from the previous discourse

1. when the referent in question is anticipated by the speaker to be a main participant in the discourse for a while, i.e. it is an important referent and;
2. when the referent in question is introduced by his/her proper name, regardless of whether the referent is a main participant or not.

The main function of *joku* as an adnominal determiner in these data is to introduce a specific or non-specific referent into the discourse

1. when the exact identity of the referent is not important or uncertain to the speaker or;
2. when the speaker chooses to mark that he/she is not the original source of the information passed.

In this respect, thus, *joku* seems to be used as indefinite pronouns are used adnominally in a number of languages.

The main function of *semmonen* as an adnominal determiner in these data is to function as a recognitional demonstrative, i.e. in cases where the identity of a referent is not in focus but the type or class membership is.[18]

Hence, the three determiners indeed show signs of functional specialization. This specialization should not, however, be interpreted as an either or choice. Instead, it should be interpreted as a possibility, a means for the speaker to actively construct the discourse entities in accordance with the desired pragmatic effects.

A note on grammaticalization

It is almost imperative for a study of functional differentiation nowadays to make a note on grammaticalization. The most common source for indefinite articles is the numeral 'one', even if the indefinite pronoun 'some' has also been pointed out as a source in e.g. English (Hawkins 1991), as has the demonstrative 'this' for a number of languages (Wright & Givón 1987). Hence, all the elements studied here are possible sources for indefinite articles.

---

18   Whether it has specialized to fulfill this function in comparison to the other Finnish demonstratives remains so far an open question.

According to Heine (Heine 1997, especially pp. 72–76; see also Givón 1981) the grammaticalization cline from the numeral 'one' to an indefinite article goes generally through the following stages, with my brief characterisation in parenthesis:

Stage I: The numeral
Stage II: The presentative marker
                     (Introduction of main participants)
Stage III: The specific marker
                     (Singular nouns, specific to speaker)
Stage IV: The non-specific marker
                     (Singular nouns, non-specific to speaker)
Stage V: The generalized article
                     (Basically all nouns, including mass and plural nouns)

Heine talks specifically only about indefinite articles originating from the numeral. The numeral *yks* as a determiner is in these data used in functions typical of his stages I–III.[19] Thus, in his terms, it has clearly reached the specific marker stage. However, as noticed above, it can also be used with plural nouns – a feature associated with stage V – but not in stage IV functions. The fact that *yks* is in these data inflected for number but does not appear with mass nouns, nor with singular non-specific nouns, may not be as exotic a characteristic as one might think: all Finnish numerals have plural forms, used for example with plurale tantum words as in *kahdet tai kolmet sakset*, 'two-PL or three-PL scissors', i.e. 'two or three pairs of scissors'. Hence, as the pattern of inflection in number already exists for numerals in Finnish and, as the indefinite *yks* clearly originates from the numeral *yksi*, the step to inflecting the indefinite marker ought to be shorter for Finnish than languages that do not inflect numerals in number. The apparent gap in the grammaticalization cline may, thus, be understood as a language specific deviation from a general pattern.

Even though Heine does not discuss a possible grammaticalization path for the other elements studied here, it is interesting to notice, that both *joku* and *semmonen* are used in all functions but the numeral above. (See also Givón 1981; Wright & Givón 1987 for a similar treatment of other than numeral elements.)

So are there indefinite articles in spoken Finnish? The question of when it is meaningful to postulate the existence of a new grammatical category in a language is not a simple one. I have previously suggested (Juvonen 1996; Juvonen 2000a; Juvonen 2000b) that we use obligatoriness in specific linguistic contexts as the limiting case, given a typologically and historically plausible candidate for a specific category. If we can find a context where the marker occurs in the speech of native speakers and where omittance of the marker changes the meaning of the phrase or makes it ungrammatical – then it is meaningful to say that in this context

---

19   Unfortunately, Heine's description of the stages is so general that it is hard to apply to individual items. I have had especially difficult in trying to find a way to distinguish his presentative uses (stage II) from the following stage III specific uses.

the use of the marker is grammaticalized. Without exploring the nature of the markers studied here in this respect in depth, suffice it to say that there are, as exemplified e.g. by Vilkuna (Vilkuna 1992: 128–132) contexts that would fit this criterion as regards the adnominal *yks*, even though these contexts were not found in the present data. For the other adnominal indefinites, I have not encountered any such contexts. The use of the three adnominal indefinites in the functions described here is thus optional, and the reasons for their use pragmatic rather than syntactic.

Concerning reduction of form, loss of inflexion or affixing commonly but not necessarily associated with grammaticalization, there are no signs whatsoever in these data for any of the markers studied other than the common shortening of the numeral *yksi* 'one' to adnominal *yks*.

Further, and finally, members of one and the same grammatical category cannot usually co-occur within a single lexical element or within a phrase. For example, a verb is typically marked for either present or past tense, not both. In a similar fashion, unbound grammatical markers for the same category tend not to co-occur. As regards the three adnominal indefinites *yks*, *joku* and *semmonen* studied here; there are no examples of *yks* and *joku* co-occurring within one single phrase and indeed, I cannot imagine them co-occurring other than in repair sequences where one is replacing the other. There are, however, a number of examples of either of them co-occurring with a demonstrative adjective. This is illustrated in examples (14) and (15).

(14) (Double determiners. Bilingual boy, age 12. Interview data.)

```
1    em        mä     muista.  /  me  / sem-/      vuokrattiin
     NEG-1SG   1SG    remember /  1PL / interrupted hired
     I don't remember. We (interrupted) hired

2    joku      semmonen   pikku    mökki.
     JOKU      SEM        little   cabin
     this small cabin
```

(15) (Double determiners. Monolingual boy, age 12. Retelling data.)
```
1    sit    tuli   vielä,  ku    ne     kilpapyöräilijät                  Oli  menny,
     then   came   further when  SE-PL  competition.bicycle.rider-PL      COP  went
     Then came yet, when the bicycle riders in the competition had passed,

2    niin   tuli   vielä   yks    semmonen   pyöräilijä        ja    se
     then   came   further YKS    SEM        bicycle.rider     and   SE
     then yet another this kind of bicycle rider came and he
```

Hence, in this respect it seems that *yks* and *joku* indeed are each other's alternatives in those functions that both occur in, whereas the demonstrative adjective seems to belong to a different category.

To sum up: the three adnominal determiners studied, *yks*, *joku* and *semmonen*, fulfill pragmatically different functions in the data studied. Based on these data, there is, however, little reason to postulate any new grammatical categories in spoken Finnish.

REFERENCES

Ariel, Mira. 1988. Referring and accessibility. *Journal of Linguistics* 24: 65–87.
Ariel, Mira. 1990. *Accessing NP antecedents.* London: Routledge.
Chesterman, Andrew. 1991. *On definiteness. A study with special reference to English and Finnish.* Cambridge: Cambridge University Press.
Diessel, Holger. 1999. The morphosyntax of demonstratives in synchrony and diachrony. *Linguistic Typology* 3(1): 1–50.
Epstein, Richard. 2002. The definite article, accessibility, and the construction of discourse referents. *Cognitive Linguistics* 12(4): 333–378.
Fauconnier, Gilles. 1994. *Mental spaces : aspects of meaning construction in natural language.* Cambridge: Cambridge University Press.
Fraurud, Kari. 1990. Definiteness and the Processing of NPs in Natural Discourse. *Journal of Semantics* 7: 395–433.
Givón, Talmy. 1981. On the development of the numeral 'one' as an indefinite article. *Folia Linguistica Historica* 2(1).
Givón, Talmy. 1983. Topic Continuity in Discourse: An Introduction. In T. Givón (ed.) *Topic Continuity in Discourse: A Quantitative Cross-Language Study.* Amsterdam: John Benjamins.
Givón, Talmy. 1995. *Functionalism and grammar.* Amsterdam: John Benjamins.
Glaser, E. 1996. Morphologie und Funktion des unbestimmten Artikels im Bairischen. In H.-W. Eroms and H. Scheringen (eds.) *Sprache an Donau, Inn und Enns,* Universität Passau und Adalbert-Stifter-Institut des Landes Oberösterreich, Linz.
Harder, Peter. 2003. Mental spaces: Exactly when do we need them? *Cognitive Linguistics* 14(1): 91–96.
Haspelmath, Martin. 2000. *Indefinite Pronouns.* New York: Oxford University Press.
Hawkins, John A. 1978. *Definiteness and Indefiniteness-A Study in Reference and Grammaticality Prediction.* London: Groom Helm.
Hawkins, John A. 1991. On (in)definite articles: implicatures and (un)grammaticality prediction. *Journal of Linguistics* 27: 405–442.
Heine, Bernd. 1997. *Cognitive Foundations of Grammar.* New York: Oxford University Press.
Helasvuo, Marja-Liisa. 1988. *Subjekteina ja objekteina toimivat nominilausekkeet puhutuissa teksteissä.* Doctoral dissertation, University of Helsinki: Editor.
Himmelmann, Nikolaus P. 1996. Demonstratives in Narrative Discourse: A Taxonomy of Universal Uses. In B. Fox (ed.) *Studies in anaphora.* Amsterdam: John Benjamins.
Himmelmann, Nikolaus P. 1997. *Deiktikon, Artikel, Nominalphrase: Zur Emergenz Syntaktischer Struktur.* Tübingen.
Jackendoff, Ray. 1991. Parts and boundaries. *Cognition* 41: 9–45.
Juvonen, Päivi. 1996. Språkkontakt och språkförändring: om användningen av demonstrativa pronomen i en sverigefinsk kontaktsituation. In L. Huss (ed.) *Många vägar till tvåspråkighet.* Uppsala: Centre for Multi-Ethnic Research, Uppsala University.
Juvonen, Päivi. 2000a. *Grammaticalizing the definite article. A study of definite adnominal determiners in a genre of spoken Finnish.* Stockholm: Dept of Linguistics, Stockholm University.
Juvonen, Päivi. 2000b. Om bestämdhetsmarkering i ett tvärspråkligt perspektiv - har finskan en bestämd artikel? In U. Melander-Marttala (ed.) *Denna – den här – den där. Om demonstrativer i tvärspråklig belysning. En minnesskrift till Elsie Wijk-Andersson* (pp. 57–92). Uppsala: ASLA Information.
Kolmer, Agnes. 1999. *Zur MASS/COUNT-Distinktion in Beirischen: Artikel und Quantifizierung.* Köln: Arbeitspapier, Institut für Sprachwissenshaft, Universität zu Köln.
Koptjevskaja-Tamm, Maria. 2001. "A piece of the cake" and "a cup of tea": Partitive and pseudo-partitive nominal constructions in the Circum-Baltic languages. In Östen Dahl (ed.) *Circum-Baltic Languages.* Volume 2: Grammar and Typology. Philadelphia, PA, USA: John Benjamins Publishing Company.

Koptjevskaja-Tamm, Maria. In press. 101. Mass and collection. In Geert Booij, Christian Lehman and Joachim Mugdan (eds.). *A Handbook on Inflection and Word Formation*. Berlin and New York: Walter de Gruyter.

Larjavaara, Matti. 1986. *Itämerensuomen demonstratiivit I: Karjala, aunus, lyydi ja vepsä*. Helsinki: SKS:n toimituksia 433. Suomalaisen Kirjallisuuden Seura.

Larjavaara, Matti. 1990. *Suomen deiksis*. Helsinki: Suomalaisen Kirjallisuuden Seura.

Laury, Ritva. 1997. *Demonstratives in interaction. The emergence of a definite article in Finnish*. Amsterdam: John Benjamins.

Lepäsmaa, Anneli. 1978. *Tunnettuuden ilmaisemisesta Helsingin puhekielessä*. Doctoral dissertation, University of Helsinki: Editor.

Lindström, Eva. 2000. Some uses of demonstratives in spoken Swedish. In S. P. Botley and A. M. McEnery (eds.) *Corpus-Based and Computational Approaches to Discourse Anaphora*. London: UCL Press.

Lyons, Christopher. 1999. *Definiteness*. Cambridge: Cambridge University Press.

Löbner, Sebastian. 1985. Definites. *Journal of Semantics*, 4: 279–326.

Maes, A. A. and L. G. M. Noordman. 1995. Demonstrative nominal anaphors: a case of nonidentificational markedness. *Linguistics* 33: 255–282.

Nivre, Joakim. 2002. Three Perspectives on Swedish Indefinite Determiners. *Nordic Journal of Linguistics* 25(2): 34-47.

Pajusalu, Renate. 2004. Viron üks ja kõik. *Virittäjä* 1/2004: 2–23.

Prince, Ellen. 1981. Toward a Taxonomy of Given-New Information. In P. Cole (ed.) *Radical Pragmatics*. New York: Academic Press.

Vilkuna, Maria. 1992. *Referenssi ja määräisyys suomenkielisten tekstien tulkinnassa*. Helsinki: Suomalaisen Kirjallisuuden Seura.

Wright, S., and Talmy Givón. 1987. The pragmatics of indefinite reference: quantified text-based studies. *Studies in Language* 11(1): 1–33.

Contributors

OUTI DUVALLON
ATER, Institut national des langues et civilisations orientales, Paris, France

MARJA ETELÄMÄKI
University lecturer, University of Helsinki, Finland

PÄIVI JUVONEN
Assistant professor, General Linguistics, Stockholm University, Sweden

ELSI KAISER
Graduate Student, University of Pennsylvania, Philadelphia, USA

LEA LAITINEN
Professor, Department of Finnish, University of Helsinki, Finland

RITVA LAURY
Associate professor, Department of Linguistics, California State University, Fresno, USA and University lecturer, Department of Linguistics, University of Helsinki, Finland

RENATE PAJUSALU
Associate Professor, University of Tartu, Estonia

EEVA-LEENA SEPPÄNEN
University lecturer, University of Helsinki, Finland

Subject index

A
accessibility 8, 135, 137, 144, 148, 158–159, 191, 192
accusative 77, 80
activation (see also discourse status) 72, 140, 143, 144ff
activity 7, 12, 15, 16, 18–34, 42, 60, 66, 68–69, 70, 71
adverb 13, 14, 45, 108, 110–111, 127–130, 133, 166
anaphora 57, 127, 163–165
animacy 8, 15ff, 79, 93, 96–101, 103, 110–126, 130–133, 193, 194, 211
antecedent 58, 62, 81, 83, 133, 135–139, 142–143, 145–158
assessment 19, 25, 26-28, 32–34

C
case marking 78–80, 108–110, 117–132
characterizing features (see also referential features) 14–15
competing referents 153–154

D
definiteness 23, 190
demonstrative 7, 12–15, 38, 39, 56
dialect 75–77, 78–79, 80–103, 139ff,
discourse referent 25, 60, 66, 192, 199, 202
discourse status (see also activation) 140ff, 149–153, 157–158
distal 59, 68, 110, 164

E
emphasis 108, 121, 131, 132
evidentiality 72–73, 75, 93, 96–102

F
first mention 56–73, 165, 194
focus of attention 60–62, 72, 165, 207
footing 68, 69

G
gaze 7, 42, 46–49
grammatical/syntactic role 8, 133, 135–137, 138, 139, 141, 143, 144–158, 159
grammaticalization 72, 81, 98, 101–102, 207–29

H
host construction 9, 16, 163, 182–184
hän 38, 39, 41, 75–104, 141–159

I
identifiability 15, 23–24, 62, 192
    sufficiently identified 15
indefiniteness 190–209
indexicality 12, 20, 32ff, 34–35, 38, 78–80, 97–98, 102–104
    indexical ground 8, 12–13, 15, 18, 25, 34, 64–66, 69
        asymmetric 15, 22, 24, 32, 68
        symmetric(al) 15, 18, 24, 28, 34, 65, 70
    indexical features (see also referential features) 14–15, 23, 24–26
        open 14, 15, 18, 22, 23, 32
        closed 14, 15, 23, 37, 60, 66
inferability 58, 62
interaction 7–8, 12–35, 38–49, 57, 59, 60, 65, 87, 91–92, 95, 100, 103–104, 164
interpretation source 25, 164, 172, 179, 183–184

J
joku 193–194, 197–202, 204–206, 208–209

L
lexical description/designation 9, 163–164, 170–176, 179, 182, 184–185
locative 13, 110, 127–130, 133, 166, 168, 177, 181
logophoricity 8, 75–77, 80–96, 98–101, 103

M
main clause 80, 83, 86–89, 118–119, 142
metalinguistic sequence 164, 172–182
metapragmatic function 79–80, 87, 100

N
necessity constructions 78–80
non-referentiality 35, 93, 98–102
non-standard 75–79, 165,

P
paradigmatic axis 167–172, 211
parenthetical insert 182–184
participant roles/framework 7, 15ff, 33–35, 38–42, 45–49, 57, 59–60, 67–69, 76, 79–99, 174ff
person 7, 8, 23ff, 38–41, 45–49, 68, 75, 77–91, 100, 103, 107–108, 113,

213

116, 120–121, 124–127, 132–133, 136, 193ff
pointing 15–20, 59
politeness 83–84, 87
possessive suffix 77–78, 86, 139ff
possessor 127
pragmatic meaning 35
presentational clause 120, 132
Pronominal Approach 9, 165–166
protagonist 8, 75, 93–96
psycholinguistics 8, 135, 138–139, 144–153, 159

R
recognitional 20, 198, 204, 297
rection place 165–185, 211
reference
    resolution 165, 179, 185
referential
    anchoring 165, 168, 179–182, 183, 185
    features 14–24
    form 39, 41–42, 59, 71–72, 86, 136, 143, 148
    hierarchy of NP types 79–80, 97, 137, 139, 148, 152, 158
    indexical 12, 14–35, 38, 79, 78–93, 98
    meaning 15, 96
reflexivity 12–13, 59
relative clause 20, 119, 155, 156ff, 183, 184
right-dislocation 22, 102, 168

S
salience 8, 23, 34, 46, 60, 112, 117, 135–139, 144–159, 179
script 58, 62
se 13–15, 18ff, 19–20, 22, 23–24, 25, 28, 33, 34, 38, 39, 59–60, 65–66, 71, 76, 163–185
seal 107, 127, 130

sealt 107
see 107, 108, 109, 110, 111, 112, 114, 115, 116, 117, 118–122, 124–125, 127, 129–133
semmonen, 193–194, 198–200, 202, 204–207, 208–209
sequence closing sequence 28
shifters 34–35
socio-centric 35
spatial opposition 108
specificity 191–192, 194–201
speech act persons 7, 39, 49, 68, 76–78, 79–85, 91–93, 103–104
syntactic rupture 175–182, 185
syntagmatic axis 167–179

T
ta 107–112, 114–118, 121, 122, 125–127, 132–133
tema 107–112, 117, 118, 121, 126, 132–133
textual domains/organisation 165, 183–184
topic framework 23
too 108, 113
tracking 8, 20, 107–132, 165, 184
troubles-telling 28–34
tuo (toi) 13–15, 18, 23, 25, 39, 46, 59–60, 68–71
tämä (tää) 13–15, 22, 23, 24, 25, 32, 38, 39, 40–49, 59–60, 66–68, 71, 76, 141–159

U
uncertainty 93, 99–100

W
word order 101, 136, 138–141, 142, 144–156

Y
yks 193–194, 196–197, 199–201, 203–207, 209

Name index

A
Agha, Asif 34
Airila, Martti 166
Apothéloz, Denis 172
Ariel, Mira 60, 137, 165, 191, 192
Arnold, Jennifer 137, 158

B
Benveniste, Emile 40, 78
Berrendonner, Alain 183
Birner, Betty 140ff
Blanche-Benveniste, Claire 9, 165, 166, 167, 168, 169, 171, 172, 185
Bolinger, Dwight 73
Brennan, Susan E. 138
Brinton, Laurel J. 81, 88
Brown, George 39, 57

C
Campbell, Lyle 79ff
Cannelin, Knut 81ff
Cantrall, William A. 75ff
Chafe, Wallace 15, 60, 71, 72, 138, 165
Chambers, Craig 136ff, 154
Chesterman, Andrew 140, 190
Chodorow, Martin S. 138
Clements, G. N. 76
Comrie, Bernard 76, 88
Cornish, Francis 25, 169, 179
Crawley, Rosalind J. 138, 149

D
Dahl, Östen 190ff
Davidson, Herbert 96
Diessel, Holger 107, 198
Du Bois, John W. 15, 56
Dubois, Danièle 172
Duvallon, Outi 8, 9, 38, 57, 65, 70, 129, 171ff, 174ff, 183, 198ff

E
Ehlich, Konrad 165
Epstein, Richard 192, 203
Erelt, Mati 107, 110, 113
Etelämäki, Marja 7, 12, 38, 57, 59, 60, 64, 65, 66, 68, 69, 70, 71, 79, 107, 136, 141, 164, 182ff

F
Fauconnier, Gilles 192
Ford, Cecilia 39
Fox, Barbara 39, 57, 58, 62, 165

Fraurud, Kari 192
Friedman, Marilyn A. 138

G
Garrod, Simon C. 57
Gernsbacher, Morton Ann 144ff
Gilliom, Laura A. 138, 139
Gilman, A. 39
Givón, Talmy 72, 137, 158, 165, 191, 193, 199ff, 201, 207, 208
Glaser, E. 203
Goodwin, Charles 7, 19, 33, 39, 42, 46, 47, 48, 174
Goodwin, Marjorie Harness 19, 33, 39, 42, 46
Goffman, Erving 7, 59
Gordon, Peter C. 138, 139
Greenberg, Joseph 23
Grosz, Barbara J. 138, 139
Gundel, Jeanette K. 57, 58, 60, 62, 107, 137, 165

H
Hagège, Claude 75, 76, 87
Hahn, Udo 139 149, 151, 158
Hakulinen, Auli 20, 28, 93, 102, 164, 166, 168, 174, 178
Halmari, Helena 141, 142, 143
Hanks, William 7, 8, 12, 13, 14, 15, 34, 35, 59, 64, 65, 66ff
Harder, Peter 199ff
Haspelmath, Martin 191, 193
Hawkins, John A. 191, 207
Heath, Christian 12
Hedberg, Nancy 137
Heim, Irene 57
Heine, Bernd 193, 199, 208
Heinonen, Mari 19
Helasvuo, Marja-Liisa 78, 79ff, 136, 140, 166, 198
Heritage, John 13
Herlin, Ilona 90
Hiirikoski, Juhani 140
Himmelmann, Nikolaus P. 20, 107, 111, 198
Hindmarsh, Jon 12
Hoffman, Beryl 139
Hyman, L. M. 76, 88

I
Itkonen, Terho 38, 59, 164

J

Jackendoff, Ray 206
Jakobson, Roman 35, 167
Jefferson, Gail 29, 33, 40, 170
Jespersen, Otto 34, 79ff
Joshi, Aravind K. 138
Juvonen, Päivi 14, 24, 171ff, 175ff, 190, 191, 193, 197ff, 208

K

Kaiser, Elsi 15ff, 59, 76, 107, 113, 133, 137, 140ff, 141, 142, 143, 145, 150, 152, 154, 155, 159, 190, 192
Kalliokoski, Jyrki 141
Kannisto, Artturi 81ff, 88ff, 100
Karjalainen, Merja 141
Karlsson, Fred 139, 156ff, 166
Kelly, John 172
Kenttä, Matti 82
Kolmer, A. 203, 205
Koptjevskaja-Tamm, Maria 190ff, 203, 205, 206
Koster, J. 81
Kuiri, Kaija 85, 175
Kurhila, Salla 178

L

Laitinen, Lea 32ff, 38ff, 78, 79ff, 81, 93, 102, 110, 136, 139, 141, 142, 165
Larjavaara, Matti 38, 59, 65, 67, 68, 107, 164, 171ff, 193, 198
Latvala, Salu 81ff, 88ff
Laury, Ritva 14, 15, 20, 24, 38, 41, 46, 59, 66, 67, 68, 70, 71, 78, 85, 107, 128, 140ff, 164, 165, 168ff, 171ff, 182ff, 190, 198, 204
Lee, John R. E. 33
Lepäsmaa, Anneli 197
Lerner, Gene 39, 40, 45
Leuschner, Torsten 100
Levinson, Stephen C. 40
Lindström, Eva 198, 201
Löbner, Sebastian 206
Local, John 172
Lyons, Christopher 190, 191, 193ff, 203
Lyons, John 12, 40, 49, 60, 78, 110

M

MacWhinney, Brian 138
Maes, A. A. 192
Maillard, Michel 184
Matthews, Alison 138
McDonald, Janet L. 138
Metslang, Helle
Milner, J.-C. 165
Mondada, Lorenza 172, 183

Mägiste, Julius 82

N

Nivre, Joakim 193ff
Noordman, L. G. M. 192
Nuolijärvi, Pirkko 78, 82

O

Ochs Keenan, Elinor 19
Ogden, Richard 172

P

Pajusalu, Renate 15ff, 38, 108, 110, 113, 116, 123, 130, 192ff
Parkvall, Mikael 190ff
Paunonen, Heikki 38ff, 78, 82
Peirce, Charles 35
Penttilä, Aarni 38, 59, 164
Pohjanen, Bengt 82
Pollard, Charles J. 138
Pomerantz, Anita 19
Pool, Raili 107, 126, 127
Prasad, Rashmi 139
Prince, Ellen F. 58, 62, 138, 140ff, 157, 192ff
Putnam, Hilary 78

R

Raevaara, Liisa 27
Rambow, Owen 139
Ravila, Paavo 183
Reichler-Béguelin, Marie-José 172, 179, 183
Reuland, E. 81
Roberts, Craige 57
Rojola, Lea 32ff
Rosch, Eleanor 169
Routarinne, Sara 172, 183

S

Saari, Mirja 174, 178
Saarimaa, E. A. 141
Sacks, Harvey 18ff, 21, 27ff, 39, 40
Salo, Juha 177
Sands, Kristina 79
Sandström, Caroline 96
Sanford, Anthony C. 57
Saukkonen, Pauli 93, 164
Saussure, Ferdinand de 167
Schegloff, Emanuel A. 22ff, 24, 27ff, 28, 39, 40, 172, 174ff
Schieffelin, Bambi 19
Seppänen, Eeva-Leena 15ff, 32ff, 33, 38, 41, 46, 48, 59, 65, 66, 68, 69, 70, 71, 78, 85, 92, 107, 136, 139, 142, 158, 164

Setälä, Emil Nestor 38, 59, 81, 164
Silverstein, Michael 34, 35, 79
Sirelius, U. 81ff, 88ff
Sheldon, Amy 136ff, 154
Siro, Paavo 166
Smyth, Ron 136ff, 154
Sorjonen, Marja-Leena 21, 32ff, 171
Stevenson, Rosemary J. 138, 146, 149
Strube, Michael 139, 149, 151, 158
Sulkala, Helena 141
Suojala, Marja 175
Suomalainen, K. 83ff

T
Tarvainen, Kalevi 166
Tetreault, Joel 138
Tiainen, Outi 82
Tiainen-Duvallon, Outi 23, 57, 165
Trueswell, John 145, 152, 159
Turan, Ümit Deniz 137, 139

U
Urbanowicz, Agnieszka 138

V
Varteva, Annukka 76, 141, 149
Vilkuna, Maria 14, 18, 79ff, 102, 136, 139, 140, 170, 174, 190, 191, 192ff, 196, 197, 198, 200, 201, 203, 209
Vilppula, Matti 83, 100, 141

W
Walker, Marilyn A. 138
Ward, Gregory 57, 58, 60, 62, 140ff
Wright, George Henrik von 80
Wright, Suzanne 199ff, 207, 208

Y
Ylikahri, Kristiina 93
Yule, George 57

Z
Zacharski, Ron 137
Zay, Françoise 179, 180, 183, 184
Ziv, Yael 57, 58, 62, 165

www.ingramcontent.com/pod-product-compliance
Lightning Source LLC
Chambersburg PA
CBHW080805300426
44114CB00020B/2834